Modernity & Consumption

THEORY, POLITICS, AND THE PUBLIC
IN SINGAPORE AND MALAYSIA

Modernity & Consumption

Theory, Politics, and the Public in Singapore and Malaysia

Antonio L. Rappa

World Scientific
New Jersey • London • Singapore • Hong Kong

Published by

World Scientific Publishing Co. Pte. Ltd.
5 Toh Tuck Link, Singapore 596224
USA office: 27 Warren Street, Suite 401-402, Hackensack, NJ 07601
UK office: 57 Shelton Street, Covent Garden, London WC2H 9HE

British Library Cataloguing-in-Publication Data
A catalogue record for this book is available from the British Library.

MODERNITY AND CONSUMPTION
Theory, Politics, and the Public in Singapore and Malaysia

Copyright © 2002 by World Scientific Publishing Co. Pte. Ltd.

All rights reserved. This book, or parts thereof, may not be reproduced in any form or by any means, electronic or mechanical, including photocopying, recording or any information storage and retrieval system now known or to be invented, without written permission from the publisher.

For photocopying of material in this volume, please pay a copying fee through the Copyright Clearance Center, Inc., 222 Rosewood Drive, Danvers, MA 01923, USA. In this case permission to photocopy is not required from the publisher.

ISBN-13 978-981-238-009-8
ISBN-10 981-238-009-4
ISBN-13 978-981-238-029-6 (pbk)
ISBN-10 981-238-029-9 (pbk)

Preface

Why are we habitual consumers? What does it mean to be a consumer in the first quarter of the 21st century, and to occupy public space in relatively advanced, cosmopolitan, and capitalist states in late modernity? Is our penchant for consumption due to political socialization, a cultural and material logic for survival; or an irrationality and impulsiveness over anachronistic traditions, cultures, and social belief systems? Could our affinity for goods be traced to a desire to amass things for the sake of the *thing*-in-itself? And to what extent are we the products of the "things" that we consume? Do we become less human as we consume more, or do we increase our humanity with variegated levels of consumption? What, in effect, has human life got to do with consumption and how can we make theoretical sense of it?

We know, for example, that a significant proportion of our time in the human reproductive-life-cycle is devoted to acting in concert with the sale and purchase of goods and services for the sake of acquisition, ownership, proprietary transfers, pure profit, greed, and basic physiological survival. The act of consuming and the nature of consumption in late modernity involves at the minimum a complex political economy of patents, copyrights, legalese, consumer advocacy, policy regulations, governmental standards, official guidelines, the vertical and horizontal integration of firms worldwide, marketing, advertising and business development within regulated and semi-regulated markets. Apart from these consumer markets, the other main actors that figure in the neoliberal international political economy include sovereign governments, NGOs, religious and non-religious organizations, civil society associations, consumer protection agencies, investment corporations, the financial and banking sectors, and the corporate agents of pan-national trading activities.

Consumption is therefore a universal phenomenon with regional, sub-regional, national, and local effects. One such deleterious effect on consumers is information overload. This effect causes consumers to resist:

after a specific level of tolerable data has been absorbed, additional information becomes background noise, and no further data can be optimally processed. This results in the increasing desensitization of consumers to their environment. Another effect is the commodification of tradition and culture into goods and services for sale and purchase that screens like a vivid videotape across global centers of cosmopolitanism. Subsequently, rural areas have increasingly experienced the impact of consumption that is catalyzed through infrastructural "development", "internal" migration, and policy changes and program development.

Modernity in this book refers to the temporal and spatial processes generated since the Industrial Revolution in the West. *Late Modernity* represents the contemporary experience and consciousness of globalization and technological transformation within the neoliberal international capitalist economy. But modernity also refers to theories that explain the processes within its ambit making it difficult to develop clear distinctions between theories of modernity and acts of modernity. Modernity *as* political practice cannot be understood apart from the seemingly illusory conceptual engagements that approximate what has come to be associated with Michel Foucault's notion of "discursive formations":

> From Wolin's perspective, Foucault's theory engenders an optical illusion. By focusing on the microcontext where regimes of power-knowledge prevails ... rather than on the operations of the state *per se*, it looks as if Foucault is scaling down the pretensions of theory and making it more amenable for purposes of personal and social reconstruction. It shows, the truth, however, is the opposite of what this appearance suggests (Botwinick and Connolly, 2001, p. 132).

The scaling down of appearances within consumer discourses are directly linked to the nature of the beast itself. It renders its users into a totally dependent relationship where power-knowledge hierarchies are structured within consumer culture itself. Consequently, consumers cannot help not consuming, and are singularly culpable of encouraging the spread of consumerism in late modernity. This is because consumption is positively associated with wealth: the more one earns, the greater the wealth, the higher the consumption. Part of the problem of consumption in late modernity is also found in changing habits, different tastes, mutable patterns of life, socialized behavior, and the remnant effects of 20th century politics and culture. We are increasingly imprisoned by the prejudices, stereotypes, and biases that help us survive the late modernity of globalization and technological change. Consumption is about choices over ranges of tangible and intangible goods and services. Yet the central paradox of consumption is that the more choices we have and the more choices we make ironically leaves us with much less room to make those choices. This is partly because the compression of space by the speeding up of time in late modernity has resulted in a narrower avenue for choices, a shorter amount of time for decision-making, and a contracted field of view for thought. In fact some would argue that we do not have to bother about thinking any longer: all we have to do to survive this place (and being displaced) is to follow the *Herd of Consumption*, deadening our instinct for adaptation, survival, and creativity.

The thinking has already been done for us. The decisions about making complex choices in modernity have been scaled down by "industry professionals" to the extent that we only have to "trust" the gurus of marketing and advertising, the specialists and experts who produce and reproduce, the sales persons who exploit that thin space between our activities to catch our attention and passionately convince us of the strengths and benefits of products we know we don't really care about, and don't really need.

No one escapes consumption. Regardless of ideological belief, religious orientation, ethnicity, class, culture, or political rhetoric, the majority of citizens are indubitably tied to the processes of globalization. Consumers exchange. That's what its all about.

Yet very often such exchanges are inclusive in the sense of containing not only purely economic dimensions but also political, cultural and social ones. These multi-dimensional exchanges of the things and services that we produce and consume make for different, interesting, and contesting bonds between and among individuals in groups and communities to the extent of influencing the nature and formation of community life and community culture. Sometimes such exchanges result in the breaking and hardening of old and, or imagined differences between and among groups. Such social bonding and social breakage also reflects a certain reliance on a common currency that are themselves agencies of exchange: language, national culture, national ideals, religion, and ethnicity.

There appears to be a general belief that the possibility of present and future survival — of individual, group, and community identities — is becoming increasingly dependent on economic growth. Greater economic performance and productivity seems to equal greater goods for the greater number. Resources that are available in state and civil society are often channeled towards various instrumentalist advancement of economic activities that not only create niches in world market, but are also extended and widened to capture a bigger market share, a larger portion of the international stock of wealth, and generate greater economic chances of surviving modernity. Or so it seems. The development, maintenance, and advancement of identity is partially dissolved, partially mired, protuberantly suspended within ascriptive ties to religion, the state, the nation, class, ethnicity, culture, and economic development. These agents of consumption are ironically contingent on the changes that they deliver. If the foregoing description generally describes our behavior as consumers within the international neoliberal political economy, then we deserve to call ourselves *modern*. And if we agree that the description above represents a fairly accurate snapshot of the world in which we live, then we are consciously and conspicuously experiencing modernity. This *is* what it means to be modern. Hopefully, most of the readers of this book would by now have rejected the modern but onerous thesis of uneven global development because of its optimistic posture, its promise of producing wealth; its value-added, time-constraining, speed-increasing, and epoch-advancing vocabulary. But for those who still believe in it, this book helps explore the meaning of modernity in terms of the way in which *things* (goods and services, both tangible and intangible) are being consumed in Singapore, Malaysia, and indeed, the late modern world. This work hopes to remind us to think (before we consume and as we consume) about how the ways in which we consume life in late modernity determines how meaningful or empty consumption makes us. Consumption is the critical agent that forces and coerces individuals, groups, and communities to engage in ways that appear to make and break the very same individual, social, and political identities in question.

The method used in this book frames five themes from the contemporary political theory of William E. Connolly, Gianni Vattimo, Theresa Brennan, Stephen K. White, and Wendy Brown with regard to (1) the fundamental value in modernity is being modern argued by Vattimo; (2) exclusionary goods decrease the private value while increasing the private costs; exclusionary goods also accentuate social costs to the detriment of the social environment; and increases the costs to the state and hence the general public burden as exemplified by Connolly's work; (3) that consumption involves a Faustian foundational fantasy of horror depicted by Brennan; (4) White's analysis that the greater awareness of the conventionality of what has been taken for certain in the modern west ought to be further interrogated especially since domestic public space is not invulnerable; and, (5) the work-gender contradiction thesis enacted by Brown. These five concepts provide the major conceptual themes used to explain the complex politics of modernity and consumption as Lyotard argues in his *Political Writings* (1993),

> capitalism tries to incorporate the dynamic of needs ever more strictly within its global economic dynamic: this incorporation operates both in the form of prediction, henceforth indispensable to the functioning of the system, and in the form of a control effectively, adjusting needs to production possibilities.

The functioning of the systems are built deep within the social structures that uphold modernity's machines, and that is why Lyotard is correct in asserting the critical and formative links between structure, function and control in production. One argument for the enviable successes of modernity and its attendants ironically comes from an alternative tradition. Thomas L. Friedman wrote an article in the New York Times (January 2002) where he quoted a Pakistani writer and businessman, Izzat Maheed on modernity and Islam:

> Without a reformation in the practice of Islam that makes it move forward and not backward, there is no hope for us Muslims anywhere. We have reduced Islam to the organized hypocrisy of state-sponsored mullahism ... for more than a 1,000 years Islam has stood still because the mullahs, who became *de facto* clergy instead of genuine scholars, closed the door on *itejhad* (reinterpreting Islam in the light of modernity) and no one came forward with an evolving application of the message of the Holy Quran ... All the Mullahs tell you today is how to go back a millennium.

The political retardation suggested by Izzat is not startling when one considers the kinds of things that are done in the name of religion, and for the sake of partially understood, partially digested, and partially manufactured interpretations of Holy Scripture though the millennia. For Friedman and Izzat, the main lament above is similar to the greatest fear of "Western" modernity. The horror in the mirror of modernity is that it might eventually stagnate and degenerate into the past, and into tradition: it might "go out of style" and be replaced. Yet Foucault's opening quote reminds us that we possess the "most complex system of knowledge and the most sophisticated structures of power". Does contemporary this make us any better than the ancient Chinese and Hindu traditions; the citizens of the Greek poleis, the new world citizens of the *Pax Romana*, or the caliphs in the gold age of Islam? Perhaps if we conceive of late modernity as being the vanguard and portal of a truculent modernity it might shed alternative nuances to the meaning of life in neoliberal international capitalist economies. The postNietzscheans in our midst are likely to be a little more skeptical about the plausibility of *a better* life in late modernity as opposed to the ancient belief in a better life after death. Negative postNietzschean thought concentrates on the analytical reconfigurations of the discontented dimensions of modernity — consumption, languages of terror, religious violence, cultural cleansing and ethnic pogroms, technologies of fear, and neoliberal attempts to re-master the international economic system. Consumers are developing a reliance on the absence of an ethical public philosophy, a commonality of morals, a nonexistent genealogy that some believed existed in the recent and remote past. Consumerism *is* the new religion that has taken over the public sphere of our lives and over taken the private dimensions of our thoughts. The majority of consumers who cease to think because it is just "too hard", and who have stopped caring about the world are those who have succumbed to the juggernaut of modernity; they are the ones who successfully negotiate late modern life in virtual ignorance. Lest we be heretics to consumption and burn at the stake of neoliberal capitalism.

Contents

Preface	v
Acknowledgements	xiii
Chapter 1 Modernity	1
Chapter 2 Consumption	27

Part I Singapore

Chapter 3 Consuming Singapore	63
Chapter 4 Family & Education	83
Chapter 5 Narrative & Public Space	115

Part II Malaysia

Chapter 6 Consuming Malaysia	145
Chapter 7 Family & Education	167
Chapter 8 Narrative & Public Space	195
Chapter 9 Consumption & Its Discontents	231
Bibliography	253
Author Index	265
Subject Index	269

Acknowledgements

The idea for a book began at an international conference in Leiden, the Netherlands (25 June to 28 June 1998) organized by ICAS and IIAS. The first draft took shape at the Institute for Governmental Studies (IGS), University of California, Berkeley in the summer of 2000. I thank Eunice Park, Bruce Cain, and the UC Berkeley's Department of Political Science doctoral students for their support and hospitality. The second draft was only revised after the late spring/early summer of 2001 as a visiting assistant professor at the Department of Political Science of the Johns Hopkins University in Baltimore, MD. Bill Connolly and Jane Bennett were very gracious hosts. I also benefited from the stimulating debates with the (informal and formal) political theorists at Mergenthaler Hall: Kellee Tsai, Adam Sheingate, Dick Flathman, Matt Crenson, Mark Blythe, Siba Grovogui, and Dick Katz. I especially thank Kellee, Bill, Jane, Joel, Mary, and Mark for their warmth and encouragement. And for the wonderful breakfast, lunch, and dinner conversations. The study leave for the trips to Berkeley, Palo Alto, Santa Monica, and Baltimore was approved by the NUS Faculty of Arts and Social Sciences; and, several concepts that are used in this book were developed out of publications arising from two NUS-FASS-funded research grants: R108-000-002-112, "A Political Ethnography of Eurasian Families", and R-108-000-004-112, "Modernity and Public Space" for which I am much obliged.

I would especially like to thank Peter J. Katzenstein, Aryeh Botwinick, Joel B. Grossman, and Douglas Mao for reading and criticizing the final manuscript; the two anonymous readers; the wonderful tech-team at World Scientific; and, my former and current students and colleagues at NUS who continue to teach me about the politics of consumption in late modernity.

Our civilization has developed the most complex system of knowledge, the most sophisticated structures of power: what has this kind of knowledge, this kind of power made of us? In what way are those fundamental experiences of madness, suffering, death, crime, desire, individuality connected, even if we are not aware of it, with knowledge and power? I am sure that I'll never get the answer; but that does not mean that we don't have to ask the question ... my knowledge of Nietzsche certainly is better than my knowledge of Heidegger. Nevertheless, these are the two fundamental experiences I have had ... I think that it is important to have a small number of authors with whom one thinks, with whom one works, but about whom one does not write...In the end for me there are three categories of philosophers: the philosophers that I don't know; the philosophers I know and of whom I have spoken; and the philosophers I know and about whom I don't speak.

Michel Foucault, Politics, Philosophy Culture:
Interviews and Other Writings, 1977-1984

A commodity is never just a commodity but, as the effect of the complex and dissimulating activity of commodification, always remains itself a social force as well as the condensed site of social forces.

Wendy Brown, States of Injury: Power and Freedom in
Late Modernity

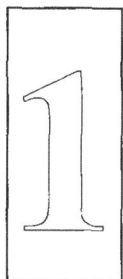

Modernity

Modernity generally refers to a set of theories that try to explain the meaning of contemporary civilization. These theories are concerned with explanations that engage and encounter the capitalist, neoliberal international world system in order for civilizational survival, maintenance, progress, and advancement as seen in the enlightenment project that ostensibly began with the Industrial Revolution in the west. However, the experience, consciousness and modality of modernity has itself gone through three main reinventions and rejuvenations over the past two hundred years. These are the information, communications, and the consumption revolution. While the information and communications' revolution are intimately interwoven, the one facilitating (while simultaneously implicating) the other as seen in third and fourth generation Global Positioning Systems (GPS) and nano-biotechnology, the consumption revolution is itself a larger and massive reinvention of how goods and services are simultaneously traded and consumed across the globe. Indeed, the consumption revolution in modernity as we experience it today is often called globalization. A principal characteristic of the consumption revolution is its homogenizing effect on consumers; an effect of capitalism, the driving force of modernity that widens and deepens the modernists' control over the political, social, cultural, and economic environment.[1] Modernity tends to homogenize identity and commodify all goods and services into products for sale and purchase; and as a result, homogenize those who identify with these goods and services. This chapter introduces the main conceptual themes and background to modernity and consumption in Singapore and Malaysia and is organized into the following sections: this book's intention, modernity and political theory, the three major prevailing debates in the literature on modernity, and the Modernity/Resistance (mRf) frame used for explanation and analysis in the book. This chapter concludes with the meaning and nature of consumption, highlights some work done on consumption, and introduces a quantitative description of consumption patterns in Singapore and Malaysia.

Synopsis

Richard Rorty suggests in *Contingency, Irony, and Solidarity* (1989:xiii) that the Platonic endeavor to fuse "public and private" space similarly motivated the search for an answer to "Why is it in one's interest to be just?" and Christianity's claim that "perfect self-realization can be attained through service to others...Ever since Hegel however historicist thinkers have tried to get beyond this familiar standoff... there is nothing 'beneath' socialization or prior to history which is definatory of the human. Such writers tell us that the question, 'What is it to be a human being?' should be replaced by questions like 'What is it to be rich and inherit a rich twentieth-century democratic society?' and 'How can an inhabitant of such a society

---

[1] See for example the excellent commentary and the significant political question raised by Melissa A. Orlie, "Political Capitalism and Consumption" in Aryeh Botwinick, and William E. Connolly, (eds.), *Democracy and Vision: Sheldon Wolin and the Vicissitudes of the Political* (Oxford and Princeton: Princeton University Press, 2001), pp. 138-160.

be more than an enactor of a role in a previously written script?' ... But even after this substitution takes place, the old tension between the private and the public remains". (Rorty, 1989) Given Rorty's position, it seems to me that the classical foundationalists, and both groups of historicists who freed us from "theology and metaphysics" (and whom that Rorty valiantly tries to reconcile) leave little room for understanding private choice and private consumption today in the early twenty-first century. However, Rorty's Northcliffe lectures (University College, London) and Clarke lectures (Trinity College, Cambridge) certainly provide a useful point of departure for this book.[2]

By accepting the Rortyian dynamic, it would be prudent, I think, to reject the Habermasian one, especially the latter view in *The Structural Transformation of the Public Sphere* (1985). Rather, we see that Rorty illustrates the differences between Foucault (for us) and Habermas (against us) in stark terms:

> Michel Foucault is an ironist who is unwilling to be a liberal, whereas Jurgen Habermas is liberal who is unwilling to be an ironist...and sees [Nietzsche] as leading us to a dead end (Rorty, *Contingency, Irony, and Solidarity*, 1989:61-2).

The deadening effect of Nietzsche's *telos* is the unseen philosophical guide of this book which proffers a non-Marxist, theoretical approach, the modernity-Resistance-frame (mRf), for examining consumption based on concepts developed in the work of William E. Connolly, Stephen K. White, Gianni Vattimo, Theresa Brennan, and Wendy Brown within late modernity.

Late modernity — the experience and consciousness of global and technological transformation today — does not result in the fusion of "public and private" spaces but in the penetration of private space by public space to the extent that private space becomes conditional, ephemeral, and decrepit. What appears in *Private* is ironically contingent on what is determined by the *Public*. Decisions about consumer goods and services no

---

[2] See Michael J. Shapiro, *Reading the Postmodern Polity: Political Theory as Textual Practice* (Minneapolis and Oxford: University of Minnesota Press, 1992), pp. 46-47.

longer represent the conscious choices of private, interest-seeking, wealth-maximizing individuals but are symbols of "social status", "public prescription", and "public constructions" that are grounded in a foundational fantasy of modernity that involves the theoretical work of Connolly, Vattimo, Brennan, White, and Brown.

Intention

This book focuses on the way in which things are consumed in Singapore and Malaysia in terms of how the patterns of consumer behavior contingently abrogates, qualifies, and affirms the meaninglessness (and meaningfulness), the emptiness and vacuity, and the power and discipline of consumption in late modernity. It promotes the need to think critically about the patterns of consumption across the globe, and in Singapore and Malaysia, and how these public patterns determine the meaning of life in late modernity.

Modernity & Political Theory

The modern period in the disciplines of political philosophy, political theory, and political science may be traced to the writings of John Locke, George Berkeley, and David Hume who were grouped together and known as the "enlightenment" theorists although many political theorists recognize that the study of politics in the modern period began with the publication of the work of Thomas Hobbes' *Leviathan* in 1651. For the purposes of this discussion, Hobbes and the enlightenment theorists are considered modern theorists but are not thought of as theorists of modernity.

The difference between "modernity" and "modern" is clear. Modernity is both a civilizational period, and a set of theories that try to explain contemporary civilization. The concept of the "modern" on the other hand is that which is neither traditional nor backward. In the 1950s and 1960s, positivist political science suggested that the world about us could be quantified and systematically illustrated through a reliance on objective observation and deductive reasoning (of political, social, cultural, and economic phenomena) through the scientific method. Modernization theory provided political scientists with simple conceptual and pedagogical devices that separated tradition from modernity: that tradition was associated with backwardness, subjectivity, irrationality, and bias; while modernity and the modern period is characterized by advancement, progress, objectivity, rationality, technology, and logic. There were two main failures of positivist political science that dominated the study of modernity in the early years of the Cold War: (1) human beings could not be placed in neat boxes for observation and examination, and neither could human beings be reduced to numbers, digits, and data (almost without consequence) as seen in the early empirical theory and research of Dahl, Easton, Lipsett, Almond, Verba, Wildavsky, Cnudde, and Neubauer; and, (2) positivist political science cannot effectively predict human behavior or the outcome of even the most simply held democratic elections. It would be a major victory for neo-positivist political scientists all over the world and punters alike had they predicted the outcome of the 2000 U.S. presidential elections, perhaps even without the benefit of the New Hampshire primaries.

By the 1970s and 1980s, positivist political scientists began a period of hyper-entrenchment of their research in elegant, and highly sophisticated equations that continued deep into the turn of the last century. These quantitative refinements lend an aura of "authority" and "factual" legitimacy to the *science* of politics. The strength of neo-positivist political science (lead by academics such as Gary King at the Center for Basic Research in the Social Sciences at MIT-Harvard University) suggests that quantitative political science remains an important and significant minority within the academic discipline of political science.[3] This is not to imply that positivists

---

[3] The seductive language of the "positivists" continues to sound wonderfully "retro" today, and as pro-canonical as it was in its heyday in the late 1950s and early 1970s, seen for example, in the very early work of Michael J. Shapiro, "The House and the Federal Role: A Computer Simulation of Roll-Call Voting", *The American Political Science Review* (1968), 62 (2): 494-517; Michael J. Shapiro, "Rational Political Man: A Synthesis of Economic and Social-Psychological Perspectives", *The American Political Science Review*, (1969), 63(4): 1106-1119; and Paul M. Sniderman, and Jack Citrin, "Psychological Sources of Political

and neo-positivists did not possess their own internal mechanisms for self-critique and development as part of a movement towards general theory-building.

Rather than being anti-positivist for the sake of critical exposure, I think that it becomes increasingly important for political scientists interested in quantitative political science and "formal theory" to see for themselves the shortcomings of their chosen methods and practices; while at another part of the methodological spectrum, political scientists who are likely to be more concerned with normative movements and methods in the discipline of political science — consumers of work that consumes us — ought to recognize that even quantitative political science has a place under a plural political cosmology, though it appeared to have rapidly emptied itself out of vigor sometime in the middle of the last century. This work rejects the metanarratival belief systems propagated by the rhetoric of the power elite; discards the universal claims of scientism; and cautions modernists against ephemeral positivist explanations of reality (through enumeration, mathematical reductionism, econometric symbolism, and foundationalism) that serve to seduce the mind while diminishing the mind's capacity for creative reasoning and thoughtful explanations of modernity.

Modernity and Consumption: Theory, Politics and the Public in Singapore and Malaysia is about being comfortable with "contingency, and indeterminacy" (after White, 2000:6-9) and being satisfied with "less" rather than "more", ambiguity rather than clarity, and an increasingly blurred division of labor between fact and fiction. This position is allied with a recent and decontextualized ontological turning point in contemporary political theory itself:

> ...The sense of living in late modernity implies a greater awareness of the conventionality of much of what has been

---

Belief: "Self-Esteem and Isolationist Attitudes", *The American Political Science Review*, (1971), 65(2): 401-417. The relatively unique language of the "positivists" has ironically become commodified by modernity itself and may now be bought and sold across libraries, institutions, and other institutional marketplaces.

taken for certain in the modern West. The recent ontological shift might then be characterized generally as the result of a growing propensity to interrogate more carefully those "entities" presupposed by our typical ways of seeing and doing in the modern world.[4]

Stephen K. White's position makes the assumption that in order for life to exist in late modernity there must exist, at least some level, a certain sense of connectivity between the living being and her modern universe especially with regard to recognizing the largesse of western conventions and certitude. Other scholars however, conceive of the modern universe quite differently.

In the case of Gianni Vattimo, for example, the familiarity of being "modern" is the fundamental value in modernity; and that the central location of such a value in modern interpretation, in modern sense-perception, in modern worldviews, and in modern prescriptions of reality makes being modern invaluable to a point. That point is where the value of "being modern" is centrally located and sited in public spaces everywhere there are reminders of the modern epoch. The need to escape from the problems that beset modernity however does not diminish the central value of being modern. There is nowhere to escape but to modernity and to the value of being modern. This makes vital sense in Vattimo's work especially where attendant ethical considerations are eventually devalued in the face of modernity, and while universal resources find their way slowly but surely towards the modern public centerpiece, diminishing in their own private identity while increasingly adapting and adhering to the modern public one. Where the only alternative for intellectual empowerment might be through his concept of *pensiero debole* or "weak foundationalist thought".

Similarly, White's articulations are unequivocally and eloquently borne out in the hermeneutical discourse of his most recent work, *Sustaining Affirmation* (2000), where he reminds us of the distinction between strong and weak ontology. Strong ontologies such as the premodern and modern

---

[4] Stephen K. White, *Sustaining Affirmation: The Strengths of Weak Ontology in Political Theory* (Princeton and Oxford: Princeton University Press, 2000), p. 4; pp. 119-120.

ones are preferred by those communities and individuals who desire deep, metaphysical, epistemological anchors in a basic set of values, and beliefs that provide certitude and the promise of progress and advancement. But there appears to be a shortcoming to this articulation, and if I read White correctly, he argues that strong ontologies provide answers and solutions that potentially offer to "solve" the problems in late modernity. Yet such ontological resolution(s) "demands too much initial forgetfulness of contingency and indeterminacy...strong ontologies involve too much 'metaphysics'"(White, 2000:8). The problem here for the proponents, interlocutors, interrupters, investigators, and interpreters of late modernity is that they are more likely than not to entangle themselves and get caught between such strong and weak ontological designs as and when they (in effect, us) continue to negotiate and encounter modernity through a theoretical triple-link skein between White's weak ontology in *Sustaining Affirmation* (2000); Vattimo's *pensiero debole*, or weak foundationalist thought in *La fine della modernita* (1985), and Kathy E. Ferguson's conception of "mobile subject[ivitie]s" in *The Man Question: Visions of Subjectivity in Feminist Theory* (1993). Their complex theoretical persuasions are linked via a set of shared commonalities grounded by cultural symbols and economic signs, the political markers of a seemingly ageless modernity.

Modernity & the Mark of Men

The genealogical origins of culture reveal ancient man as marked by fear of the unknown. Unexplained events in nature were attributed to the presence of some divine or superior power. Truth was to be found in knowledge about the divine; as the interlocutors of such secret knowledge, the priesthood became as powerful as (the) god(s). The universe was small and limited to spatial metaphors based on vague abstractions of the sky, sea, and land. Public and private space were idealism and realism conflated. There were no distinctions or differences to be made between one kind of space and another, and if indeed such differences did exist, they were simple and uninteresting. Theory had no place in the ancient world. The dominant mode of knowledge involved ritual and sacrifice as expedient measures of simple social, political and cultural organization.

Medieval man was marked by faith in the unknown. Unexplained events in nature were attributed to the presence of a larger, secret, and divine-inspired master narrative, a larger and humanly unknowable masterplan that mortals could not conceivably understand nor were expected to understand. Truth was built on knowledge of religious and quasi-religious dogma that was founded on blind faith. Everything conceivable, and every conceivable thing in life, death, and the afterlife had been predestined by a greater power and an unseen entity. Fate was all that medieval man could rely on. As the interlocutors of faith, the priesthood remained powerful but were not as powerful as God since God was removed to the security of a secondary place and an infinite time zone where He could not be seen, nor heard, nor faulted. The earth was at the center of the universe and God's image was in a central position. Public space was occupied by God while private space was occupied by man. God could however visit man in his private space, though this was not possible in the other direction. The distinction between the public and the private was also seen in the division between the Church (or Mosque or Synagogue or Temple) and the State. Theory was based on criticism within the pre-Enlightened religiosity, theological doctrine and canonical dogma.

Modern Man is marked by science. Unexplained events in nature are explained by several competing and competent physical and emotive theories that quantify and diagnose civilization. The Divine masternarrative was displaced and replaced by the Scientific masternarrative. Truth was to be found in knowledge about science and technology, communications' revolutions, systemic, and informational analyses. The modern epoch displaced God and replaced him with Man. As the new interlocutors of the new faith, the scientists assumed power from the religious priests. The earth was no longer at the center of the Enlightened universe, although Man's image now occupied a central position in that cosmology. Man was considered the generic term for women. The distinction between public and private space was clear. Politics stopped at the door, and private space visited itself upon a public to the extent that it could not and should not remonstrate or violate the private space of another person. The critics of the modern period are postmodern theorists. However, such contemporary theorists as Michael J. Shapiro and William E. Connolly differ by the pastiche of their patterns while offering similar conceptual reflections under different shades of theoretical light. Shapiro for example, once argued, "Whereas contemporary modernists have sought to replace the destabilized bases of objectivity and subjectivity with alternative stabilities — for example, a reliable, universal, and felicitously aimed intersubjectivity in the case of Jurgen Habermas — critical postmodernist thinking is based on an acceptance of instability".[5]

Postmodern thought and postmodern thinkers — whether they be of the critical, non-Marxist, high octane, or regular "persuasions", and as Shapiro's title suggests, "intimations" — tend to accept unstable situations as a tacit recognition of the shifting background of serious and playful narratives that bear the marks and scars, for example, of urban life and urban legend — terrorism, crime, delinquency, husband-beating, murder, rape, arson, loss of property, loss of life, some Acts of God, and most acts of men. Some narratives are partially inherited while other narratives are partially understood and conceived in making sense of the world and of other possible worlds. Unexplained events in nature are always shifting and static. There is no need to explain anything in the natural world because it is mostly unnatural. The postmodern person resents masternarratives and possesses a high sense of disbelief in systemic productions of truth and reality. Truth no longer exists as singular theme but a plural one. There is no universe but multiple layers of multi-verses within the limitations of our three dimensional world. The existence of other worlds is not possible because our entire modern belief system is built and designed on a three-dimensional model of everything. If we could only perceive in six, eight or nine dimensions, death and the afterlife, our systems of morality and ethics, our modes of discipline and punishment would no longer exist. Public space,

---

[5] Michael J. Shapiro, "Eighteenth Century Intimations of Modernity: Adam Smith and the Marquis de Sade", *Political Theory* (1993), 21(2): 289-290.

rather than being fused, collapsed, conflated, or periodically separated in the past is now the primary determinant of private space. The public and private roles of contemporary political theory include: (1) the deconstruction of the discontinuities, inconsistencies, and contradictions in analytical philosophy (2) weakening the weak claims of foundationalism and reductionism in grand narratival strategies; (3) challenging and criticizing post-Enlightenment movements against the romantic movement, the reformation, metaphysical speculation and theology; (4) encountering and disparaging the modern penchant for positivism and the secular support for the quantification of the world and the enumeration of persons; (5) and to reintroduce pathos and pastiche as exemplars of passion, color, plurality, difference, and verve in the late modern post-digital age.[6]

Reviewing Modernity

Jean- Francois Lyotard argues, "Modernity consists in working at the limits of what was thought to be generally accepted, in thought as in the arts, in the sciences, in matters of technology, and in politics."[7] How do we know what public and private spaces are about apart from what we receive from our five(-to-six biological) senses? How can we effectively predict "quotidian" activities, and negotiate "immediate" tasks before us with some degree of reliability? How might it be possible to measure with discretion what it means to be modern? These three questions suggest that there must at least exist in language some degree of reasonable expectation on our part that demands a primary dissatisfaction — even disaffection — with our inherent, ordinary, and congenital means of understanding consumer life today. These questions are more than mere doubtful questions about modernity. These

---

[6] Consider the import of Shapiro's treatment of "Politicizing Ulysses — Rationalistic, Critical, and Genealogical Commentaries", Ch. 2, Michael J. Shapiro, *Reading the Postmodern Polity: Political Theory as Textual Practice* (Minneapolis and Oxford: University of Minnesota Press, 1992), pp. 18-36.

[7] Jean-Fancois Lyotard, *Political Writings* (Minneapolis: University of Minnesota Press, 1993), p 24.

doubts pressure us to consider alternative ways of gaining access to knowledge while we simultaneously gain access to the ways of understanding the knowledge that we are rapidly acquiring. Modern people (the moderns) are dependent on modes of measurement, pre-written scripts, complete stereotypes, name-card holders, and prefabricated structures to hold us in place. We are merely moving abstractions of life. We need speed, but can't go too fast for fear of flying-off the handle; we need reliability, but are not always reliable ourselves; we have a need for security, though we make others insecure; we need certitude, but that often detracts certainty from others; and we need perspective, but not too much lest it throws us off balance. Some people want more of modernity, some less, others, none at all, mainly because it is too troublesome and difficult to do the thinking ourselves. Modernity, in that sense, is about revealing perspectives on life. The three questions also require an ability to step back and take a second view of life. The second view is like looking at the scenery, as Neil Postman once mentioned, through the rear view mirror of a speeding car as opposed to looking at it through the windshield. It is about a quest for knowledge over our shoulders. The quest for knowledge in the history of ideas is similar to looking for things but with temporary glances to images of a recent past. These glances fill the little blank spaces between confronting the immediate reality that we face, and the disappearing reality behind us, the disappearing view behind us, the view that eventually becomes so small as to be unrecognizable. The quest for *sophia*, knowledge, or *scientia*, is an expedition that requires a certain sense of disbelief, and a strong sense of the present. The quest for knowledge seems to require a certain sense of disbelief, or at least the temporary suspension of our belief systems because we have to be able to doubt the world around us and not immediately accept whatever might be placed before us. There is a need for a strong sense of the present to "ground" us in some reality at some point in time and space.

Variations on the theme of modernity are not new. The history of ideas suggest an accumulation of different fragments in the disparate work of St. Augustine of Hippo, St. Thomas Aquinas, Immanuel Kant, Sören Kierkegaard, Friedrich Nietzsche, and Jean-Paul Sartre. Their political, social, and cultural philosophies continue to resound within and among the interpretations held variously by Gilles Deleuze, Felix Guattari, Sheldon S. Wolin, Charles Taylor, Jurgen Habermas, Judith Butler, Michael J. Shapiro, William E. Connolly, Aryeh Botwinick, Stephen K. White, Susan Moller Okin, Kathy E. Ferguson, Wendy Brown, Quentin Skinner, Charles Larmore, Gianni Vattimo, Thomas L. Dumm, and J. Donald Moon — to name several but not the entire list of proponents of theoretically deep voices that apodictically interrogate modernity on a daily basis. The following section, here and below, reflect some of these voices with the main themes that tie the chapters of this book together.

CONNOLLY

While Shapiro tends towards "language" and "media" centered theoretical analyses of discursive formations, William E. Connolly has carved out his career on a "pluralism-plus" motif.[8] Connolly believes that a crucial aspect of cosmopolitanism's modernity works in a complex matrix involving the correlatives of speed, cosmopolitanism and concentric cultures (Connolly, 2000:596-618). Connolly's says that we are short on time, but potentially long on the plurality of cosmopolitan complexity. He makes a crucial and succinct distinction of modern cosmopolitan life where the political culture of cosmopolitan cities is contingent on the ways in which (1) "time is being sped up" (Connolly, 2000:597); and (2) "the [greater] speed at which we perform tasks today tends towards softening up universal explanations of life" (Connolly, 2000:609). The "speeding up of time", and the "softening up of universal categories" makes it difficult, indeed, almost impossible to sustain the value and applicability of universal laws. However, Connolly is a serious and skeptical optimist. For him, cosmopolitan modernity lives in the ironic metaphors that center on concentrated images of culture (Connolly, 2000:602).

In an earlier work on the *Ethos of Pluralization* (1995) Connolly speaks of two main kinds of consumption in modernity: exclusionary goods and

---

[8] This is stridently different from the younger Connolly as seen in the first edition of the award winning *Terms of Political Discourse* (1974).

inclusionary goods. Connolly's interpretation of exclusionary and inclusionary goods falls under the rubric of Foucault's architectonic unities of systems that are concerned with "internal coherences, axioms, deductive connexions, compatibilities" (Michel Foucault, *The Archeology of Knowledge and the Discourse on Language*, 1972:5). This ties in his concepts with the ontological strategy of postmodernism that is closely associated with Foucault. The synchrony between Connolly's concepts and Foucault's projections in the "Analysis of Wealth" is uncanny. It is exemplified in the American political economy:

> built around the illusory promise of universalizing exclusionary goods. As it becomes increasingly clear to a variety of constituencies that they are losing ground in this elusive quest, they either drop out of institutional politics or vent their anger on the most vulnerable scapegoats available. An economy built around the elusive promise to generalize exclusionary goods eventually turns against the promise of pluralism, as many caught in the binds it creates respond with restrictive versions of family life, sexual practice, gender authority, race relations, consumption practices, and norms of self-sufficiency rooted in rosy memories of the past.[9]

Carefully constructed and stilted with style, this instructive verse bends our thoughts towards states and economies outside America, contributing to a re-interrogation of the foundational questions of the modern commitment to political power. We do not have to go far to witness the extent of the successes, and the depths of the global impact of these exclusionary goods in the private stores of wealth of the political, social, cultural, and economic

---

[9] William E. Connolly, *The Ethos of Pluralization* (Minneapolis and London: University of Minnesota Press, 1995), 83.

elite of Singapore and Malaysia.[10] Is there an alternative, a panacea, to such exclusivity? Connolly suggests that,

> An inclusive good reverses these pressures. It is susceptible to generalization because its private value increases as it is extended; because its unit social costs are reduced through extension; because state supports for its development and extension reduce the per capita public costs of meeting consumption needs in its domain; and because it curtails economic sources of the politics of revenge against vulnerable constituencies.[11]

Connolly goes on to exemplify his arguments with illustrations from health care in the United States, the shift from private insurance programs to universal state-sponsored medical political economy; and the re-concentration of public monies towards infrastructural development "in-between" urban and rural America through rapid, people-mover systems. His suggestions regarding the differences between the mass desire for exclusive goods is part of an argument about redirecting our thoughts away from individual expenditure patterns towards taking note and radicalizing the way in which public consumption takes place.

Connolly's concept is useful for the study of consumption in Singapore and Malaysia where the problems of modernity are stridently similar within a milieu of traditional, cultural and religious resistance to western modernity. Connolly offers all irascible and petulant moderns a powerful and radical pluralist strategy for reconciling the use of private and public time, space, and money in modernity. His strategy continues to evoke important and instructive devices for unlearning the problems that currently appear in the west. Although Connolly has not designed nor designated his

---

[10] Compare with the analyses of Russell J. Dalton, "Generational Change in Elite Political Beliefs: The Growth of Ideological Polarization", *The Journal of Politics* (1987), 49(4): 976-997.

[11] Connolly, *The Ethos of Pluralization, ibid.*

strategy for use worldwide, I think that his strategy provides a parsimonious theoretical concept for understanding Southeast Asian modernity and consumption in general, and, for understanding theory, politics, and the concept of the public in Singapore and Malaysia. With the Asian putsch for modernization built on modified versions of the advanced industrial west, the problems that now exist in western modernity will eventually arise in Singapore and Malaysia regardless of how traditionalists and fundamentalists try to subvert the processes of modernity in Southeast Asia. We can already see partial images of Southeast Asia's future in the present political economies of North America and many (former western) European countries. Connolly's strategy on consumption is this: Connolly argues that exclusionary goods decrease the private value while increasing the private costs; exclusionary goods also accentuates the social costs to the detriment of society; and increases the costs to the state and hence the general public burden (Connolly, 1995: 82). Therefore, the state and civil society organizations must cooperate to reduce the consumption of exclusionary goods over inclusionary ones in terms of state and civil society measures and policy implementation (especially of large infrastructural projects) vis-à-vis the *ways* in which goods and services are likely to be consumed rather than the *type* of goods and services that are likely to be produced if only to avoid advanced economic recidivism in these countries.

VATTIMO

In *The End of Modernity* (1988) Gianni Vattimo defines modernity as "that era where the modern becomes a value, or rather, it becomes *the* fundamental value to which all other values refer" (Vattimo, 1989:99).[12] Therefore if the modern is in fact the main value, and consumption — in theory and in practice — becomes subordinated to "the modern" than we have "consumption" embracing all the traits that are considered modern: this

---

[12] Gianni Vattimo, *The End of Modernity* (Baltimore: Johns Hopkins University Press, 1988), p. 99.

leads to a situation where material and non-material consumption patterns exist for the sake of representing modernity. Therefore consumers continue to consume goods and services because these material and non-material goods and services make the consumers modern, and to be modern is to remain relevant, and to remain relevant is to continue to be needed. Where the definition of modernity as the primus inter pares value is highlighted, we immediately see the importance of consuming material and non-material goods as emblematic of staying alive, staying relevant, controlling. For Vattimo, the end of modernity refers to the belief — in his conceptual method of *pensiero debole* or weak foundationalist thought — that all values are meshed and work themselves into the single value of the modern. There is no need for any other value in the world of consumption, indeed, in modernity, since all past, present, and future values are united in the value of "the modern".

BRENNAN

Theresa Brennan offers similarly didactic work, though apparently less compassionate, in her recent book, *Exhausting Modernity* (2000). Brennan argues that we now have faster and more efficient means of extracting the surplus value of natural substances needed for capitalist production (Brennan, 2000:118) that is evidently built on consumption in terms of her interpretation of a Faustian foundational fantasy:

> The desire for instant gratification, the desire to be waited upon, the envious desire to imitate the original, are more troubling in that their universality is more difficult to locate...the desire to know by dismembering and destroying...or the denial of time in relation to power and control.[13]

---

[13] Theresa Brennan, *Exhausting Modernity: Grounds for a New Economy* (London and New York: Routledge, 2000), p.160.

Building on the calculated desires of unthinking moderns, the supporters of neoliberal institutionalism and capitalist reproduction continues to reap huge benefits from mass produced goods and services maintaining the essence of the Faustian fantasy as it is reiterated in consumer behavior and reified in the minds of modern consumers.

WHITE

Stephen K. White's *Sustaining Affirmation* (2000) offers the modern imagination "a greater awareness of the conventionality of what has been taken for certain in the modern West".[14] How do we know for sure that convention is sufficiently knowledgeable a guide as to comfort our belief in the future, and more importantly to act as the harbinger of advancement and progress? Agreeing with Connolly's assessment of late modernity in the latter's *Ethos of Pluralization*, White argues that the conditions of late modernity have "accelerated the drive for further cultural pluralization" and secondly, there is more "aggressive fundamentalization of existing identities".[15] It isn't so much that together, these two theorists have given Americans, and indeed, all non-violent human beings a complex cautionary ontology that engulfs the events surrounding September 11, 2001, in New York City's World Trade Center, the bastion and symbol of global consumption, and global capitalism, if we interpret their work as offering us contemporary philosophical precautions and reminders against the fundamentalization and resistance that terrorism proffers. Rather, the point here is that Connolly and White reveal that domestic public space is not invulnerable to the power of identities, ignorant and unenlightened, that embrace religious fundamentalism, fascism, ultra nationalism, and hyper-communalism despite our search, and Connolly's optimism for discovering — and at some level, disavowing — an affective, self-sustaining disaffection with (the conditions of late) modernity.

---

[14] White, *Sustaining Affirmation*, *ibid.*
[15] White, *ibid.*, p. 120.

BROWN

In her excellent overture to Nietzsche's concept of *ressentiment* in *States of Injury: Power and Freedom in Late Modernity* (1995), Wendy Brown reminds us that "Foucault takes modernity's most pervasive mode of social power" to be disciplinary power (brown, 1995:19). The power of Brown's assessment however derives not from her reading of Foucault exposure of crime, discipline, and punishment; nor his re-conceptualizations of the discursive formations of power, truth and madness of this, "our" civilization. Rather, we are drawn to Brown's comment and sustained energy in terms of the deconstruction of familial hierarchies of control:

> Within a general sexual division of labor — female labor within and male outside the household — two roughly contradictory tendencies unfold in the course of capitalism's development. On one side as household production shrinks and (increasingly industrialized) socialized production takes its place, women's varied tasks associated with the double-sided reproduction of labor — generating the new, replenishing what exists — are increasingly privatized and confined to the household, while men's work is increasingly socialized and removed from the home. The steady widening of the spatial separation between "home" and "work" has significant indirect effects: women's work in the home becomes less visible as work, and the constitutive values of the realm of civil society are distinguished form the order of the family...on the other side, the steady movement of "women's work" into the market (production of food and clothing, education and socialization of children, service work of every variety) increasingly reduces women's work in the home to service functions and also erodes the separation between home and market, rendering the membrane between them highly permeable in both directions (Brown, *States of Injury*, 1995: 144).

The disappearance and gradual invisibility of (the recognition of the value of) women's work (and of women *per se*) contradicts the movement of women's work into public spaces and the market spaces where much of consumption takes place. The contradiction arises because the incongruent arrangements of the international neoliberal political economy have resulted in a mismatched, lopsided, and gendered division of labor in late modernity: women cannot be "physically" present at two places at the same time. Yet with the technologization of the home and the market place, it is now possible to be in two places at the same time at least theoretically or cyberspatially: a human being can potentially monitor the household with internet-web cameras positioned in the private/home space while at work any where else in the world. The permeability that Brown suggests increasingly burdens the role and gendered division of labor in the politics of consumption because the structure of patriarchal discursive formations annihilate the need for men to serve home-bound functions (although there appear to be well advertised detractors) and for women to be expected to carry their "traditional" burdens in addition to the expectation of entering the work force and market places of consumption. The net result, says Brown, is the erosion of the familial structure in (what I have paraphrased as the work-gender contradiction thesis). The socio-pathetic contradictions have indeed resulted in feminism as being an historical outcome of such eroded arrangements.

Summary

This introduction helped what Lyotard calls the ability to "distinguish intelligence from the paranoia that gave rise to 'modernity'"[16] and provided the general theoretical background of modernity, the movement within the classical and historicist debates on the public/private tension, and introduced the major writers and the concepts who influenced the concepts used in this book. The following chapters explain the theories, politics, and the idea of "the public" in terms of the hierarchies of political discourses within the discursive formations of the family, education, narrative, and public space that are explained and analyzed within the modernity/resistance frame (mRf).

---

[16] Jean-Fancois Lyotard, *Political Writings,* "Tomb of the Intellectual" (Minneapolis: University of Minnesota Press, 1993), p. 7.

References

Bianchi, Marina. ed. 1998. *The Active Consumer: Novelty and Surprise in Consumer Choice*. New York: Routledge.

Bocock, Robert. 1993. *Consumption*. London and New York: Routledge.

Brennan, Theresa. 2000. *Exhausting Modernity*. London and New York: Routledge University Press.

Brown, Wendy. 1995. *States of Injury: Power and Freedom in Late Modernity*. Princeton, N.J: Princeton University Press.

Bryant, W. Keith. 1990. *The Economic Organization of the Household*. Cambridge and New York: Cambridge University Press.

Burk, Marguerite C. 1968. *Consumption Economics: A Multidisciplinary Approach*. New York: Wiley.

Campbell, Colin. 1987. *The Romantic Ethic and the Spirit of Modern Consumerism*. Oxford and New York: Basil Blackwell.

Connolly, William E. 1995. *The Ethos of Pluralization*. Minneapolis and London: University of Minnesota Press.

Connolly, William E. 2000. "Speed, Concentric Circles and Cosmopolitanism", *Political Theory,* **28**(5): 596-618.

Dalton, Russell J. 1987. "Generational Change in Elite Political Beliefs: The Growth of Ideological Polarization", *The Journal of Politics*, **49**(4): 976-997.

Deaton, Angus. 1992 *Understanding Consumption*. Clarendon Press, Oxford and Oxford University Press, New York.

Foucault, Michel. 1972. *The Archeology of Knowledge and the Discourse on Language*. New York: Pantheon Books.

Frith, Katherine Toland. 1996. *Advertising in Asia: Communication, Culture, and Consumption*. Ames: Iowa State University Press.

Galbraith, John Kenneth. 1996. *The Good Society: The Humane Agenda*. Boston: Houghton Mifflin.

Green, H. A. John. 1971. *Consumer Theory*. Harmondsworth: Penguin.

Habermas, Jurgen. 1985. *The Structural Transformation of the Public Sphere: An Inquiry into a Category of Bourgeois Society*, Cambridge, MA: MIT Press.

Henderson, David K. 1993. *Interpretation and Explanation in the Human Sciences*. Albany: State University of New York Press.

Jackson, Stevi and Shaun Moores. eds. 1995. *The Politics of Domestic Consumption: Critical Readings*. London and New York: Prentice Hall-Harvester Wheatsheaf.

Kamal, S. 1988. *The New Economic Policy After 1990*. Kuala Lumpur: Malaysian Institute of Economic Research.

Karni, R. S. 1980. *Bibliography of Malaysia & Singapore*. Kuala Lumpur: Penerbit Universiti Malaya.

Lee, Martyn J. 1993. *Consumer Culture Reborn: The Cultural Politics of Consumption*. London and New York: Routledge.

Lyotard, Jean-Fancois. 1993. *Political Writings*. Minneapolis: University of Minnesota Press.

Mahathir, Mohamed. 1998. *The Way Forward*. London: Weidenfeld & Nicolson.

Miller, Daniel. 1987. *Material Culture and Mass Consumption*. Oxford and New York: Basil Blackwell.

Moffat, Robert Scott. 1878. *The Economy of Consumption: An Omitted Chapter in Political Economy*. London: C. K. Paul.

Nystrom, Paul Henry. 1929. *Economic Principles on Consumption*. New York: Ronald Press.

Orlie, Melissa A. 2001. "Political Capitalism and Consumption" in Botwinick, Aryeh, and Connolly, William E. eds. *Democracy and Vision: Sheldon Wolin and the Vicissitudes of the Political.* Oxford and Princeton: Princeton University Press.

Pearce, Ivor F. A. 1964. *Contribution to Demand Analysis.* Oxford: Clarendon Press.

Roche, Daniel. 1998. *France des Lumires* (France in the Enlightenment) trans. by Arthur Goldhammer. Cambridge, Massachusetts: Harvard University Press.

Rorty, Richard. 1989. *Contingency, Irony and Solidarity.* Cambridge: Cambridge University Press.

Sack, Robert David. 1992. *Place, Modernity, and the Consumer's World: A Relational Framework for Geographical Analysis.* Baltimore: Johns Hopkins University Press.

Shapiro, Michael J. 1968. "The House and the Federal Role: A Computer Simulation of Roll-Call Voting", *The American Political Science Review*, **62**, 2: 494-517.

Shapiro, Michael J. 1969. "Rational Political Man: A Synthesis of Economic and Social-Psychological Perspectives", *The American Political Science Review*, **63**(4): 1106-1119.

Shapiro, Michael, J. 1992. *Reading the Postmodern Polity: Political Theory as Textual Practice.* Minneapolis and Oxford: University of Minnesota Press.

Shapiro, Michael J. 1993. "Eighteenth Century Intimations of Modernity: Adam Smith and the Marquis de Sade", *Political Theory*, **21**(2): 273-293.

Shutz, Eric A. 2001. *Markets and Power: The 21st Century Command Economy.* Armonk, New York: M. E. Sharpe.

Sniderman, Paul, M. and Citrin, Jack. 1971. "Psychological Sources of Political Belief: Self-Esteem and Isolationist Attitudes", *The American Political Science Review*, **65**(2): 401-417.

Vattimo, Gianni. [1985]1988. *La Fine Della Modernita. The End of Modernity.* Baltimore: The John Hopkins University Press.

White, Stephen K. 2000. *Sustaining Affirmation: The Strengths of Weak Ontology in Political Theory.* Princeton and Oxford: Princeton University Press.

Xenos, Nicholas. 1989. *Scarcity and Modernity.* London and New York: Routledge.

Consumption

The first thing is that in studying the rationality of dominions, I try to establish interconnections which are not isomorphisms. Secondly, when I speak of power relations of the forms of rationality which can rule and regulate them, I am not referring to Power — with a capital P — dominating and imposing its rationality upon the totality of the social body. In fact, there are power relations. They are multiple and have different forms, they can be in play in family relations, or within an institution, or an administration – or between a dominating and a dominated class power relations having specific forms of rationality, forms which are common to them.

Michel Foucault
Politics, Philosophy, Culture: Interviews and Other Writings (1988)

28 Modernity and Consumption

> If greed was taken to be the fuel of the capitalist engine, then surely rationality was the driver...competition in the market place requires that the buyer knows not only what is good for him but also what is good. If the seller produces nothing of value, as determined by a rational marketplace, then he loses out. It is the assumption of rationality among buyers that spurs competitors to become winners, and winners to keep on winning. When it is assumed that a buyer is unable to make rational decisions, laws are passed to invalidate transactions, as, for example, those which prohibit children from making contracts. In America, there even exists in law a requirement that sellers must tell the truth about their products, for if the buyer has no protection from false claims, rational decision-making is seriously impaired.
>
> Neil Postman
Amusing Ourselves to Death (1985).

Foucault's notion of multiple power relations in the quote above is interpreted as bearing the cautionary tale of dividing the structure of consumption into two distinct processes. The first process being the language of the dominant bourgeois class, the economic and political elite, who as Marx said, are the owners of the factors of production. The second process reveals the language of the dominated class, an apparently seamless neo-proletarian "corps" that exists as a class in itself unable to transform itself by the bootstraps into a class for itself because it speaks a pigeon variety of the dominant language of the bourgeoisie. The pigeon that is spoken is self-limiting in its imitation of the master vocabulary weakening potential efforts to challenge its subalternity, its inferior position. The powerful framing structure of consumption arises out of the Postman quote where rationality and legal-rational discourses permeate the relations between the processes of the structure of consumption. A high rate of return is earned on consumption practices that are constituted around the vocabularies of domination.

Analysis and Consumption

Public consumption is one of the most under-analyzed and most easily overlooked characteristic of modernity as indicated and clearly illustrated in the work of David Kolb (1986);[1] Zygmunt Bauman (1989; 1990);[2] Anthony Giddens (1990;1991;2000);[3] John Tomlinson (1991);[4] Louis K. Dupre (1993);[5] Arjun Appadurai (1996);[6] José Maurício (2000);[7] and Theresa Brennan (2000).[8]

There are many ways to interpret "consumption" in modernity but most work tends to fall within four broad categories: (1) empirical studies by government and official state agencies; (2) empirical studies by NGOs and

---

[1] David Kolb, *The Critique of Pure Modernity: Hegel, Heidegger, and After* (Chicago: University of Chicago Press, 1986).

[2] Zygmunt Bauman, *Modernity and the Holocaust* (Ithaca, N.Y.: Cornell University Press, 1989); his *Modernity and Ambivalence* (Oxford: Polity Press, 1991); and Zygmunt Bauman, "Modernity, Racism, Extermination" in Les Back and John Solomos (eds.), *Theories of Race and Racism* (New York : Routledge, 2000).

[3] Anthony Giddens, *The Consequences of Modernity* (Stanford: Stanford University Press, 1990); his *Modernity and Self-Identity: Self and Society in the Late Modern Age* (Polity Press, 1991); and his "The Globalizing of Modernity" in David Held and Anthony McGrew (eds.) *The Global Transformations Reader: An Introduction to the Globalization Debate* (Malden, MA: Polity Press, 2000).

[4] Tomlinson, John. *Cultural Imperialism* (London: Pinter Publishers, 1991).

[5] Louis K. Dupre, *Passage to Modernity: An Essay in the Hermeneutics of Nature and Culture* (New Haven: Yale University Press, 1993).

[6] Arjun Appadurai, *Modernity at Large: Cultural Dimensions of Globalization* (Minneapolis and London: University of Minnesota Press, 1996).

[7] José Maurício, *Social Creativity, Collective Subjectivity, and Contemporary Modernity* (New York: St. Martin's Press, 2000).

[8] Theresa Brennan, *Exhausting Modernity: Grounds for a New Economy* (New York: Routledge, 2000).

academic institutions; (3) advanced qualitative techniques that range from scientific accounting to empirical ethnographic methods; and (4) a mixture of the preceding three techniques. Naturally, these four categories are not independently autonomous and tend to overlap one another as if their public boundaries and private spaces were artificial and porous. This itself leads us to acknowledge that:

> The homologous logic of modernity constructs spaces in private and in public that are monochromatic, bland, and efficient where "expertise" indicates "precision"; "substance" implies "knowledge"; and "norm" signifies "value". The homology of modernity allows us to recognize one another — despite differences in technological dependence — this is because of a common genealogy traceable to rational thought, empiricism, and the scientific method".[9]

These characteristics of rationality, empirical thought, and the scientific method are may be tied into three main approaches in the study of consumption in the social sciences in general and in political science in particular.

Most social scientific approaches both yield and project three argentiferous dimensions: the economic dimension, the cultural dimension, and the political dimension (Nystrom, 1929; Burk, 1968; Green, 1971; Sack, 1992; Bocock, 1993; Bianchi, 1998). Burk's approach, for example, was born out of positivist social science in the late 1950s and early 1960s, and represents a rudimentary attempt at a multidisciplinary approach to modern consumption as reflected in the work of Ivor Pearce (1964) and captured over thirty years later in the examination of "theory-dependent" and "transcendent preferences" justifications — for example — within the human sciences (Henderson, 1993).

More recent work by Bryant and Roche adopt a Western historical orientation in *France des Lumires* (France in the Enlightenment), analyzed

---

[9] See the "Introduction" in Antonio L. Rappa, "Modernity and the Politics of Public Space", *Innovation: European Journal of Social Science Research*, Vol. 15, No. 1 (2002).

the microcosm of daily, city-life as the Ancient Regime unfolded and enfolded 18th century Europe through quotidian activities that consumed both aristocrat and peasant in the expansion and contraction of public and private spaces (Bryant, 1990; Roche, 1998).

The wisdom of conventional social science suggests that modernity is perhaps best explained in three general hypotheses:

1. politics determines economics;
2. economics determines politics; and,
3. culture determining economics and politics

The Political Argument (Politics Determines Economics)

In the "political argument", modernity is about realist power and liberal "control". This position highlights the importance of political decision-making over economic output; or elite structural analyses of the bureaucracy in the regulation of financial markets for example. The "political argument" tends to focus on problems in the political structures and institutions themselves: the bureaucracy, the legislature, the executive, and the judiciary. One end of this school of thought involves policy analyses where the public policy processes, research and other activities in advanced industrialized countries are considered knowledge *de rigueur* in academic circles. As Deborah A. Stone argues in *Policy Paradox and Political Reason*, "Policy is centrally about classification and differentiation about how we do and should categorize in a world where categories are not given…policy arguments are convincing to the extent that they give a satisfying account of the rightness of treating cases alike or differently" (Stone, 1991:308). This argument suggests the following aphorism, "resistance and consumption are appropriate means to political objectives in modernity". The political and social scientists associated with this approach include luminaries such as Alvin Gouldner, Gabriel A. Almond, Murray Edelman, Peter J. Katzenstein, G. Bingham Powell, Seymour Martin Lipsett, Robert A. Dahl, Guillermo O'Donnell and Robert Keohane.

The Economic Argument (Economics Determines Politics)

There are two main branches in the social science literature when the argument "economics determines politics" is used. The first argument tends to employ classical Marxist and neoMarxist modes of analyses involving the class, social structure, new proletarianism, and the events surrounding the international capitalist system. The second branch uses non-Marxist statistical and econometric analyses to determine the equilibrium position for the best possible outcomes under various economic models. When problems arise in this case, the demonization tends to involve the political ideology of capitalism and the liberal state in the first branch, and market imperfections, structural faults, and market failure in the second branch. This argument suggests the aphorism, "resistance and consumption are the means to (historicized) economic objectives in modernity". This position is often associated with the work of the "third" generation of the Frankfurt School; and similar work offered by Tom Bottomore, James O'Connor, Terrell Carver, John Maynard Keynes, John Kenneth Galbraith, and Robert Reich.

The Culture Argument (Culture Determines both Politics and Economics)

This set of explanations in the social sciences tends to focus on the softer side of society. Society is seen as a series of competing cultural interests that override and modify the political and economic structures of society. Scholars belonging to this school of thought tend to magnify and aggrandize such cultural norms such as the existence of a "Confucian belief system", a "Protestant Ethic", "an obedient and compliant public", or the "Society above Self". A subset within the culture argument is the motif of mass cultural consumption, commodity fetishization (with neo-Marxist elements), and the commodification of traditional culture into goods and services for sale and purchase. At one end of the culture spectrum, work on consumption tends to move into the area of Cultural Studies. This argument suggests the aphorism, "resistance and consumption are the primary cultural determinants in modernity", and is often associated with the work of Edward W. Said, Charles Taylor, Roland Barthes, Paul De Man, Rey Chow, and Aijaz Ahmad to name a few.

mRf: Sub-Hypotheses

The modernity/Resistance frame (mRf) is a necessary and sufficient theoretical method that is made up of five central concepts (described in detail below) that helps examine and analyze any given text while simultaneously maintaining the importance of the themes of (1) the public and private tension, (2) marginal resistance, and (3) discipline and punishment within discursive formations.

Political, economic, and cultural analyses are necessary but not sufficient conditions for the study of consumption because there is too much "slippage" due to their narrow, unidirectional foci. The Modernity/Resistance frame however takes into account much of the "slippage" and, in a sense, "picks up the slack" made by the preceding three arguments. There are four premises in mRf:

Sub-Hypotheses:
1. Modernity is about power and coercion;
2. Consumers cannot escape the homogenizing effect of modernity;
3. Resistance to modernity occurs at many levels within the political, economic, and cultural structures;
4. Consumption is a form of resistance against modernity.

mRf

Modernity's homogenizing effect pressures the political, economic, and cultural institutions to fragment sites of resistance across all modes of resistance and consumption. Therefore, the study of modernity necessitates the study of ethnic, class, gender, and language dimensions as sites of consumer resistance.

The most dogmatic of moderns would reject the mRf as a method of analysis simply because it exposes the vacuity of their moral authority and delegitimizes their fraudulent cosmological belief system. The dogmatists and their dogmas would have us believe that there can be no transplantation of political and social software from one point on the globe to another, especially if (1) the software was invented overseas; and (2) the software entails reworking and re-looking at the ways in which tangible and intangible goods and services are consumed and how these modes and patterns of consumption are affecting and impacting consumer life, and more importantly the political life of human beings within cosmopolitan sites on a daily basis.

The mRf is based on the work of contemporary political and social theorists studying life in late modernity. There is a large pool of political and social theorists from which one might approach and attempt to understand late modernity. However, the ones that are most relevant to this cause are Gianni Vattimo, William E. Connolly, Theresa Brennan, Stephen K. White, and Wendy Brown and the conceptualizations that were untimely, perhaps somewhat unfairly, plucked from their investigations of modernity from the earlier section on 'Reviewing Modernity'.

mRf Concepts

(1) The fundamental value in modernity is being modern (Vattimo).
(2) Exclusionary goods decrease the private value while increasing the private costs; exclusionary goods accentuate the social costs to the detriment of society; and increases the costs to the state and the overall public debt and burden (Connolly).
(3) Consumption involves a Faustian foundational fantasy of horror (Brennan).

(4) Greater awareness of the conventionality of what has been taken for certain in the modern west ought to be interrogated: domestic public space is not invulnerable (White).
(5) The work-gender contradiction thesis (Brown).

This book does not intend to replicate the basic data found in statistical information of Singapore and Malaysia, but rather explore further considerations that arise out of these two countries' political, cultural and economic matrices. The following section reveals how the book is organized while the section at the end of this chapter highlights several generalizations of consumption patterns in Singapore and Malaysia based on the following conceptual themes symbolized by **FV, EG, IG, FH, VP, WG**.

(1) **[FV]** = fundamental value (after Vattimo)
The fundamental value in modernity is being modern (Vattimo).

(2) **[EG]** = exclusionary goods (after Connolly)
Exclusionary goods decrease the private value of consumption goods in Singapore and Malaysia while increasing the costs to private consumers; exclusionary goods accentuate the social costs to the detriment of the Singapore and Malaysian environment; and increases the costs to the Republic of Singapore and the Federation of Malaysia in terms of total public debt and burden (after Connolly). Note that **[IG]** = inclusionary goods.

(3) **[FH]** = the foundational Faustian fantasy of horror (after Brennan)
Consumption involving a Faustian foundational fantasy of horror: the extent to which the punitive state is willing and capable of ordering its coercive agencies (the powerful) against criminals (the powerless) who then form the

foundational fantasy of horror for the majority upholders of the law in Singapore and Malaysia that they wish to avoid.

(4) **[VP]** = vulnerability of the public consumer (after White)
Greater awareness of the conventionality of what has been taken for certain in the modern west ought to be interrogated: domestic public space is not invulnerable and is similarly challengeable and contestable in Singapore and Malaysia as the examples will illustrate.

(5) **[WG]** = work gender imbalances and contradictions (after Brown)
The work-gender contradiction is especially present for women consumers in Singapore and Malaysia as the examples will show.

These symbols indicate the meaning of the concepts against the evidence in the context of Singapore and Malaysia modernity and consumption. These 5 concepts come together with the (1) public and private tension, (2) marginal resistance, and (3) discipline and punishment within discursive formations to form the major conceptual themes examined in this book. The following section deals with the local nature of Singapore and Malaysian modernity and the specific work done on these countries.

Singaporean and Malaysian Modernity

Within the area of purely economic consumption studies of Singaporean modernity and Malaysian modernity, similar methods of research are used as seen in terms of social scientific strategies and methods used and advanced by Western countries and those in the "First World". An outdated pamphlet, *Test of Leser's Model of Household Consumption Expenditure in Malaysia and Singapore* was published by the Institute of Southeast Asian Studies in Singapore (Arief, 1980a). This was followed by a longer study titled, *Study of Household Consumption in Malaysia and Singapore* (S. Arief, 1980b). Clearly the work thus far has been restricted to government reports, descriptions and narrow econometric analyses of the topic. An interesting socio-cultural approach to consumption appeared in an edited volume by B. H. Chua, titled, *Consumption in Asia: Lifestyles and Identities* (2000). An interesting, four volume edited work by Daniel Miller, *Consumption: Critical Concepts in the Social Sciences* (2001), traces the nature of consumption across a wide spectrum of consumption specialists across the globe. The four volumes provide in-depth analyses that begin with the theories and issues in the consumption studies; trace the histories and regional developments of consumption; examines the various disciplinary approaches to consumption; and, concludes with the "objects", "subjects" and "mediations" of consumption. However, there is currently no specific work to account for how political science, and indeed, social and political theory might begin examining consumption in terms of the nature of the public in Singapore and Malaysia. The following section explains why consumption is political, and what the basic nature of consumption reveals.

What Makes Consumption "Political"?

What makes consumption political in Singapore, Malaysia or in any other part of the globe? While there can be no comprehensive tome to comprehensively represent the consumption patterns of any state or region perfectly, there are proto-theoretical possibilities. One such possibility arises out of the idea that consumption rewards the consumer and privileges her with a certain amount of power — the power of purchasing or selling a product or service — in addition to the satisfaction derived from consuming that good or service at that point in time and space across economic markets (Shutz, 2001). For every sale and purchase of a good and service, something is gained and something lost in terms of the quantum of satisfaction derived at the point of sale and purchase. This politicizes the issue of consumption because of the limited value that markets and their users place on products and services: raising and lowering or edging products and services out of the markets, while allowing new entrants at the same time. This push and pull tension of markets and their makers creates opportunities for the existence of those who advance the cause of progress and change, and those who resist such transformations.

The propensity to consume generates a hierarchy of social and cultural influence(s) which are imbalanced and differential because consumption goods and services are differentially priced. Product differentiation, product life-span and life-cycles; the influence of civil society associations (including cultural, religious, and traditional forms of resistance to modernity); the volatility of markets; the regulatory effects of state, regional and national governments; an ever widening range of goods and services; and political activism represent significant contributory factors to the creation of status, class and image construction that are needed, indeed, required in order to survive modernity.

There is a politics of consumption where the resulting vectors hinge on the premises described earlier: where there can be no genuine disengagement from international consumption society (and the anachronism of autarkic economic arrangements and systems found in contemporary politics of Laos, Myanmar, Cuba, and North Korea) non-consumers in modernity that seeks homogeneity; the development of resistance within the structures that uphold modern complexes of consumption — from tangible stock and trade markets to intangible e-commerce and cyberspatial ones; and the ironic use of consumption as a way of resisting modernity — by consuming as little as possible and in ways that do not invite further consumption, or further need for consuming goods and services against future time: a movement against modernity that subverts the possibilities for environmental and cultural degradation. There is a politics of consumption because of relative deprivation that cuts across class, culture, language, and ethnicity: persons who are relatively deprived have to settle for cheaper basket of goods, for a cheaper set of services are more likely than not to feel relatively deprived *vis-à-vis* those who appear to possess such goods and services.

Consumption in modernity is political because it creates a desire to possess and project images of social, cultural and political status. While traditional societies tended to accord status by age, experience, or along familial lines, societies in late modernity (after 1945) tend to reject such simplistic allocation of cultural and social ranks. Rather, consumption in modernity has created a class-based system which is fractured along social, ethnic, cultural, and political lines wherein which the need to project a certain identity, and a specific social status is via a recognition of an outer, superficial appearance of what one possesses. Therefore, there is a politics of consumption because there are power differentials in society that accrue to consumption, and consumer-related activity which pressures individuals and groups to project images that can be constructed out of the consumption of goods and services. This is part of the reason why credit card debt is so high in the both "advanced" industrial countries and in "developing" ones: the politics of consumption creates a tax on future income, income that might not ever be earned. The political conundrum is in the irony that the juggernaut of modernity prevents individual consumers from avoiding present consumption (purchases) on future unearned income in order to survive. The politics of consumption forms part of what Zygmunt Bauman describes as modernity's ambivalence (Bauman, 1991).

The Nature of Consumption

The nature of consumption is premised on dynamic consumer choices from a range of goods and services. For most consumers, the selection of such goods and services depend inherently on three factors: (1) current disposable income; (2) past spending patterns; and (3) taxes on current and future income. We are less concerned with bean-counting issues of consumer choices in Singapore and Malaysia. Rather the work involves the political, cultural, and economic considerations and arrangements of consumers in both countries with people tied by blood and history. The review of literature conducted for this book on the politics of consumption in Singapore and Malaysia resulted in a scarcity of analyses. This is because of three reasons: (1) both countries' economies are often treated separately in terms of their political sovereignty; (2) both countries are significantly different in terms of population size, Singapore having close to 4 million persons, and Malaysia over 23 million;[10] and (3) most reports are primarily empirically-based yearly summaries of economic performance in various sectors.

A Divided Modernity

The division of the book in two highlights the differences, similarities, and the effects of these differences and similarities in which things are consumed in Malaysia and Singapore. But because this book is about a politics of consumption, it evokes a natural comparison between the two countries that continues to be represented in the subject matter of all cross-Straits work. At another level, this book is divided in two because Singapore and Malaysia are divided in two. No matter how much effort that is poured into melding relationships between the two countries, there continues to be periodic eruptions of political differences despite endeavors by these very leaders to mend political and economic ties. Both countries are in perpetual competition, for land, resources, and human talent. Both endeavor to attract foreign capital towards it and away from the Other. Most books on Singapore and Malaysia tend towards a kind of utopianism, an ideal desire that some day both countries will be united. The other kinds of books on Singapore and Malaysia tend towards a kind of pessimistic determinism that curses both sovereign states to remain mutually separable.

The political dimension of consumption has often been marginalized if not completely omitted from consumption, apart from the material, cultural and economic dimensions discussed above, and from within the discipline of non-Marxist political science in spite of Moffat's writing on the narrow confines of an early and relatively crude form of political economy at the *fin de siecle* (Moffat, 1878). On the other hand, multidisciplinary studies in Southeast Asian consumption are not common. While much is being produced within Asia for Asians and the rest of the world, there appears to

---

[10] Department of Statistics, Government of Malaysia, April 2001 Release; Department of Statistics, Government of Singapore, May 2001 estimates.

be little work designed at capturing alternative aspects of understanding the nature of modern consumption in Southeast Asia. Consumption has made deep inroads in the foundations of the Singaporean and Malaysian societies. Business marketing, stupendous advertising, political rhetoric, the Internet, and continuous supplies of information throughout the 24-7 period fuels a cyclical desire among consumers of language, culture and politics to become less aware, more alienated, and increasingly vulnerable to systems of mass consumption. Perhaps when we realize that we are ourselves at some level, a commodified species, "living" consumer goods for sale and purchase in the marketplace of ideas, will we be able to answer what makes consumption the political common denominator for human activity in Singapore and Malaysia. Table 4 at the end of this chapter illustrates the consumption patterns by preferred choice of brand across seven Asian countries, while the following section briefly compares the choices made by Singaporean and Malaysian consumers.

Comparing Consumption Patterns

A. Singapore

The *CIA World Factbook* on Singapore describes the country's economy in the following manner:

> Singapore is blessed with a highly developed and successful free-market economy, a remarkably open and corruption-free business environment, stable prices, and the fifth highest per capita GDP in the world. Exports, particularly in electronics and chemicals, and services are the main drivers of the economy. The government promotes high levels of savings and investment through a mandatory savings scheme and spends heavily in education and technology. It also owns government-linked companies (GLCs) — particularly in manufacturing —

that operate as commercial entities and account for 60% of GDP. As Singapore looks increasingly marked by globalization, the country is positioning itself as the region's financial and high-tech hub.

The main criticisms include: (1) the relative size of Singapore when compared to other states as an advantage rather than a disadvantage to progress; (2) market consumption provides sufficient levels of wealth to generate sufficiently high levels of disposable income [**IG/EG**]; while at the first instance, housing and automobile loans in Singapore appear to be inclusionary goods in the short term, they are effectively exclusionary goods because they increase the private cost to consumers who have to pay high prices to consume the same quality and quantity of good in the long term; (3) the statement that Singapore is 'corruption free' is too presumptuous as there have been cases in the past where public officials have been caught for corrupt practices. It is perhaps fairer to state that corruption levels are relatively low in Singapore because of social discipline, fear of punishment, and observance of the law by such coercive agencies as the Singapore Police Force (SPF), the Commercial Affairs Division (CAD), and the Corrupt Practices Investigation Bureau (CPIB). Levels of corruption are uneven and are overtly present in some departments such as the Customs, Excise, and Immigration departments than others [**FH**]. This is an example of a Faustian foundational fantasy of discipline and punishment where corrupt persons are deemed to exhibit "the horror" of anti-social behavior. Singaporeans tend to shun corrupt behavior than to indulge in it, but whether it is because of the prospect of severe penalties by law or a social consciousness, or a combination of the two, is not currently known yet it might be part of the fundamental value of being modern if traditional local practices had encouraged corrupt behavior. [**FV**]. There are two main implications of the low levels of corruption for the politics of consumption: (a) less money is wasted on petty bribes and "connections by goodwill"; and (b) lower levels of slippage among the general consuming population implies greater prospects for efficient collection by tax collectors of the Inland Revenue Authority of Singapore (IRAS) [**FV**]. These are clear examples of the fundamental value of modernity in operation, one that supports the in-flow/out-flow of public money where the belief is that such systemic movement keeps the economy afloat, and helps the people survive.[11] This is quantified in Table 1 which illustrates the changing patterns of Singaporean consumers over a period of twenty years in terms of expenditure d istribution by goods and services over a twenty years period in support of the fundamental value of what is considered "modern". What does this tell us about the pattern of consumption in Singapore? There are three main implications that can be drawn out from Table 1, viz.,

> (1) a significant percentage of total monthly income is devoted to housing and transport/communications. **[FV]** This is because Singapore is among the most expensive places to buy/rent a home in Asia outside Hong Kong and Tokyo; **[EG]**
>
> (2) the section on transport and communications belies the fact that Singapore is the most expensive place to buy a car for four main reasons: (a) exorbitantly high customs duties, additional registration fees, goods and services tax (GST), and the cost of the certificate of entitlement (COE); (b) the profit-motivated, very high "mark-up" rates for various makes of cars that are brought into Singapore in order to make it "worthwhile" to the local distributors which vary from S$5,000 to S$80,000. These "mark-up" prices are over and above the open market value (OMV) of the car; it is only a recent consumer phenomenon in Singapore when the State modified the oligopolistic situation where a single-

---

[11] Consider the comments and compare the results in, for example, Peter J. Katzenstein, "International Interdependence: Some Long-Term Trends and Recent Changes", *International Organization* (1975), 29(4): 1021-1034; see also, David Henderson, "International Economic Integration: Progress, Prospects and Implications in Integrating Economies", (1992), *International Affairs*, 68(4): 638; and David K. Henderson, *Interpretation and Explanation in the Human Sciences* (Albany: State University of New York Press, 1993).

distributor would control one to several brands of popular vehicles; there was some lowering of prices when the oligopolistic franchise deadlines ran out and parallel importers entered the market; [EG] (c) a large proportion of status conscious Singaporeans who continue to be willing to pay enormously high prices for cars that are worth a fraction of the total cost in neighboring countries, despite the limiting influence of the high, market-derived costs of the Certificates of Entitlements (COE) that help reduce the physical number of cars and number of years (ten years in the first instance) [EG];

Table 1: Household Expenditure Survey (1978 to 1998)

	Average monthly income per household (S$)	
	1978	*1998*
Lowest 20%	362	1368
Second quintile	571	2588
Highest 20%	2403	12685
All households	1066	5262
	Distribution of expenditure by type of goods and services (%)	
	1978	*1998*
Food	44.7	23.7
Clothing	5.6	4.1
Housing	15.6	21.6
Transport & Communications	13.0	22.8
Education	3.8	6.9
Health	1.7	3.3

Source: Department of Statistics, Singapore, 2001.

this is an exclusionary good because there is a regional social cost forming when the 10-year old cars are no longer consumed in Singapore and exported to the region; this is an exclusionary good because Singaporeans generate so much relative economic wealth as to be willing to pay such high prices; however, the willingness on their part to pay high prices for cars in Singapore does not indicate the level of affordability as much as the importance of social status associated with car ownership in Singapore; (d) a government that is unwilling to regulate downwards these high mark-ups by distributors.[12] It is possible that the medium term loans tie down vehicle consumers' disposable income to the domestic market.

The third implication from Table 1 is the fact that a significant proportion of the Singaporean consumer income is distributed towards food. However, the statistics do not reveal immediately the high rate of savings among Singaporeans, and the other fact that it is ironic that Singaporeans desire and purchase expensive cars (that vary from low quality to high quality vehicles) when an excellent public transport system has been in place since the 1970s. It would not be too presumptuous to hypothesize that the majority of Singaporeans are highly conscious of their social status and believe in conspicuous consumption in terms of what is colloquially known as the five "Cs": cash, credit card, car, condominium, and career [FV] [EG] [WG]. The five Cs illustrate the materialistic attitude that many Singaporeans have, and is one of the clearest examples of the belief in progress, advancement, and the fundamental value of modernity where being modern means possessing cash, credit facilities, cars, condominiums, and careers to support these modernist emblems of success and of being modern.

What have government and state agencies recently achieved in terms of influencing other patterns of consumption in Singapore? According to the official representations to UN sessions on Sustainable Development (January 1999), the Singapore government through the Ministry of the Environment performs waste minimization audits and recycling schemes for consumer-related businesses. A quasi state agency, the Economic

---

[12] Karamjit Kaur, "What Are You Paying For?" *The Sunday Times*, April 8, 2001, p. 3.

Development Board (EDB) which was created as a statutory board, "provides tax incentives and financial assistance schemes to encourage the adoption of energy-efficient technologies and the installation of energy-efficient equipment"; another agency, the Singapore Productivity and Standards Board (PSB) "promotes waste minimization through the promotion of Green Productivity". At the ministerial level, there was a Green Labeling scheme that was implemented in 1992 which determines which product categories — with the help of consumer representatives — are to carry the Green label:

> The Green Labeling Scheme helps consumers to identify environmentally friendly products and enable them to exercise their choices more objectively in order to influence producers and suppliers to take into account the protection of the environment when producing goods. The Scheme applies to most products, excepts foods, drinks and pharmaceuticals. It does not apply to services and processes.[13] **[IG]**

The intention of the Singapore Green Plan at the national level is to reduce domestic (and commercial) consumer waste to less than 0.9 kg per capita of population. In order to help achieve world standards in sustainable consumption, the government has promoted the minimal use of packaging for consumer durables and consumer produce to influence the nature of their consumption patterns. **[IG]** This is a positive example of an inclusionary good because costs to the public, and the "measurable" extent of environmental degradation are tend to be reduced in the long run.

---

[13] "Singapore Government Report on Sustainable Development", 5th and 7th sessions of the UN Commission on Sustainable Development, January 1999.

A. Malaysia

According to the *CIA World Factbook*,

> Malaysia made a quick economic recovery in 1999 from its worst recession since independence in 1957. GDP grew 5%, responding to a dynamic export sector, which grew over 10% and fiscal stimulus from higher government spending. The large export surplus has enabled the country to build up its already substantial financial reserves, to $31 billion at yearend 1999. This stable macroeconomic environment, in which both inflation and unemployment stand at 3% or less, has made possible the relaxation of most of the capital controls imposed by the government in 1998 to counter the impact of the Asian financial crisis. Government and private forecasters expect Malaysia to continue this trend in 2000, predicting GDP to grow another 5% to 6%. While Malaysia's immediate economic horizon looks bright, its long-term prospects are clouded by the lack of reforms in the corporate sector, particularly those dealing with competitiveness and high corporate debt.

There are three implications of these observations: (1) the country's economy has attained a sufficient level of economic maturity to sustain the cyclical patterns of global economic pressures with minimal damage to the infrastructural software in the country. More specifically, the constrictive impact on the economy in the initial two years after the recent crises have abated consumer demand, and up till the September 11, 2001 crisis in New York City, public choices had actually almost returned to the pre-recession levels of 1997/8; [**FV, VP**]. Clearly the economic maturity and the general belief among the population that there continues to be hope of progress and advancement in spite of the September 11 crisis and the 2000-2002 global recession which are indicative of a strong belief in the fundamental value of modernity; (2) the low level of inflation and employment indicates that sufficient real wages left over from surplus labor are available for investment, savings or quotidian expenditure; and (3) optimistic economic forecasts indicates that the economy is more likely to perform well than not in the short term, while economists and econometricians are still unable to accurately predict long-term economic development. [FV] Again, this is another example of the belief in the modern value of progress and economic advancement despite the global recessionary pressures. The belief in the modern value means that people are generally hopeful that the recession will eventually pass, and new wealth will again be created for all.

In Malaysia, the Malaysian government's department of Statistics (*Jabatan Angkaan*) calculates the Consumer Price Index (CPI) on the Laspeyres principle aimed at the average rate of change over a fixed basket of 430 goods and services over a period of time with the base year in 1994.

Table 2: *Indeks Harga Pengguna* (CPI) (1999 to 2000)

Region\CPI	1999	2000
Semenanjung	1.7	1.6
Sabah	0.6	0.8
Sarawak	1.5	1.2
Federation Total	1.6	1.5

Source: *Jabatan Perangkaan Malaysia*, Malaysia (March) 2001

Monthly consumer price collection are carried out by 116 collection centers in Peninsular Malaysia, 15 in Sabah and 13 in Sarawak. Table 2 illustrates the CPI over two years after the 1997/1998 economic recession. There are three implications from Table 2: (1) the cost of consumer prices has stabilized since the 1997/1998 economic recession; (2) consumer prices in the State of Sarawak are almost as high as those found in Semenanjung, while, ironically, the state of Sabah continues to return the lowest CPI levels.

What has the Malaysian government done to change and influence patterns of consumption among its Malaysian consumers? The primary strategy stems from the New Economic Policy (NEP) and New Development Policy (NDP) that allocated national resources towards poverty eradication and had the objective of lowering the level of poverty and the association of ethnicity with occupation. While the Malays are not specifically mentioned in these long term strategies, the intention was to overtly secure at least a 30% equity stake for Malays bumiputra (son of the soil) in the national economy (Kamal, 1988). In order to achieve these goals without eroding the real wages of non-Malay bumiputra Malaysians, and non-bumiputra Malaysians, the federal government encourages increased savings through rises in income tax relief for insurance contributions; acts as a facilitator of purchases of new, low-waste "clean technology" for manufacturing, waste management and air pollution control through exemptions of import duty, sales taxes and excise duties for companies producing consumer goods that use pollution control technology.[14] Unlike Singapore, the Malaysian government does not have a "green plan" strategy and continues to use ethnic bias based on the NEP and now, the NDP, in public policy formulation, implementation, and evaluation. Although it has one of the highest per capita GNP in the region, the level is significantly lower when compared to the Singapore case. However, consumer durables and cost of living indices indicate lower levels when compared to Singapore. It continues to be cheaper to live in Malaysia. In addition, there continues to be a large number of Malay bumiputra Malaysians — virtually unable to effectively participate in consumer decision making — living at or under the poverty level despite the affirmative action NEP and NDP. This case is especially true in the poorer northern Malaysian states in the *Semenanjung* or Peninsula (formerly known as West Malaysia). [**FV, FH, WG**] The general and highly successful Malaysian economy over a forty year period, 1963-2003, since its political independence under *Yang Teramat Mulia Tunku* Abdul Rahman Alhaj is a clear illustration of the

---

[14] Malaysian Government Submission, 5th Session, *United Nations Commission on Sustainable Development*, April 1997.

belief in "the modern" as the fundamental value of modernity. Yet, the existence of Opposition-held states in the north that wrested political power from the incumbent national government is a site of political, social, cultural, economic, and especially religious resistance. These Northern states are relatively less developed when compared to the other Malaysian states and have a higher rural population with the vast majority embracing Islam. This means that modernity/resistance occurs and continues to occur through the validation of religious differences between what the power elite in the federal capital of Kuala Lumpur (KL) and the Oppositional power elite in Kelantan and Trengganu on both sides. This continues to remain a threat to the relatively moderate KL policies of the incumbent government under Barisan Nasional (BN, the National Front) with its policies of moderate Islam, religious tolerance of Christianity, Hinduism, and other religions (perhaps with the possible exception of Judaism), series of economic successes since 1963, and political legitimacy of the popular vote in Malaysia's general elections, with the last one resulting in a landslide victory for Mahathir and his Cabinet in all but the two Opposition-held states. The people in the poorer, Muslim-dominated, rural Northern states are more likely than not to remain steadfast to their religious beliefs rather than subscribe to modern modes of advancement and progress mooted by KL. There are significant differences in the way that Muslim men and women are expected to behave in Malaysia in general. There are clearly stated religious laws and a kind of religious "police" with an entire coercive structure of support who keep watch over Muslims who detract from proper social conduct and behavior. For example, Muslim men and women who are not legally married cannot be found in close physical proximity as this is considered taboo (*khalwat*), and must observe the legally-defined religious regulations during the Holy fasting month of *Ramadan*. Those Muslims who flout the laws are liable for prosecution by religious authorities. The situation in the Northern states is much more severe in the sense that the legitimately elected Opposition state governments of Kelantan and Trengganu are moving towards a kind of Islamic state. No *hudud* laws have yet been implemented although public songs and dances are disallowed as the chapter on Malaysian narratives illustrates. The religious motif seeks to garner and engender a greater Islamic religiosity among the believers and those who are also domiciled in those parts. These are states where just slightly over 95% embrace Islam as their religion, hence the pressure to conform to Islamic teaching, Islamic dress, and the Islamic view of the world — at least according to the interpretation of the power elite in Kota Bahru (capital of Trengganu) and Alor Setar (capital of Kelantan) — exerts a social pressure of its own. This reveals at least a century-old interpretation of the Holy Koran and an Islamic value and belief system of knowledge that existed within the socio-cultural structure of Kelantanese-Malay, and Trengganu-Malay hierarchy of values that resisted the limited Christianizing effects of western colonialism of the three colonial powers — Portuguese, Dutch, and British — that ruled a significant part of the peninsula since the Portuguese invasion and sacking of Melaka on the indentured West coast. Religious fervor is encouraged and magnified throughout all aspects of life in Kelantan and Trengganu and led by powerful Imams, Ulama, and other religious teachers with influence in Kelantan and Trengganu in the various *madrasah* or colloquially, the "pondok" school of thought.

The idea of multiple power relations divides the structure of consumption in Singapore and Malaysia into two broad processes. The first broad process is the language of the Singaporean and Malaysian economic and political elite whose language of neoliberal capitalism is empowered by the international neoliberal economic system.[15] The second broad process imitates the first. This process engulfs the majority of workers whose main aim in life appears to revolve round the consumption of images: social, cultural, and economic intimations of those who are traditionally held in high esteem in society, perhaps, the economic and political elite whose partial consumption patterns are illustrated in Fig. 1 across Asia that indicated a small fall in the total amount spent in the aftermath of the 1998

---

[15] See Katzenstein's analysis of capitalism as a parallel to Malaysia and Singapore in the international political economy. Peter J. Katzenstein, "Capitalism in one Country? Switzerland in the International Economy", *International Organization*, 1980, 34(4), pp. 507-540.

"Asian" recession although elite consumers in Singapore and Taiwan increased over the same period when compared to Hongkong and KL.

This is V. S. Naipaul's metaphor of the "mimic man" writ large in late modernity. There is no one language but multiple languages bearing multiple power relations within the two main structures of consumption that engulf and weaken traditional forms of economic resistance. The idea of modernity and consumption as explained in the introduction delivered the main theoretical background and concepts drawn primarily from the work of Gianni Vattimo, William E. Connolly, Theresa Brennan, Stephen K. White, and Wendy Brown. The following table on the Consumption patterns across several Asian countries provides a rough estimate of the kinds of brand names that people working and living in these Asian countries, including Singapore and Malaysia, appear to prefer (Table 3). While it illustrates a certain preference for certain brand names in these countries, the findings are not entirely representative of all consumers in these countries nor of the availability of choices in these countries. Rather, such an illustration often raises more questions than providing answers. Here are just six possibilities: (1) which Asian countries were included, and which omitted? (2) what is the

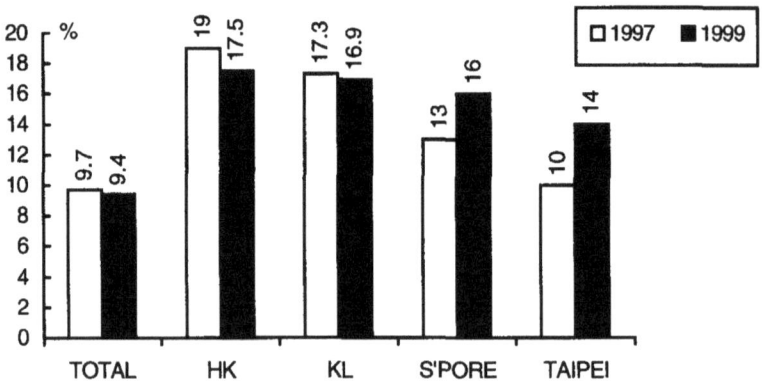

Fig.1: Consumption Patterns Among Asia's Elites
Source: Modified from M. Chew, *Business Times*, October 22, 1999

basis of the comparison? (3) what kind of research instrument was used to conduct the survey? (4) is the sample statistically representative? (5) are all these brand names available as choices in all these countries? (6) did the researcher, statistician, or journalist correct for differences in GNP per capita, cost of living, currency differences, quality of life, and cultural differences?

Table 3: Consumption Patterns in Asian Countries

Product	Asia*	Malaysia	Philippines	Singapore	Thailand
Car	Toyota	Toyota	Toyota	Mercedes Benz	Toyota
Hotel	Shangri-La	Shangri-La	Holiday Inn	Shangri-La	Regent
Airline	Singapore Airlines	Malaysia Airlines	Philippine Airlines	Singapore Airlines	Thai Airways
Computer	Acer	Acer	IBM	Compaq	Acer
Printer	Hewlett .P	Canon	Epson	Hewlett. P	Epson
Scanner	Canon	Canon	Canon	Hewlett. P	Canon
Fax machine	Cannon	Canon	Panasonic	Canon	Panasonic
Photocopier	Cannon	Canon	Xerox	Canon	Xerox
Mobile Phone	Nokia	Motorola	Nokia	Ericsson	Nokia
Television	Sony	Sony	Sony	Sony	Sony
VCR	Sony	Sony	Sony	Sony	Sony
CD/MD Player	Sony	Sony	Sony	Sony	Sony
VCD/LD/DVD	Sony	Sony	Sony	Sony	Sony
Camera	Canon	Canon	Canon	Canon	Canon
Video Camera	Sony	Sony	Sony	Sony	Sony
Watch	Rolex	Rolex	Seiko	Rolex	Rolex
Quality Pen	Parker	Parker	Parker	Parker	Parker
Designer	Versace	Versace	Moreno	i Versace	Versace
Water	Evian	Spritzer	Wilkins	Evian	Aura
Soft drink	Coca-Cola	Coca-Cola	Coca-Cola	Coca-Cola	Coca-Cola
Tea	Lipton	Lipton	Lipton	Lipton	Lipton
Instant coffee	Nescafe	Nescafe	Nescafe	Nescafe	Nestle
Milk	Nestle	Nestle	Nido	Nestle	HKI
Cereal	Campbell's	Nestle	Nestle	Nestle	Nestle
Soup	Maggi	Campbell's	Knorr	Campbell's	Knorr
Instant noodles	Knorr	Maggi	Maggi	Maggi	Ma Ma
Beer	San Miguel	Carlsberg	San Miguel	Tiger	Singha
Whisky	J. Walker	J. Walker	J. Walker	J. Walker	Black Label
Brandy/Cognac	Hennessy	Martell	Fundador	Martell	Hennessy
Vodka	Absolut	Smirnoff	Absolut	Smirnoff	Smirnoff
Shampoo	Pantene	Pantene	Pantene	Pantene	Sunsilk
Toothpaste	Colgate	Colgate	Colgate	Colgate	Colgate
Cosmetics	Avon	Avon	Avon	Estee Lauder	Avon
Baby products	Johnson	Johnson	Johnson	Johnson	Johnson

Source: Modified by the author from *The Straits Times* May 25, 1999

Summary

This chapter lays the methodological foundation for the book in three main ways. Firstly, the literature review in this chapter covers the major debates in modernity beginning ostensibly with the positivist movement in the 1950s and the advances in the social sciences in the post World War 2 era. Secondly, this chapter describes the three prevailing categories of argument in the political and social sciences in their approaches to modernity. The political argument on modernity being about realist power and liberal "control"; the economic argument employing both classical Marxist and neoMarxist modes of analysis as well as non-Marxist econometric analyses, with different implications for each. The latter argument suggesting resistance and consumption as the means to economic objectives in modernity. The third intention of this chapter was to introduce the mRf based on the following 5 concepts: [FV] fundamental value; [EG, IG] exclusionary and inclusionary goods; [FH] foundational Faustian fantasy of horror; [VP] vulnerability of the public consumer; [WG] work gender imbalances and contradictions.

References

Appadurai, Arjun. 1996. *Modernity at Large: Cultural Dimensions of Globalization.* Minneapolis and London: University of Minnesota Press.

Belshaw, Horace. 1956. *Population Growth and Levels of Consumption.* (with special reference to countries in Asia). London: Allen & Unwin.

Bianchi, Marina. ed. 1998. *The Active Consumer: Novelty and Surprise in Consumer Choice.* New York: Routledge.

Bocock, Robert. 1993. *Consumption.* London and New York: Routledge.

Brennan, Theresa. 2000. *Exhausting Modernity: Grounds for a New Economy.* New York: Routledge.

Bryant, W. Keith. 1990. *The Economic Organization of the Household.* Cambridge and New York: Cambridge University Press.

Burk, Marguerite C. 1968. *Consumption Economics: A Multidisciplinary Approach.* New York: Wiley.

Campbell, Colin. 1987. *The Romantic Ethic and the Spirit of Modern Consumerism.* Oxford and New York: Basil Blackwell.

Deaton, Angus. 1992. *Understanding Consumption.* Oxford: Clarendon Press, and New York: Oxford University Press.

Dupre, Louis K. 1993. *Passage to Modernity: An Essay in the Hermeneutics of Nature and Culture.* New York: Yale University Press.

Foucault, Michel. 1988. *Politics, Philosophy, Culture: Interviews and Other Writings, 1977-1984.* New York: Routledge.

Frith, Katherine Toland. 1996. *Advertising in Asia: Communication, Culture, and Consumption.* Ames: Iowa State University Press.

Giddens, Anthony. 1990. *The Consequences of Modernity.* Stanford: Stanford University Press.

Giddens, Anthony. 1991. *Modernity and Self-Identity: Self and Society in the Late Modern Age.* Cambridge & Oxford: Polity Press.

Giddens, Anthony. 2000. "The Globalizing of Modernity" in David Held and Anthony McGrew (eds.) *The Global Transformations Reader: An Introduction to the Globalization Debate*. Malden, MA: Polity Press.

Government of Malaysia. 1969-2001. "Department of Statistics Reports" (various).

Government of Singapore. 1978-2001. "Department of Statistics Reports" (various).

Green, H. A. John. 1971. *Consumer Theory*. Harmondsworth: Penguin.

Henderson, David. 1992. "International Economic Integration: Progress, Prospects and Implications (in Integrating Economies)", *International Affairs*, **68**(4): 633-653.

Henderson, David K. 1993. *Interpretation and Explanation in the Human Sciences*. Albany: State University of New York Press.

Howard, G. S. 1997. *Ecological Psychology: Creating A More Earth-Friendly Human Nature*. Notre Dame, IN: University of Notre Dame Press.

Jackson, Stevi and Shaun Moores. eds. 1995. *The Politics of Domestic Consumption: Critical Readings*. London and New York: Prentice Hall-Harvester Wheatsheaf.

Kamal, S. 1988. *The New Economic Policy After 1990*. Kuala Lempue: Malaysian Institute of Economic Research.

Karni, R. S. 1980. *Bibliography of Malaysia & Singapore*. Kuala Lumpur: Penerbit Universiti Malaya.

Katzenstein, Peter J. 1975. "International Interdependence: Some Long-Term Trends and Recent Changes." *International Organization*, **29**(4): 1021-1034.

Katzenstein, Peter J. 1980. "Capitalism in one Country? Switzerland in the International Economy." *International Organization*, **34**(4): 507-540.

Kolb, David. 1986. *The Critique of Pure Modernity: Hegel, Heidegger, and After*. Chicago: University of Chicago Press.

Salih, K. 1988. *The New Economic Policy After 1990*. Kuala Lumpur: Malaysian Institute of Economic Research.

Lee, Martyn J. 1993. *Consumer Culture Reborn: The Cultural Politics of Consumption*. London and New York: Routledge.

Mahathir Mohamed. 1998. *The Way Forward*. London: Weidenfeld & Nicolson.

Mauricio, Jose. 2000. *Social Creativity, Collective Subjectivity, and Contemporary Modernity*. New York: St Martin's Press.

Miller, Daniel. 1987. *Material Culture and Mass Consumption*. Oxford and New York: Basil Blackwell.

Miller, Daniel. ed. 2001. *Consumption: Critical concepts in the Social Sciences*, vols. I – IV. London & New York: Routledge.

Moffat, Robert Scott. 1878. *The Economy of Consumption: An Omitted Chapter in Political Economy*. London: C. K. Paul .

Nystrom, Paul Henry. 1929. *Economic Principles on Consumption*. New York: Ronald Press.

Pearce, Ivor F. A. 1964. *Contribution to Demand Analysis*. Oxford: Clarendon Press.

Postman, Neil. 1985. *Amusing Ourselves to Death: Public Discourse in the Age of Showbusiness,* New York: Penguin Books.

Rappa, Antonio L. 2002. ed. Thematic issue on "Modernity and the Politics of Public Space", *Innovation: The European Journal of Social Science Research,* **15** (1).

Roche, Daniel. 1998. *France des Lumires* (France in the Enlightenment), trans. by Arthur Goldhammer, Cambridge, MA: Harvard University Press.

Sack, Robert David. 1992. *Place, Modernity, and the Consumer's World: A Relational Framework for Geographical Analysis*. Baltimore: Johns Hopkins University Press.

Shutz, Eric A. 2001. *Markets and Power: The 21st Century Command Economy*. Armonk, NY: M. E. Sharpe.

Sritua, Arief. 1980a. *Test of Leser's Model of Household Consumption Expenditure in Malaysia and Singapore*. Singapore: Institute of Southeast Asian Studies.

Sritua, Arief. 1980b. *Study of Household Consumption in Malaysia and Singapore*. Kuala Lumpur: Meta for Sritua Arief Associates.

Tomlinson, John. 1991. *Cultural Imperialism*. London: Pinter Publishers.

Xenos, Nicholas. 1989. *Scarcity and Modernity*. London and New York: Routledge.

Zygmunt, Bauman. 1989. *Modernity and the Holocaust.* Ithaca, NY: Cornell University Press.

Zygmunt, Bauman. 1991. *Modernity and Ambivalence.* Oxford: Polity Press.

Zygmunt, Bauman. 2000. "Modernity, Racism and Extermination" in Les Back and John Solomos (eds.) *Theories of Race and Racism.* New York: Routledge.

PART I
SINGAPORE

Consuming Singapore

This chapter illustrates the nature of modernity, consumption in terms of national security and the distribution of wealth in Singapore. The idea here is not to tie national security to the distribution of wealth but to show how each constitutes a different kind of consumption in Singapore and how both these public forms of consumption are effectively determined by the "public" to the extent that "private" space in Singapore becomes conditional, ephemeral, and decrepit.

Simple forms of consumption were first imported into Southeast Asia as a process of proto-modernization activity that began most prominently and ostensibly with the influence of Chinese and Hindu commercial activity in South China and the Southern parts of Asia about a thousand five hundred (1,500) to two thousand three hundred (2,300) years ago. This period of "early commerce" was succeeded by the Islamic influence and the rise of western forms of colonialism. The postcolonial map of Southeast Asia today

64 Modernity and Consumption

is a production of these early political forms and those of the archipelagic traders in and around the region, a social, economic and cultural confluence of Eastern and Western tension. The onset of modernity may be directly tied to the metropole-satellite and dependency school theses (1960s-1970s) that explained the materialist-based, lop-sided arrangements between colonial master and colonial subject.[1] These neo-Marxist arguments are only part of a larger competing pattern of intellectual interpretations of modern Southeast Asia.

The idea of a consumption-driven modernity as an intellectual slice of public space cuts deeper into the private space of citizens that is nominally perceived. Modernity may be partially explained through the meaning of things are represented, their points of references, and the relationships between syntax, meaning, identity, and society. [FV] While Homi Bhabha's *Nation and Narration* (1990) illuminates the discussion of interstitial and liminal spaces in late modernity, these architectonic forms are even further complicated in *The Location of Culture* (1994) that examines the "in-between" ways in which powerful discursive formations and disempowered discursive formations survive. Like Fanon, Foucault, Baudrillard, and Derrida, Bhabha cannot accept the limitations of reductionist perspectives on the formation of cultural identities within public space and public time. For Bhabha, liminal spaces occur between the real and the reel, between the imagined and the imagination; among virtual-, written-, and hyper-texts that confide in each other and in between the spaces of sociological code-switching within traditional substance and modern forms within urban structures.[FV, EG] Liminal spaces themselves represent sets of public economic exchanges of social formations and cultural formulations. The existence of the liminal landforms is reflected within the surface structures that uphold and hold up the values and interests that are ordinarily seen as symbols of representation (Edelman), emotively charged condensation symbols (Sapir) and objectively neutral referential symbols (Sapir). George

---

[1]See Georg Simmel, "Culture and Quantitative Increase in Material Culture", in Daniel Miller, ed. *Consumption, Critical Concepts in the Social Sciences*, vol. I, *Theory and Issues in the Study of Consumption* (London & New York: Routledge, 2001), pp. 89-94.; see also Daniel Horowitz, "Consumption in Antebellum Life and Thought", in *ibid.*, pp. 75-88.

Lakoff's important work on metaphor also draws similar parallels within the language of language, as does Berman's *All That is Solid Melts Into Air*, V.S. Naipaul's *The Enigma of Arrival*, R. K. Narayan's *The Guide*, and, Douglass's and Friedman's *Cities for Citizens: Planning and the Rise of Civil Society in a Global Age*. A favorite approach of mine that effectively captures aspects of modernity in the urban marketplace of ideas and contests is Mike Davis's *City of Quartz*, a public-consumerist pastiche of greater and lesser Los Angeles at the end of the last century.

Singapore's consumption-driven modernity appears to be relatively simple to identify in general terms: land-use policies, urban renewal projects, and urban preservation and conservation work by state and non-state authorities.[EG] A reason for the apparent simplicity, apart from the outpouring of scholarly articles and serious journalism on urban life within the without the region, lies in the increasing awareness among scholars who live and work within urban centers also growth centers and are often co-located with centers of political power, and have large, dense concentrations of citizens. However, there are many problems of the rural past, the urban future and urban present that are not immediately evident at the general level; problems that become increasingly complex and complicated when confronted at the micro-level. Again, Bhabha's interstitial concept finds use in the overlap of social and economic domains. Overlapping domains are inherently complex and made worse by a hubris of information, a false consciousness and insecurity that generates from the virtual inability to mete out effective control over urban populations. The urban center is the creation and by-product of modernity that reflects Prometheus unbound, a kind of postmodern Frankenstein for a postindustrial age that is simultaneously duplicitous, articulate, sensuous, vibrant and seductive. Modernity at the 2000-2001 *fin-de-siecle* cannot be understood without a certain familiarity and knowledge of the Ages that have come before our time. Modernity today cannot be understood without the experience of ambiguity, logic, reason, passion, emotion, success and failure. Modernity is at the end, a shifting replication of the consciousness of complicated bodies of being human. Developments in scholarship point towards the traits that characterize modernity: simulacra; the emptying out of meaning; alienation and atomization; and an unfulfilled and unfulfilling series of personal and group achievements. For example, the pressure on the youth of Singapore, a direct result of the city-state's economic wealth, appears to have made Singapore youth old before their time. They are overburdened with school work — as a point registered by the information overload society — and schoolbags with texts that are outdated as soon as they are printed. Sometimes politicians berate them; parents abuse their own children; unwanted children are abandoned. Male Singaporeans who turn 18 years old are not yet allowed to vote for their future, but bear the national burden of two-years compulsory military training (National Service). Is it better to have a daughter instead of a son? How does it make a difference for public consumption?

"Older" Singaporeans today who grew up in the 1940s and 1950s cannot completely relate to the experiences of today's youth with their own memories of Malaya and early postcolonial Singapore. Through the 1970s and 1980s, Singapore youth were labeled "McDonald's Kids", " Centrepoint Kids", and "Latch-Key Kids". To keep with the times of change, what used to be known as "disciplining the child" in 1960s' and 70s' Singapore is now considered abuse by law, a move by public interest, into the realm of the private. Parents and grandparents themselves have become increasingly involved in this society of conspicuous consumption of branded goods[2], ungrammatical English, blank stares, and incivility as some of the residual effects of the *instant gratification society*. The new generation of the "Ugly Singaporean" is seen in the need to continue the annual Courtesy campaign, a Singapore Kindness Movement and "Kindness Week", and a "Speak Good English" campaign by the State's bureaucracy. The ugliness of some Singaporeans is not unique to all Singaporeans in general, but interestingly runs parallel to Michael J. Shapiro's interpretation of the magic Kingdom as

---

[2]See Mary Douglas, "Why Do People Want Goods?" in Daniel Miller, ed. *Consumption, Critical Concepts in Social Sciences,* vol. I, *Theory and Issues in the Study of Consumption* (London & New York: Routledge, 2001), pp. 262-271; see also Deborah S. Davis, 'Introduction: A Revolution in Consumption", in *ibid,* vol. II, pp.283-307; Kim Humphery, "Living the Transformation", in *ibid,* vol. II, pp. 384 – 402; Richard R. Wilk, "Houses as Consumer Goods: Social Processes and Allocation Decisions", in *ibid,* vol. II, pp. 133-154.

a kind of "burlesque of the Snow White story".[3] These Disney-ification of the world and the deeper effects of global modernity appear to characterize Singapore and make it not too dissimilar from Paris, London, New York (City), Seattle, Mumbai, Kuala Lumpur, Bangkok, Seoul, and Tokyo.[VP]

Singapore citizens bear two main burdens: firstly, they have to live and work in one of the smallest and most densely populated areas in the world with over 10,000 people per km^2. This increases the level of stress in densely populated areas, an unseen and often easily overlooked stressor within the urban center (Glass and Singer, 1972; Martin, 1982; Gottdienner, 1986; and Goldsmith and Villasen, 1986).[4] Secondly, unlike the classical Greek model, the Singapore city-state is a state in itself and cannot depend on other city-states. All male citizens, who make up about half the population, have to perform compulsory military service or civil defense service that lasts between two to two and a half years; this is in addition to the "reserve service" period that comes after the compulsory service period. The reserve service may last up to a maximum of 40 days per annum until the reservist completes his thirteen year cycle in his given vocation (SAF Act, 1995).[5][WG] The vocation may either be in the Army, Navy, Air Force, Civil Defense or Special Constabulary (part of the "regular" Singapore Police Force). Modernity has become the rationalization and justification for the political rhetoric of the state. This chapter focuses on two ways in which consumption modernity has been achieved in the Singapore city-state: (1) national security; (2) wealth distribution.

Singapore has a very small market for domestic consumption. While the cost of living in Singapore is low when compared to first world urban

---

[3] Michael J. Shapiro, *Reading the Postmodern Polity: Political Theory as Textual Practice* (Minneapolis and Oxford: University of Minnesota Press, 1992), pp. 149-150.

[4] See for example, Joan K. Martin, *Urban Financial Stress: Why Cities Go Broke* (Dover, MA: Auburn House, 1982); David C. Glass and Jerome E. Singer, *Urban Stress: Experiments on Noise and Social Stressors* (New York: Academic Press, 1972); Mark Gottdiener (ed.), *Cities in Stress: A New Look at the Urban Crisis* (Los Angeles: Sage Publications, 1986); and the introductory chapter by Michael Goldsmith and Soren Villadsen (eds.), *Urban Political Theory and the Management of Fiscal Stress* (Brookfield: Gower, 1986).

[5] See also the Singapore Armed Forces Act (Revised) (1995) in *The Statutes of the Republic of Singapore*, Volume 10, Chapter 295.

centers in Asia, North America and Western Europe, Singapore's costs are relatively high when compared to Malaysian cities. The cost of living is very high when compared to Indonesia, Thailand, the Philippines, and Myanmar. These cost increases appear to have been driven by rising differences in mean incomes between the countries than by rising inequalities within countries. The most important contributors were: rising urban-rural differences in China, and slow growth of rural purchasing-power adjusted incomes in South Asia compared to several large developed market economies.[FV]

The National Security Good

The Southeast Asian region has consistently been a contested site for the expansion of empire and the control of sea-lanes. Mainland Southeast Asia was the battlefield of Burmese, Vietnamese, Cambodian, and South Chinese empires for at least eight hundred years before the rise of the Siamese kingdoms. The golden ages of Hinduism and Islam followed and heavily influenced the nature of Malay settlement patterns in Riau, Melaka, and parts of maritime Southeast Asia. The 15th and 16th century Portuguese conquests of Goa in India and Melaka in the Malay peninsular were countervailed by the Spanish King Philip II's invasion and colonization of the Philippines. The Spaniards would dominate Philippine politics, economics, and society for almost 350 years till the late 19th century when the economic and political interests of the United States of America ran afoul of the Spanish establishment in Southeast Asia. US activities in Cuba, a Spanish colony, and the Cuban rebellion in February 1895 ended Spanish colonialism in Southeast Asia.[6] Mainland and maritime Southeast Asia was the site of Portuguese, Dutch, British and French colonial re-mapping and production. The assassination of Archduke Ferdinand in 1914 was the catalyst for World War I, primarily a Western European war with colonies in Southeast Asia playing a supporting role. The Pacific war broke out with

---

[6] See "Spanish-American War and Philippine Resistance" in US Army Area Handbook, US Department of the Army, Chapter 1.05.

the bombing of Pearl Harbor signaling the advent of a new era of mass mechanized warfare in Southeast Asia between the Axis, Allies and their dependents. The old sea town of Temasek, then known as Singapura (the word "Singapore" being the result of Anglicization) with less than 150 people was ushered into the modern period in 1819 by Stamford Raffles. The naturally deep harbor made Singapore a site that would have a greater impact over the region and the Straits as Melaka had been in the preceding centuries. In the fall of 1897, Singapore (like Hong Kong) was the site of US negotiations with the Philippine rebel/resistance leader Aguinaldo. By the late 1920s Singapore had already been developed by the British as a Fortress designed to protect British interests from seaward attack. The city was also influenced by the activities from the opposite side of the world. For example, Winston Churchill's UK-centric decisions (when he was British Chancellor of the Exchequer) and General Percival's cowardice and weakness as the Allied commander against General Yamashita's shrewdness, and the Japanese general's battle-fatigued, lightly equipped, and (grossly) numerically inferior Japanese "bicycle" army resulted in the loss of the "fortress" city. Singapore was also the site where the fall of Malaya to Japan was signed at the old Ford Motor Factory along Bukit Timah Road. By the late 1960s and early 1970s Singapore would gain economically from the Vietnam War, as it was the primary center for the export of Malaysian rubber needed for the conduct of battle. There are two main military arrangements: the Five-Power Defence Arrangement (FPDA) that includes the UK, Australia, New Zealand, Malaysia, and Singapore; and the Australia-New Zealand-United States (ANZUS). When bilateral ties between Singapore and Malaysia cooled, Malaysia decided not to take part in the FPDA, but later rejoined the exercises.[7][FH]ASEAN is a political forum, but not a military one that has weakened since Suharto's fall from power in 1999. When the British army units in Singapore withdrew in the early 1970s causing both a loss of jobs and a larger security vacuum, the fledgling city-state's diplomats consistently stressed the importance of a

---

[7] See Ian Stewart, "KL Reveals Review of Defence Pact Membership," *South China Morning Post*, Oct 28, 1998.

70 Modernity and Consumption

strong US presence (in the form of the Seventh Fleet) in Southeast Asia based at Clarke AFB and Subic Naval Base in the Philippines to countervail Vietnamese and Soviet intentions and successes in the 1970s and early 1980s.[FH] Since the fall of Berlin Wall and the end of the Cold War, US military units moved out of Clarke and Subic, although the Pacific Fleet based in Okinawa and headquartered in Honolulu, Hawai`i, continues to maintain a "watching brief". This security complex includes the presence of US units in several Southeast Asian cities including a 15 man logistic team in Singapore. Singapore has bilateral military arrangements with other states in the region that are "open secrets" and indicate formal and informal modes of military deterrence through formal military exchanges within ASEAN countries and in the Asian region.[FH]

The post-Cold War era is possibly the most peaceful in the history of political violence in Southeast Asia (with the exception of internal state violence in Batam, Jakarta, Jogjakarta, Medan, and Kuala Lumpur as a result of the change in Indonesian leadership and the sacking of Anwar Ibrahim). However, there continues to be concern with several issues: the future of the large, sophisticated Soviet-built naval base at Cam Rahn Bay in Vietnam; India's desire to build a blue-water fleet; Chinese military strategy over the next fifty years if the current economic successes persist; the possible break-up of Malaysia and Indonesia; the tension between Singapore and Malaysia over territorial and other claims; the Philippine claim over the Malaysian state of Sabah; and the Islamic fundamentalist movements in the region.

Military strategy in the post Cold War period has shifted from military secrecy and a quasi-arms race to military openness and renewal and rejuvenation in the post Cold War scene. Based on the garrison mentality of a small state surrounded by unpredictable larger, Islamic states, the city-state continues to explore various ways of using science and technology as alternatives to mass military manpower. For example, the amount of state dollars in the annual budget allocated to military expenditure in terms of government expenditure and revenue, was S$4.41 billion in 1993. This amount almost doubled over the subsequent five years to 7.19 billion. For example, the Republic of Singapore Air Force (RSAF) has the most modern and sophisticated aircraft for attack operations; while the Republic of Singapore Navy (RSN) has recently acquired submarines. Information technology continues to alter the course of strategy, tactics, counterintelligence, and combat force multipliers. This will trickle down to paramilitary forces that are designed as combat force supplements. The amount of the annual budget spent on security includes non-military unit activities and programs in support of a national integrated defense philosophy known as Total Defence. This includes Military, Civil, Psychological, Economic, and Social Defence. Civilian control over the military continues to be a primary principle of the defense of the city-state. The city-state went through three phases of defense evolution: 1959-1967 under British advisement;1967-1975 under Israeli consultation; 1975-1989 under US consultation; & from the 1990s onwards, yet not without severing

Table 4: Government Revenue and Expenditure

	1993	1997	1998
REVENUE (Billion S$)			
Total Govt Revenue[8]	19.53	30.61	28.21
Income Tax	7.2	11.4	10.97
Fees & Charges	3.02	4.03	3.35
Vehicle Tax	1.88	1.77	1.55
GST (April 1, 1994)	NA	1.99	1.69
Betting Tax	0.82	1.26	1.27
Other Receipts	1.06	2.14	2.7
EXPENDITURE			
Security	4.41	6.67	7.19
Public Housing	0.11	0.19	0.17
Operating	9.14	**15.16**[9]	14.24
Development	3.41	10.71	10.56

Source: Singapore Department of Statistics, Singapore, 2000.

---

[8] Does not include entire breakdown of all taxes listed by the Department of Statistics (DOS), Singapore.

[9] According to Singapore DOS, this amount includes a one-off compensation of S$1.5 billion to Singapore Telecom for early termination of its exclusive telecommunication privileges.

ties with the former allies. There are many issues in the SAF and one such issue that has reached the level of public discussion is that of the SAF and Malays. It appears to be a traditional practice in the SAF to limit the number of Malay-Muslim officers in the SAF's senior officer corps and other "combat sensitive areas" so as not to place them in situations where they have to choose between national duty and the concept of *ummah* or universal brotherhood among Muslims. However, the current Defense Minister and Deputy Prime Minister has repeatedly denied that Malay-Muslim officers face discrimination in the SAF. No official numbers have been released to prove otherwise. There is also no public or official mention of any Malay-Muslim SAF officers of the general staff rank of brigadier general to date. This is likely to continue even after July 1, 2003 (for example), the traditional promotional date for SAF officers. A Malay-Muslim of the rank of brigadier is unlikely in the future, and the prospect of such an overture might be seen as being more politically symbolic rather than ethnically substantive, and is unlikely to be sufficient to placate the critics of the regime. The promotion to one-star generalship might be one indicator of "meritocracy" at work in the military while the actual post assumed thereafter is the true mark of whether or not the promotion was politically-motivated or based on the merit of the case. Indeed, most appointments to generalship are partially motivated by political concerns, partially by political ones, given the small size of the military relative to other states in the region. The organizational culture in the SAF is intricately tied to the dynamics of the political and administrative culture in Singapore.[FV]

Between December 2001 and January 2002, fifteen people were arrested by the Internal Security Department (ISD). The ISD has been likened to the U.S Federal Bureau of Investigation (FBI), but has wide-sweeping powers including advising the Minister of Home Affairs to detain without trial any person or persons suspected of anti-state activity such as terrorism and subterfuge for a period of two years that may be extended, virtually, indefinitely. On 7 January 2002, *The Straits Times* reported under its "Prime News" section that Deputy Prime Minister and Defence Minister Tony Tan said that Singapore, "could not afford to practice discrimination...for [the]

SAF meritocracy means that so long as the person is committed to Singapore, dedicated to [the] SAF and capable of doing his job, he will have a role to play".[10] The *Straits Times* also quoted Dr Tan as saying that some of the fifteen arrested by the ISD were "national servicemen holding junior positions mainly in the support positions of the armed forces". Dr Tan said, "We have to face facts and SAF manages the realities of race and religion carefully and sensitively."[11] Given this political rhetoric, it remains unclear what exactly the minister means by the "realities of race and religion" as reality and fact are often contingent on individual and group perceptions, persuasions, and prescriptions, and are subject to prejudices and biases since Malay-Muslims, Malay-Christians, Tamil-Christians, Tamil-Hindus, Eurasian-Catholics, Chinese Buddhists, and Chinese-Christians (for example) share similar, convergent, and yet opposing world views. The point the minister should have addressed perhaps is that there can never be a singularly clear-cut distinction between one ethnic community's idea of race and another's idea of reality. The minister went on to say that, "Social cohesion in Singapore does not only depend on the Malay/Muslim community. It needs the co-operation and efforts of all communities here."[12] The political rhetoric here clearly reflects how political speeches provided for public consumption tend to revolve round the multi-cultural, multi-ethnic and multi-lingual showcase of cosmopolitan Singapore. Law and Foreign Affairs Minister S. Jayakumar said, "These are the acts of a group who do not, in my view, represent the majority of our Malay/Muslim population. I have no doubt Singaporeans will unite to express universal condemnation"[13] (see Appendix A). The call for unity expressed through the public medium or "forum" of *The Straits Times* itself represents a redefinition of the social, political, racial, and economic modes of how Singaporeans themselves publicly "consume Singapore".[**FV, EG, VP**]

---

[10] Lydia Lim, "Policy on Muslims in SAF won't change: DPM Tan", *The Straits Times*, Januray 7, 2002, p. 3.

[11] *Ibid.* See also, Lee Hsien Loong's speech on the "tudung issue". *The Straits Times*, January 28, 2002, p. 1.

[12] *Ibid.*

[13] *Ibid.*

Recent history has shown that it is possible to turn a high-ranking military officer into a politician and a civil servant into a politician. However, the old fashioned way of simply converting technocrats into politicians no longer holds, the process of political leadership and generational change in terms of party political structures in Singapore consists of a complex interplay of military and private sector arrangements as the November 2001 elections has shown. [14]

Distribution of Wealth

Incomes in Singapore have risen steadily since the country's independence in 1963 and separation from Malaysia in 1965. In 1963 Singapore had an uncertain future as a former colony of an empire in its own death throes. The Singapore city-state was a third world country with all the problems of unemployment, housing shortages, poor health care and hygiene, and low-income levels. However, as the economy grew steadily over 35 years from 1965, incomes grew accordingly. There were two periods when incomes stagnated: once in 1985/86 when the nationalized unions under then NTUC secretary-general Ong Teng Cheong managed workers and employers to make adjustments in their CPF contributions in the wake of the Pan-Electric crisis and the second time when Southeast Asian stock markets collapsed in the 1998 recession. The public intervening deeply into the private purses of the citizens, and the private citizens depending on public or State leadership. Again, Singapore workers especially in the public sector saw their wages stagnate. These wages have not yet been restored to their pre-recession levels, even though there is much political rhetoric about the full restoration

---

[14] See also, Antonio L. Rappa, (1999) "Political Pluralism and Governance in Singapore," in Frank Delmartino, Amara Pongsapich, and Rudolf Hrbek, (eds.), *Regional Pluralism and Good Governance: Problems and Solutions in ASEAN and EU-countries* (Baden-Baden: Nomos Verlagsgesellschaft); and the review of Joseph B. Tamney's "The Struggle Over Singapore's Soul: Western Modernization & Asian Culture", *Journal of Developing Areas*, 1997; 31(4): 584-586.

of incomes; and in spite of the economic recovery since the "technical recession". Several thousand workers, however, were retrenched by several multinationals over the past three years. The increase in incomes across the board for all classes of Singaporeans is no mean feat. Income levels while relatively higher than other Southeast Asian countries have not been met with equal distribution of the proportional wealth distributed for the overall population of workers of the city-state as a whole. There is no publicly available data on the incomes of Singaporeans per ethnic community, although the local press reported the deputy prime minister as having stated that in Australia that the bottom ten per cent of Singapore households earn approximately S$133 (S$1.81 = USS$1). This refers to the entire family, not individual incomes. This was in stark contrast to Singapore's total government revenue of S$30.61 billion (1997), and S$28.21 billion (1998). The ethnic breakdown of the poorest poor is not available in the public realm. Thus while standards of living have risen, costs of living have also risen in tandem. Income and wealth are very unevenly distributed in Singapore. Why would a country with year-on-year budget surpluses have the bottom 10 per cent of its households earning S$133 monthly? One hypothesis is that the greatest amount of wealth is concentrated in the top five per cent of the population, while the remaining 80 per cent of the population earn progressively, but not substantially, higher amounts than the previous cohort.[15][EG, VP]

Table 3 displays several high-profile consumer goods that have been categorized into durable and non-durable types. This is followed by a look at the kind of prices that are actually being paid by consumers. The table gives a positive though cursory snapshot of the cost of consumables in Singapore

---

[15] *The Straits Times*, June 2000, "Housing Board residents are getting more affluent, according to the latest Housing and Development Board (HDB) survey which profiled 2.7 million HDB residents. The average monthly household income had risen by about 40 per cent from $2,653 in 1993 to $3,719 in 1998. 60 per cent of households are living in four-room flats or bigger, compared to 50 per cent in 1993. Salient statistical improvements include 49.3 per cent of all households owning a personal computer (1993: 20.2 per cent) and 30.8 per cent owning a split air-conditioning unit (1993: 8.6 per cent). One in four households also has an Internet account today".

divided between consumer durables and consumer non-durables. However, the ownership of these small items mean nothing unless they are considered with the Consumer Price Index. The Department of Statistic's historical data set for CPI with a base year at 1998 (November 1997 to October 1998) year on year from 1961 to 1999 indicate a clear increase in the cost of living in Singapore for all residents.[16] While gross monthly household income of the bottom 50 per cent of all households in the year 2000 is numerically higher than the gross monthly household income was thirty years before in 1970, it cannot be equated with a similar increase in the total monthly real income for the same number of households of the same cohort for two reasons. Firstly, the cohort has changed significantly, and secondly, the lack of longitudinal studies for the 1970 to 2000 period implies that there is no factual way of knowing the actual movement between and within economic classes, and among ethnic communities in terms of gross income, real income, nominal income, and total wealth.[EG] While it is true that the basket of wealth has increased significantly for most groups it is not a claim that can be made for all groups. Disposable income must be considered alongside CPI because it allows for the relative position of consumer costs to be estimated from a particular year's perspective. For example, the Singapore Department of Statistics reported that between July – December 1999, "the Consumer Price Index for general households increased by 1.1 per cent in the second half of the year, compared with –0.3 per cent in the first half of 1999. A similar trend is noted for the three income groups. During the second half of 1999, the consumer price indices for the lowest 20% and middle 60% income groups rose by 1.5 per cent and 1.0 per cent respectively. The consumer price index for the top 20 % income group experienced the highest growth of 2.5 per cent in the second half of 1999. After registering a decline of 0.3 per cent in 1998, the general consumer price index for 1999 rose by 0.4 per cent. Households in the lowest 20% income group experienced a lower inflation rate of 1.2 per cent in 1999 compared with the previous year. The inflation rate for the middle 60% income group was half a percent in 1999, the same rate as in 1998. As a

---

[16] "Statistics Singapore," DOS, Singapore, March 30th, 2000.

result of higher car prices, the consumer price index for households in the top 20% income group went up by 0.6 per cent in 1999, as against the decline of 4.3 per cent in the preceding year". The CPI also allows for changes in tastes, even though it is an inaccurate measure, to be reflected in a new basket of goods over time. However, consumption in Singapore cannot merely be measured in terms of which economic classes and ethnic groups get what, and how much.

Cost of living indices are arbitrary measures and have to include calculations that seek to measure the quality of life. The quality of life is always more subjective and unclear and dynamic than the costs it entail. Neither can be reduced to either's terms.

Table 5: Consumption of Selected Durables and Selected Non-Durables

Item\Year	1988	1992	1997
	Percentage of Households		
DURABLES			
Air-conditioner	19.4	35.3	53.1
Car	29.8	31.1	35.8
Computer	11.2	20.2	40.8
Laser/Video/Compact Disc Players*	—	19.6	47.4
Motorcycle/scooter	13.5	10.6	9.2
Washing Machine	73.5	80.5	90.6
Television Licenses ('000)	639.139	600.382	704.296
NON-DURABLES			
Cinema Attendance (millions)	19.97	17.35	16.4
Swimming Pool Attendance (millions)	5.7	6.45	6.82
Cable TV ('000)	22.2	104.02	144.0
Newspaper Circulation (all languages) (millions)	0.98	1.02	1.05

Source: Singapore Department of Statistics, 2000
*Data not available for 1988.

Table 5 demonstrates the analytical power of Adorno and Horkheimer in Bauman's reading of the decomposition of community and the fragmentation of life, "The life-process of every agent tends to split up into a series of episodes, each episode being in principle self-confined and self-sustained. Leaving the site cleared and ready for another sensation-seeking episode is perhaps the only self-limiting consideration which the code recommends. The pursuit of no desire should undermine, let alone pre-empt, the pursuits of future desires. Adorno and Horkheimer expressed this state of affairs rather sharply: 'Individuals are reduced to a mere sequence of instantaneous experiences which leave no trace, or rather whose trace is hated as irrational, superfluous, and "overtaken" in the literal sense of the word."[17]

Summary

This chapter examined the nature of modernity, consumption in terms of national security and the distribution of wealth in Singapore. The chapter showed how public goods constitute different kinds of patterns of consumption in Singapore and how such public forms of consumption are effectively determined by the "public" to the extent that "private" space in Singapore becomes conditional, ephemeral, and decrepit.

---

[17] Zygmunt Bauman, *In Search of Politics* (Cambridge & Oxford: Polity Press, 1999), p. 77.

References

Bauman, Zygmunt. 1999. *In Search of Politics.* Cambridge & Oxford: Polity Press.

Glass, D. C. and Singer, J. E. 1972. *Urban Stress: Experiments on Noise and Social Stressors.* New York: Academic Press, Academic Press.

Goldsmith, M. and Villadsen, S. (eds.) 1986. *Urban Political Theory and the Management of Fiscal Stress.* Brookfield: Gower.

Gottdiener, M. ed. 1986. *Cities in Stress: A New Look at the Urban Crisis.* Beverley Hills: Sage Publications.

Government of Singapore, White Paper (various).

Martin, J. K. 1982. *Urban Financial Stress: Why Cities Go Broke.* Dover, MA: Auburn House.

Miller, Daniel, ed. 2001. *Consumption, Critical Concepts in the Social Sciences.* vols. I – IV. London & New York: Routledge.

Rappa, Antonio L. Review of "The Struggle Over Singapore's Soul: Western Modernization & Asian Culture", by Joseph B. Tamney, *Journal of Developing Areas.* 1997, **31** (4): 584-586.

Rappa, Antonio L. 1999. "Political Pluralism and Governance in Singapore," in Frank Delmartino, Amara Pongsapich, and Rudolf Hrbek, (eds.), *Regional Pluralism and Good Governance: Problems and Solutions in ASEAN and EU-countries* Baden-Baden: Nomos Verlagsgesellschaft.

Singapore Armed Forces Act. 1995. (Revised). *The Statutes of the Republic of Singapore*, 10, 295.

US Army Area Handbook, United States Department of the Army.

Appendix A

Mrs Ong-Chew Peck Wan, director of corporate communications at the Ministry of Home Affairs:

ST: *Is there still a threat? Should the public be concerned?*

MHA: We believe that the network has been disrupted. There is no information of any imminent threat. Nevertheless, all measures that can be reasonably taken to defend ourselves against terrorist threats have been taken.

Some are very visible and the public can see this. Others are less visible, involving our security and intelligence agencies working with counterparts in the region and other parts in the world.

As investigations are ongoing, we should avoid speculation. More details will be disclosed when investigations are completed.

The public should be assured that there is no cause for panic.

ST: *Are American establishments among those targeted for terrorist bombing?*

MHA: Yes, American establishments, including the US embassy and commercial entities, were the principal targets for attack in this case.

ST: *Is this group connected with the Kumpulan Militan Malaysia (KMM)? (Revealing the arrest of 13 terror suspects last week, Malaysian police said the KMM wanted to forcefully establish an Islamic state made up of Malaysia, Indonesia and the southern Phillipines.)*

MHA: There are clearly some links.

ST: *Is this group connected with the Al-Queda?*

MHA: There are links. However, investigations are still on-going.

ST: *Is this case connected to the increase in security measures in Singapore in recent months, especially since December last year?*

MHA: Yes, the intelligence obtained in the current case was one of the reasons why security measures were upgraded at that time.

ST: *There was a UPI report on Dec 28 of United States intelligence leading to arrests in Singapore. Was this the case? (The UPI news agency report said that the Singapore Government, acting on US intelligence gathered in Afghanistan, raided a "terrorist nest" in December and arrested 12 alleged Al-Queda members suspected of planning an attack on Singapore's deep-water Navy port.)*

MHA: The Ministry of Home Affairs responded to this earlier. The position is unchanged. We did not receive any information from the Americans or others which led to these arrests. In fact, following the arrests, we had briefed various intelligence services, including the Americans, of the case.

ST: *Is this case connected to the recent Jane's Intelligence Review Report? (The Jane's report revealed the extent of Al-Queda's reach in this region and said that Al-Queda members in Singapore were believed to have been about to launch an operation, but were stopped by terrorist Osama bin Laden for reasons not known.)*

MHA: No, although the article was obviously not wrong about Al-Queda links in the region, including Singapore. We have no information to confirm that Al-Queda plans for terrorist action in Singapore were aborted by Osama.

ST: *The Malaysian authorities reported that they have detained one Mohamed Iqbal A. Rahman for KMM activities since June last year. Is he the Abu Jibril referred to in the Singapore Government press statement?*

MHA: Yes. Abu Jibril is also known as Mohamed Iqbal A. Rahman.

Source: Lydia Lim and Steve Dawson, "American Establishments here were group's main targets", *The Straits Times,* 7 January 2002, 3.

Family & Education

It needs to be understood that in Athens marriage was not the only kind of union that was accepted; it actually formed a particular and privileged kind of union, which alone could lead to matrimonial cohabitation and legitimate offspring.

Michel Foucault
The Use of Pleasure: The History of Sexuality, vol. 2, 1985

J. S. Mill's suggestion that governments devote themselves to optimising the balance between leaving people's private lives and preventing suffering seems to me pretty much the last word. Discoveries abut who is being made to suffer can be left to the workings of a free press, free universities, and enlightened public opinion — enlightened for example by books like *Madness and Civilization* and *Discipline and Punish*.

Richard Rorty
Contingency, Irony, and Solidarity, 1989

84 Modernity and Consumption

A prerequisite to consumption in Singapore's late modernity is its conflation of, and dependence on, a modern patriarchal family structure within the narratival framework of general education, military education, and national education.

Singapore's self-government in the modern period as an independent state began in 1959 when the British agreed that the city-state and former Crown Colony would be allowed to elect its own Legislative Assembly with the Colonial Office retaining control over Internal Security, Defence, and Foreign Affairs. Singapore achieved political independence through a second step via the Federation of Malaysia concept in 1963. However, not long after the political merger with Malaysia, the federal prime minister, *Yang Teramat Mulia Tunku* Abdul Rahman Alhaj (known by his supporters as the Father of Malaysia or Bapa Malaysia) decided that Malaysia and Singapore should evolve as separate, sovereign entities two years after Merdeka in order to avoid ethnic violence between the two largest ethnic groups, the indigenous Malays and the immigrant Chinese. The decision was historically important because it would pave the way for a series of political strategies and public policies that would prove to be marked by a competition over public space on ethnic, racial, and religious grounds. J. S. Mill's suggestion in Rorty's quote above signals the crucial balancing act that governments play everywhere in the world — and in Singapore and Malaysia — between private space and public reduction of poverty. In the case of both countries, it becomes increasingly clear that consumption patterns reflect the low levels of relative poverty and that the classical notion of a modern state redistributing wealth to its citizens is in effect a net product of a generally consistent direction taken by the various prime ministers and their various cabinets since decolonization in the 1950s and early 1960s.[IG]

A Foundational Fantasy of Success and Failure

Singapore's modern political history may have begun with political success (at independence) but the threat of economic failure through the political separation from its natural market and economic hinterland overshadowed the regime's early days. There were also those who resented the belligerence of the Singapore leadership, and wanted to see it fail. Ghazalie Shafie, for example, was "the permanent secretary in Malaysia's external affairs ministry said soon after separation, after a few years out on a limb, Singapore would be in severe straits and would come crawling back — this time on Malaysia's terms" (Lee, 1998: 663) [**FV**].

The fear of economic failure was part of the modernist foundational fantasy of horror. But like all fantasies, there is always an ending and there is always space for potential closure within the public realm. In retrospect, the closure with Singapore's economic success showed that the fantasy was not as horrifying as its perpetrators would have had it. The fantasy was not as stultifying and horrific as it must have appeared to the political leaders of the day on both sides of the Singapore-Malaysia Causeway. The Singapore leadership was able to overcome the horror by deliberately reinventing Singapore because the fantasy told them that there was nothing to lose but everything. In the mind of these modern Singapore leaders, there was a need to reinvent the local view of a vulnerable, peninsula-dependent city-state to that of a global view with international links through what eventually became a multinational economic strategy. While the adult leaders were not always sure of what they were doing they did it anyway. This stemmed from a confidence, determination and a resolve to counter the challenges of modernity with modern instruments of war.[**FH**] A confidence that already existed in the political leadership with the decision to hang to the death two foreign commandos during Confrontation — a short-lived tousle with the regional hegemon, an Indonesia heavily influenced by the Indonesian communist party (PKI).

Reliance on rational thought, logical argument, and breaking away from the mindset of a colonially-constructed bureaucracy was to be the primary narrative that Lee Kuan Yew and his early cabinet embarked on. The foundational fantasy in the making was not without public displays of weakness and vulnerability. Only once did Lee Kuan Yew, the favored son and popular patriarch of the fledgling Republic, make an unexpected display of such emotions in public to the extent of his own self-deprecation of traditional Chinese ancestral expectations:

> Among Chinese it is unbecoming to exhibit such a lack of manliness. But I could not help myself ... I was emotionally overstretched, having gone through three days and nights of a wrenching experience. With little sleep since Friday night in Kuala Lumpur, I was close to physical exhaustion. I was weighed down by a heavy sense of guilt. I felt I had let down several million people in Malaysia: immigrant Chinese and Indians, Eurasians, and even some Malays. I had aroused their hopes and they had joined people in Singapore in resisting Malay hegemony, the root cause of our dispute (Lee, 1998: 16-17).

The tears of the national leader broadcast over television to a public unaccustomed to see a weak Lee resulted in nothing less than political capital for the man and his party by default not design since political capital was not his intention. The telling and sharing of sadness, just once in his long political career was enough to cause grief and worry, anxiety and fear among his supporters. This was perhaps one of the lowest points in Singapore's public narrative where the father shows weakness and vulnerability.[1][FH]

Lee knew that he had to get it over with, and to get on with government otherwise — as his pragmatic side told him — time would be foolishly wasted on a narrative of tears, emotional rhetoric, and an unnecessary distraction from the public demands of the day. Consequently, Lee and his

---

[1] See also, Kim Wah Yeo and Albert Lau, "From Colonialism to Independence, 1945-1965", chapter 7, *A History of Singapore*, edited by Ernest Chew and Edwin Lee (Singapore, Oxford and New York: Oxford University Press, 1991); Albert Lau, 1998, *A Moment of Anguish: Singapore in Malaysia and the Politics of Disengagement* (Singapore: Times Academic Press, 1998), pp. 253-265.

supporters acquired what these politicians labelled as Singapore's pragmatic approach to nation-building and state-building from 1965 to 1998, bereft of ideology, with a top-down, paternalistic government that will go down in history as a central part of Lee's political legacy. Ironically, where other states had failed, Lee's paternalistic, *father-knows-best* "philosophy" of government resulted in an unanticipated economic recovery, economic development, and economic productivity and achievement over a thirty-three year period. In a sense, and after his emotional outburst over television at the advice of P.S. Raman.[2] Lee has not broken down once then, nor let emotion sway his politics, or his politics to sway his emotions:

> I had let many people down in Malaya, Sabah, and Sarawak. They had responded to our call of a Malaysian Malaysia. Had they not done so and there was no danger of widespread racial collisions if the Malaysian government arrested us, Singapore would not have been expelled. By accepting separation, I had failed them. That sense of guilt made me break down. It was my moment of anguish (Lee, 1998:649).

However, Lee appeared to have recovered very quickly, and his Malaysian Malaysia campaign narrative quickly evolved into an enigmatic metaphor of "pragmatism" Lee Kuan Yew-style which together with his staunch supporters in the form of Toh Chin Chye (the former Chairman of the PAP), Lim Kim San (who contributed to the economy for many years till he stepped down as Chairman of Singapore Press Holdings), S. Rajaratnam (who was eventually to become the first senior minister of Singapore) decided in the tense weeks that followed that fateful day, August 9, 1965.

---

[2] I wish to thank Kenneth Anthony Rappa for sharing his inside views as one of the assistants to P. S. Raman who was at the studio scene with Lee that fateful day. In 1968, P. S. Raman was appointed Singapore's first Ambassador to Indonesia, and later became High Commissioner to Australia in the early 1970s when Dr. Benjamin Henry Sheares was the President of the Republic. Rahman played a crucial role in RTS in the early years before he became a diplomat.

They decided to make a 180 degree turn away from the days when Lee and his men argued so vociferously for merger with Malaysia, to one where Lee and his supporters began rationalization of complete and utter separation from Malaysia. Rather than return to the Federation on the latter's terms in 1965, Singapore embarked on a course of action that was publicly inconceivable at the time: being forced to go alone in a political and economic future without the Federation of Malaysia. Tungku Abdul Rahman's decision that both countries should separate would challenge the indubitable bonds that had evolved over centuries of ethnic, linguistic, religious, and familial lines on both sides of the mile-long Causeway across the Straits of Johore. [FH]

Regional and Local Family Ties & Threats

> In saying this, I do not mean to imply that adults were always aware of what they were doing or why they were doing it. To a considerable extent, developments were dictated by the nature of both books and schools. For example, by writing sequenced textbooks and by organizing school classes according to calendar age, schoolmasters invented, as it were, the stages of childhood. Our notions of what a child can learn or ought to learn, and at what ages, were largely derived from the concept of a sequenced curriculum; that is to say, from the concept of the prerequisite.
>
> Neil Postman
> *The Disappearance of Childhood*, 1982

State rhetoric promotes the belief that the family plays a central and foundational importance in Singapore's economic success. There is also the belief in the preservation of the Asian family structure will be beneficial to the economy since the family is considered the unit in society that is at the heart of the social fabric. If the family is destroyed, then the social fabric is torn and social disintegration, possible. The centrality of the Asian family structure whether or not it is perceived by western liberals as constructed in the sense of being artificial is not the question. The point is that the Asian family structure is one that is perceived to be widely accepted in and around Asia and dispossessed of particular characteristics: nuclear, independent, non-traditional, separate and autonomous. Political leaders sometimes believe that the Asian family structure is one that is built around close family ties, an extended kinship network, filial piety, and "respect" for authority; and where problems and challenges to the (ritual make-up of the) family are met head-on *by* the family as a whole.[FV]

The irony about the Asian family as perceived by such leaders is that the "Asian" family structure is not unique to Asia, but is found virtually everywhere else in the world. The idea of closeness and family ties that stretch beyond two generations is commonplace among many African societies, Scandinavian societies, and central European ones. There are three reasons why there is such a misperception within the Singapore case, if indeed it still exists, that the Asian family unit is markedly different from other family and extended family units: (1) the ancient cultural resilience of the Chinese and Indian civilizations; (2) the tendency among leaders to think they are always right leads to reification of the *status quo* within the confines of a patriarchal society where father knows best; and, (3) the power of modernity that has changed and altered the traditional structures of many American families has led to the belief that individualism has run amok and is rampant to the extent that familial ties no longer exist is untrue and often more a result of mediated broadcasting and syndicated television networks that promote and ideal that becomes a reality.[FV]

Foucault suggests that the existence of the family and its structure in terms of legal connections and consequences was already apparent in ancient Greece. Yet Singapore's political leaders who hold that the family is indeed the basic building block of society are correct in principle but are motivated by different and problematic reasons. One problem is that the political rhetoric of the family creates the dualism between an "us" and "them" which is useful as it is perceived to galvanise and bond citizens within the concept of nation-hood. The "Asian" "us" and "Foreign" "them" in terms of how a family is structured appeals to those who desire a simple prescription of what life is about and develops space between the "us" and "them". The contradiction arises when policies such as the foreign talent policy that is designed to attract foreign talent receives much media support and attention, thereby generating even more public interest where there was none. The foreign talent policy is a logical and rational policy yet it has not gone down well with Singaporeans because it runs counter to the rhetoric of the family that has been promoted for many years in order to combat what used to be perceived as "decadent western morality". The foreign or global talent policy occupies a subliminal space where the us and them used to occur. If indeed western "decadence" was part of the foundational fantasy of horror, then it becomes clear why people complain when they see the horror of job loss and that of foreigners supposedly and mistakenly "occupying" space originally held by Singaporeans. They are not. Another problem is another contradiction that occupies the subliminal space between the public and private perceptions of the family that Foucault later speaks about.[IG]

The notion of the family as the basic unit of society appears to have been promoted in terms of a typical, ethnic-centred marriage where the majority of citizens are supposed to support or believe in the ideal of husband, wife, and two children (in the initial stop at two policy) and later a "two or more if you can afford it" slogan. This "Singaporean-pragmatic" ideal is problematic because it is *not* an ideal in the first place. And neither is it unique. There are many families in Singapore who contribute productively to the economy and who pay taxes and uphold the law but because of unforeseen circumstances have only one child, or no children, or are single (female or male) parents or have children who are from divorced marriages. The state model is too conceptually blind limited to be able to reconcile the reality of families that do not subscribe to the ideal. This also increases the social stigma attached to such families.[FH]

There appears to be limited resistance to modernity in Singapore because the potential sources of resistance — across socio-economic class, ethnicity, and gender — are co-opted into mainstream pro-establishment culture through state-recognised channels such as the government Feedback Unit housed in the Ministry of Community Development and Sports; through letters to the "Forum Page" of the largest daily newspaper, *The Straits Times*; the local theatre and arts scene that comes under the "guidance" of the National Arts Council; and the ethnic self-help groups. For example, the Feedback Unit channels the views across the spectrum of Singaporeans from all social and economic classes. Views are also often sought from the various trade unions, professional associations, and ethnic self-help groups such as the Eurasian Association of Singapore (EAS) the Singapore Indian Development Association (SINDA), *Mendaki*, and the Chinese Development Assistance Council (CDAC). These ethnic self-help groups must also satisfy the criteria for an Institution of Public Character (IPC) in order to receive "dollar-for-dollar matching" for their welfare and assistance programs. This means that for each dollar that the ethnic self-help group raises, the government will match it by the same amount up to a specific quantum that can be as high as several millions of dollars. Also, these ethnic self-help groups that are run by volunteers represent pseudopolitical organizations with one foot in civil society and the other one in government. One of the central purposes of these groups is to provide support for the familial structure of the family unit by co-ethnic volunteers. The motif often used by such groups in propelling their cause is one that champions the belief that "charity" literally "begins at home". These groups work closely with community organizations such as the People's Association (PA) and Community Development Divisions run by the Community Development Councils which disburse state revenue towards community development activities.[IG]

The Singapore family unit has been pivotal in the successful evolution of a dynamic, highly efficient, literate, and economically productive labour force. Externally, the political leadership of the postcolonial state established comprehensive and integrated structures of political, military, social, and economic governance in preparation for, and in response to, the global and regional tensions of the periods, viz., negotiating with the British for a more gradual withdrawal of its military and economic activities, East of the Suez canal from 1967; preventing Mao's export communism from infiltration in Operation Cold Store; diplomatic rapprochement with Suharto's Indonesia after Sukarno's policy of megalomaniacal political confrontation (Konfrontasi); the closing down of the communist-infiltrated Nanyang University ("Nantah", the only Chinese medium university); a pro-

U.S. foreign policy as a countervailing force against the likelihood of a communist Indochina (Vietnam war and the fall of Cambodia); the use of the Internal Security Act in the 1987 Marxist conspiracy that involved some clergy and lay workers of the Catholic Church; on-going territorial claims with Malaysia over *Pulau Batu Putih* or *Pedra Branca*; and the problematic territorial relationship with Malaysia.

The first decade of political independence of the new nation from August 9, 1965, was vague, uncertain, and unknown. The most exciting thing about foundational fantasies in modernity is that no one knows what the outcome might be. The external security environment was uneasy: the distribution of regional military power and influence was dominated by Suharto's new Republic to the south, the ideological, IndoChinese hot war to the north-east, and the Sabah claim between the Philippines and the Federation of Malaysia that still exists in the first quarter of the 21st century although it is kept quietly under the diplomatic carpets of both countries. Additionally, there was a larger ideological war looming in the PRC's brand of export-communism that threatened the regional stability of the newly decolonised Southeast Asian nation-states. The Chinese Diaspora in Southeast Asia that included the relatively large population in Singapore was perceived with a certain degree of suspicion by other Southeast Asian states because of its former ties with PRC on the one hand and the KMT on the other. Singapore's "land-linked" neighbour to the immediate north, while struggling with the demands of a newly independent political economy would eventually be given the litmus test of ethnic management in 1969. The economic differentials between ethnically-Chinese citizens and the "indigenous" citizens served as a point of disaffection, an inequality that would fuel the race riots in 1969 that led to the implementation of the New Economic Policy (NEP). While the NEP was not overtly touted as an affirmative action strategy, its ultimate goal was clearly targeted at minimising the association of occupation with ethnicity in the public and private sectors, with the intention of securing at least a 30% stake-holding in the country's economy. However, these economic differentials were not exclusive to Malaysia. The 1998 economic recession gave vent to political scapegoatism against ethnic-Chinese in the Philippines and most clearly in

Indonesia under B. J. Habibie within the Southeast Asian ethnic-Chinese Diaspora, a representation of the relative deprivation across ethnic groups that had welled up over three and a half decades in a region with one of the world's highest levels of economic growth. Singapore's own position was limited to minimising its economic, military, and social uncertainties.[FH] These uncertainties could not have been placed under control without recourse to strident policies in social policing and state control of potentially subversive elements. The use-vale of the Internal Security Act itself, at the expense of complete political liberty, was instrumental in ensuring that "undesirable elements" would be kept at bay if not in check. In order to reconcile the problems of unemployment, housing, health, and defence, Singapore's elected leaders had three main tasks ahead of the new nation-state: state-building, economic viability, and nation-building.[FV] State-building was by far the simplest to achieve of the three tasks. It warranted the establishment of political institutions — Parliament, the Judiciary, and the Executive within a system of governance — that would institutionalise the three arms of government in order to represent social interests, provide a means of distributing public goods and services, and enable justice through the rule of law. The burden of state-building was made simpler because there was an old colonial model to follow. Modifications were made to the Westminster system of parliamentary democracy, resulting in a hybrid, managed democracy, Singapore-style. Managed democracy is defined as state-led reconciliation of public demand for political representation through interest articulation and agglomeration, and is characterised by paternalistic governance (the state knows best), incorporation of technocrats as political leaders (political leadership through technical skill), and committee decision-making (shared responsibility).

The Chinese majority in Singapore are often considered to be politically apathetic. This is a misnomer. While Singaporeans in general, and Chinese Singaporeans in particular are not overtly demonstrative in the political realm because of the penalties for unlicensed, non-authorised political activity, the former take the opportunity to make their opinion known at the regularly held General Elections (GE). In the 1997 GE, for example, almost 40% of voters chose not to vote for the incumbent Peoples' Action Party

(PAP). If there is a greater slide away from the incumbent party then it must be due to the absence of a social polity — public forums for expressing political dissent without penalty. An increase in the popular vote for the PAP is likely to be interpreted at the national level that the preceding years of behavior-modifying campaigns in conjunction with rational economic policies have indeed been successfully accepted by the public (and the private) in spite of the 1997-1998 recession, and 2000-2003 recession. Clearly, the 2001 General Election that saw significant swing of voters — primarily Chinese working-class Singaporeans living in the Housing and Development Board (HDB) estates (the heartlands, and the heartlanders) — towards the PAP with a massive 75% majority in the November 3, 2001 election. This indicates to a certain extent that under crisis situations, people bonded together by citizenship, ethnicity, class, a common political and economic history, and other Andersonian-type "imagined ties" are more likely than not to band together and vote solidly for a government they can trust and have trusted in the past rather than to experiment. The converse argument is that during economic upswings there is a greater likelihood towards political experimentation in the general elections of democratising states.[3][IG, FV]

The rationalisation of the political good into political stability has transformed economics into a consumer good that is much "more important" than politics, and Goh Chok Tong warned that Singaporeans and others in Singapore had to act and speak within political OB markers. Singapore is also efficiently managed because of the low levels of corruption, a high propensity for saving, mass political apathy, and ironically, the absence of natural resources. This has led to a culture that is proud of successive generations of political leaders devoted to maintaining a robust, efficient, productive, literate, non-political, non-resisting workforce.

---

[3] Antonio L. Rappa, "Economic Slowdown Seen Favoring PAP in Coming Polls", interviewed by Ca-mie De Souza, *Channel News Asia*, see the CNA website, Singapore: September 27, 2001, 1452 HRS GMT, 2252 HRS Singapore Standard Time, written by Ca-mie De Souza and Asha Popatlal; see also, Antonio L. Rappa, "*Cresco o clima de apreensao no sudeste asiatico*," (Crisis in Southeast Asia) interviewed by Mirna Queiroz, The BBC World Service – Brazil Correspondent, 1 October, 2001.

Economic Education

After separation from the Federation of Malaysia, Singapore was thrust into the pragmatic quagmire of global economics. Economic sovereignty at the time involved a large number of citizens who were unemployed or about to be retrenched by the British withdrawal, inadequate public housing, low levels of public sanitation and hygiene, and a population that was increasing at an increasing rate. The large pool of labour would be introduced to the radical concept of the multi-national economy, one based on foreign direct investment of western transnational corporations (TNCs). The first decade saw industrial policies targeted at developing a niche in the flows of international capital and global markets.[FV] The TNC-led economy was buttressed by the development of world class port facilities that would continue to ensure that Singapore remained at a major confluence of modern shipping and airline routes. The devotion of public money to these enterprises, and the enhancement of its economic infrastructure would gradually enable Singapore to gain, and retain its status as an international hub of global capital movements.[EG] In terms of social infrastructure, massive public housing plans initiated in the early 1960s replaced previous (limited) endeavours represented in part by public organisations like the Singapore Improvement Trust (SIT). The integrated, comprehensive urban planning approach to national housing provided a blueprint for the formation of a social support system that would enhance liveable space, for the maximisation of limited natural resources. For the economy, the next two phases of industrialisation shifted from labour-intensive industries to a technology-intensive one that was complemented by regional and international searches for investment and other economic policies that drew various catch phrases such as "growth triangles", "external wings", "Singapore Incorporated", "Singapore One", the search for foreign talent, as the nation-state directs itself and its energy toward "Singapore 21". The attraction of Singapore's ideal geographical position was further enhanced by infrastructural development in mass communication, transportation strategies, and a regionally-based, internationally-responsive financial sector.[FV] The overall success of the product — Singapore in 1998 — was in effect built and designed on a series of smaller successes: Neptune Orient Lines (one of the few non-conference based national shipping lines that managed to keep afloat through ebb and flow of the volatile 1970s, 1980s, and 1990s shipping markets); the Port of Singapore Authority, now renamed, redesignated, and reorganised; and the Orientalist, exotic, and capitalist Singapore Airlines Group. The basic strategy of the small, sovereign, nation-state was to maximise its limited resources, keep abreast of leading-edge technology, be constantly sensitive to changes in global demand for technology-based goods and services, and to avoid economic complacency.[FH]

Military Education

The implementation of full-time National Service (NSF) served three main purposes: to fulfil the hardware and software defence requirements of the new nation-state, to indoctrinate male Singaporeans with a sense of military duty to the nation, and to put in place a system of military reservists (NSR) who would form the core of front-line, combat-ready soldiers in times when a military solution was the "only" alternative. The short-term economic spin-off from the NSF-NSR policy in the late 1960s and early 1970s was that it kept a generation of otherwise young and impressionable men "employed", instead of contributing to the level of unemployment. As the SAF developed from a weak, vulnerable, and superficial force into a full-service, technologically advanced military machine over three decades, it became increasingly apparent that a large, full-time, cost-efficient, conscript defence force offered a viable and plausible alternative to an expensive, full-time, professional military force found in most larger nation-states. The military policy was unpopular but far-sighted.[FH] A third option to engage in an externally-dependent security arrangement with a small volunteer force may have proved to be fatal as demonstrated in the case of Kuwait in the 1990 Gulf War. The SAF policy kept the cost of maintaining and training a military force relatively low, while national energy was concentrated on economic development. This also provided the fledgling nation-state a time-tested avenue for value indoctrination that was vital for national survival and social cohesion. Since all Singapore males were enlisted, the SAF provided a site where males from different economic classes would have to work together, and be forced to work together efficiently as a team. Singapore in late modernity is about reinventing the traditional wheel unlike in the United Kingdom (at Sandhurst for example) where the presence of "royalty" and "nobility" was already a long and established tradition, and where "passing out" of military colleges was an affair *de rigueur*. Unlike Singapore, there was always a traditional officer corps on tap in Great Britain and in Malaysia, especially among the gentry. However, what was lacking in tradition was made up for in terms of the financial rewards and perks that professional (regular) combat personnel in the SAF received in the past and continue to receive in the present. The Singapore military model, initially influenced by Israeli consultants disguised, rumoured, and portrayed as Mexicans, provided and continues to provide a certain sense of masculine cohesion and bonding. National defence education, in spite of the Spartan training, has over the years become normalised as part of Singapore culture and has evolved into an important rite of passage in the education of the Singaporean male. Many parents boast of their "son's" accomplishments with the most prestigious being that of gaining a place, and perhaps even graduating from the difficult and challenging tri-service Officer Cadet School SAFTI-MI in Tuas as an SAF officer. The esprit de corps and leadership among all SAF commanders and the rank and file represents an integral part of the national education strategy.**[FH, EG, FV]**

National Education

The on-going task of nation-building is onerous, delicate, and crucial for political survival. An important aspect of nation-building is imbuing in citizens a uniformity of purpose, and singularity of belief in the national identity. The symbols of the nation — the national flag, the national crest, and the national anthem — represent the ideals upon which the body *corpora* of a nation directs itself. However, rather than adopt an ideological policy akin to its ASEAN counterparts (Malaysia's *Rukunegara*, or Indonesia's *Pancasila*) Singapore espouses a short-list of shared values, in addition to the five forms of defence/unity in diversity theme. The implementation of the ideological values of a nation-state rests with the state bureaucracy, or the civil service component within the executive arms of government. The former Ministry of Culture, Ministry of Information and the Arts, and to a certain extent, the Ministry of Communications, represent the primary agencies for implementing the national agenda.

In addition to their primary tasks, these government agencies may be directed to plan, evaluate, and implement policy programmes in direct relation to the national interest, that would ordinarily lie outside their purview and jurisdiction. This is illustrated in the Ministry of Education and the its implementation of the National Education (NE) policy that seeks to instil a sense of history among school going citizens. Part of the larger intention is to return students to a time of danger and chaos, a period in Singapore history that was fraught with modern uncertainties: political, security, economic, social, cultural, demographic, and religious. At the heart of the programme on National Education is the concept of the Singapore Story (SS). Both NE and SS involve the re-telling of historical hurdles and obstacles faced by Singaporeans and Singapore leaders intricately woven and edited into a comprehensive, coherent set of facts that is easily consumed by the masses. These themes are part of the institutional memorialization that serve to root the citizens in the nation-state and the nation-state in the citizens. The thematic launches and implementation through the school system are not new to Singaporeans, only more technically advanced, complex, colourful, authoritative, and expensive when compared to old productions like the monochromatic "Birth of a Nation". The former is targeted at the youthful generation that has grown up in relative wealth but have no feelings of danger, or fear, or alarm. The motivation behind DPM Lee Hsien Loong's call for a correction of the imbalance in NE appears to be observation that there is a deficit in valuable historical knowledge among the school-going population of Singapore. This in itself is a reflection of the low priority that the study of Singaporean history had been accorded in the past, presumably among culpable parents, and teachers themselves. The historical deficit represents a deficit in the citizenship component of the social contract among those who will eventually occupy positions of responsibility — in the public and private realms of Singapore's future. The absence of such historical knowledge, if not corrected through overt national education programmes, will severely restrict the evolution of the Singaporean identity, the national identity that bonds citizens in crisis. Previous, and current relational experiences with a vacillating Malaysia, and an unpredictable Indonesia serve to remind Singaporeans that a lack of historical knowledge will only worsen the effects of unknown variables exacerbated by potential threats.[FH]

General Education

There are four main ingredients in Singapore's General Education narrative, viz., (1) Meritocracy and Academic Streaming; (2) Internationally recognised benchmark public examinations (3) Scholarships and Bursaries (4) Singapore's Bilingual policy.[FV]

Meritocracy refers to a system of promotion and reward based on individual ability rather than ethnic considerations. Meritocracy is theoretically blind to all variables but "ability". Talent is rewarded, poor talent goes un-rewarded. However, meritocracy Singapore-style involves a complementary strategy of "Streaming" in which students are graded and placed into peer classes where they are likely to maximise their academic potential. In the 1970s, students were promoted to the next level or standard regardless of their academic performance up till the Primary School Leaving Examination (PSLE). Those who performed well at the PSLE would go onto secondary schools of their choice while those who failed would be revocationalized to non-academic training centres that came under the auspices of the Vocational and Industrial Training Board (VITB). The "vocational-industrial" graduates would complement Singapore's multi-national economy with industrial apprenticeships, and attachments to supplement the secondary and post-secondary school graduates. VITB candidates were thus farmed-out to technically-based systems of instruction, designed for students who were better able to use their hands as opposed to using their minds.[FV]

"Academic Streaming" was as serious a business in the 1970s and 1980s as it continues to be today. At the secondary school level, students in the 1970s and 1980s were streamed into science, arts or technical "streams". The policy complemented the Meritocratic policy in two main ways: by applying specialisation to task where students could opt to read subjects in which they were more proficient, and secondly, to allow for the early differentiation of students into areas of academic and, or, technical specialisation. The joint Singapore-Cambridge General Certificate of Education (GCE) "Ordinary-level" examinations were the second benchmark public examination after the PSLE in which all students who completed four years of secondary education could compete for places at pre-university centres and junior colleges. Those who did not qualify for these centres would enter the job market with their "O-level" certificates. For those who completed the two years of immediate post-secondary education at the junior colleges or three years of pre-university education at the pre-U centres could then sit for another competitive public examination known as the GCE "Advanced-level", jointly administered with the University of Cambridge in England.

The highly competitive, rigorous Singapore system of education (six years at the elementary or primary level, four years at the secondary level, and another two years for those who qualified for (what used to be called "pre-University" and now referred to as) Junior College system continues to be based on "meritocracy", specialisation via "academic streaming", and joint-administration and reviews by a renowned, former British colonial university, the University of Cambridge. This strategy had two main effects: (1) it provided a mass of educated workers who were as literate as any of their peers and counterparts around the world in the same age group; and, (2) developed a small, elite talent pool of government scholars who willingly and proudly returned to serve the nation-state in various positions in the civil and administrative services, the SAF, and the government-linked companies (GLC) after returning from their undergraduate studies in universities in the U.K., other European countries, the U.S., Australia, and New Zealand, on various scholarships that ranged from Fullbright, Rhodes, Colombo Plan, Overseas Merit Scholarships, and President Scholarships that were administered by the Public Service Commission (PSC). However, since the late 1990s, the later generation of Singapore scholars appear to be increasingly driven by material desires and expectations of rapid promotions without which they are most likely to leave the employment of the government for the private sector. This is ironic because there appears to be public sector funding of private sector ventures much of which are not found in Singapore and require the former scholar to be based overseas. In the absence of a "freedom of information act", several questions arise, viz., (1) are there gender biases in terms of the selection, recruitment, and retention of government scholars? (2) what proportion of the PSC itself is made up of women? (3) are female scholars more or less likely to return to complete their "public service" and to discharge their "public duties and responsibilities" than male scholars? (4) are there imbalances in the number of female to male scholars at specific levels of the civil service hierarchy? (5) what is the attrition rate for all scholars and what are their motivations for leaving the public service? (6) should public money be spent on scholars who are unlikely to return to Singapore or who are likely to want to settle overseas with foreign spouses? (7) what is the impact of the liberalization and relaxation of citizenship and permanent residency requirements for foreign male spouses of local female scholars? (8) with the shift to global talent and the need for foreign expertise in Singapore, are there sufficient security arrangements and clearances for foreign spouses married to local women and men who hold "sensitive positions" in the public sector? (9) to what extent should or could the state lawfully control or express a vested interest in the private behavior of scholars studying abroad in the national interest? (10) what can be said about the kind of motivation and the level of morale required by the majority of non-scholar civil servants in the SCS?[**FV, WG**]

Education at the end of 20th century Singapore is a vast and complex business with heavy state involvement in all aspects of formal education. Apart from the continuing bilingual education policy mooted by Lee Kuan

Yew and the first generation of political leaders, MOE has continued to finetune education policy with the changing dynamics and demands of the day, with each successive Minister of Education leaving a particular hallmark. Streaming today begins in primary school and the options within the streaming process involves parents, teachers, and the students themselves. There are specialised programmes like the Gifted Education Programme (GEP), and the older Special Assistance Plan schools (SAP). The 1990s has also seen a significant reshaping of the meaning of Secondary Schools. In the early 1950s and 1960s the school system was made up of three main school types: vernacular, government grant-in-aid (the Christian Missionary Schools), and government schools. Almost four decades later under the Goh Chok Tong government, there is a wide choice for parents and students: Independent Schools, Autonomous Schools, SAP schools, among others, that are differentiated by financial (in)dependence from the government, relationships with structures in civil society, modes of educational governance, religious, and moral bases of education.[FV]

Education in Singapore continues to retain a position of high priority because the state believes that education is an investment in the future. Educational governance Singapore style is one way to establish and control uncertainty and the unknown. It is also an effective means of formal political socialisation. The education of the masses is crucial in nation-building because the current cohort of students form the critical mass that makes Singapore (note Michael J. Shapiro's quote in the last chapter).

At the level of domestic politics, Singaporeans, and the family unit, became targets of population control programmes; national and sub-national language policies (speak Mandarin, not "dialect"); campaigns aimed at modifying social behaviour (spitting, courtesy, littering, smoking, chewing gum, flushing toilets). The campaign trail over the past three decades has seen varying degrees of success — the "Stop-At-Two" policy that resulted in Chinese and Other Singaporeans not reproducing themselves; the successful Speak Mandarin Campaign that marginalised the importance of Chinese "dialects"; and the "flushing of public toilets" campaign that was difficult for the authorities to monitor and police. Undaunted by the variegated successes of the national campaigns, the State has continued to propagate values through the Ministry of Education. Within the schools, the aim has always been pragmatic: use English as the medium as it is both the language of international business and the language of government in Singapore. The State needs to ensure political stability in order to enable economic success: "economics good; politics, bad". Since the majority of Singaporeans are of Chinese descent, it would be ideal for the largest ethnic group to be tractable, cohesive, and compliant. Hence the need to create a generation of Singaporean Chinese who are imbued with a moral sense of duty, character and tradition. The Ministry of Education continues to be the primary agent for political socialisation in the country, as is common in most developed States like France, Japan, the United Kingdom, the United States, and Italy. The State believes in maintaining a certain rooted-ness in certain Chinese traditions and values, and this is transmitted (because the State believes it is transmittable) through the Ministry of Education's bilingual policy. This is important for the coherence and political stability of the largest ethnic community in Singapore: a common language is more likely to bind then break a community. A primary strategy for the transmission of values is through the bilingual policy where all Singaporean students learn English as a first language, and their "Mother tongue" as the second language. Statistically insignificant communities that have made substantial contributions to governance, like the Eurasians, have the facility of choice among several languages, including Malay, Tamil, and Mandarin classes. The bilingual policy familiarises school-going children with the variegated metaphorical and symbolic issues of, for instance, the Chinese past. The Special Assistance Plan (SAP) school-children learn both languages at the first language level. The majority of these schools cater for Mandarin-speaking students, or for those whose mother tongue is Chinese. When the policy was first introduced at the SAP schools it seemed counterproductive to provide first language level teachers for non-Chinese speakers. These Eurasian, Malay, Tamil, Sikh, and Parsi students had their classes conducted elsewhere, away from the schools at specific tuition centres. The bilingual policy has been successful to a point. Many younger Singaporeans now speak mandarin more than they might have had the policy not been put in place by Lee Kuan Yew in the 1980s. The value-transmitting bilingual policy has been successful in the local arena. However, it may be too early to look for successes at the regional and international level. This is because the Mandarin spoken elsewhere in the Chinese Diaspora and on mainland China is distinctly different from that spoken in Singapore. For example, the use of Singapore Chinese does not seem to have thoroughly helped Government of Singapore Investment Corporation (GSIC) activity in China. Ironically, the Chinese market has become more exclusive than inclusive and prevented the Singapore team in Suzhou from achieving success in the 70 hectare township. The use of language in business has not completely facilitated economic intelligence gathering, and communication. In this instance, the linguistic and cultural "loopholes" resulted in the construction of a rival Chinese-managed industrial park at a mirror site instead.[FH]

The State and the Family

The informal means of political socialisation involves the family unit in Singapore. The family unit is the basic social structure in Asian and Western modernity. Cultural differences between and among family units around the world in urban centres and rural areas do exist, but the family units do not necessarily form pattern that is sufficiently distinct to support claims of a distinctively different Eastern or Western family unit. These "general distinctions" existed in the "traditional" past, even as recently as the middle of the 20th century. However, movements in global capital flows, the commodification of culture, the rapidity of communication, the pressures of democratisation, and geometrical advances in technology change across the world have limited the structural differences between and among most family units. Rather, the structure of the family unit in modernity continues to be determined by economic class, and national economic performance rather than traditional, religious or cultural values.

The foundational value of the modern ethos is clearly seen in the choice of family housing units in Singapore. As all cultures in late modernity appear to be moving steadily towards a kind of postmodern restructuralism with a wide and engaging variety of prefabricated choices that are superficially different but substantially similar. The family structure in Singapore is not distinctively different from most urban centres in the west except for the fact that the spatial layout for high-density, high-rise living achieves one of the highest and most modernist standards of precision: well thought-out and thought-through, maximising the natural limitations to land-use and land-development in Singapore in support of the foundational value of rationalistic modernity. There are two forms of property ownership in Singapore that has a direct impact on the family structure: leasehold, and freehold property.

Most family units reside in state-subsidised 99-year leasehold properties (known as public housing), with a small minority occupying 99-year or 999-year leasehold high-rises and landed properties (private housing). There has been some degree of product differentiation since the 1980s with the construction of higher quality HUDC units in addition to the massive HDB public housing programme. However, all former HUDC estates are self-run, or in the process of moving towards self-management. In order to anticipate the demand for high-quality, more exclusive condominium-type housing, the Housing and Development Board (through the Ministry of National Development) introduced the Executive Condominium or E-Condo product targeted at young working couples with new careers and young families, some of whom are known colloquially as "Dinks" (double-income, no kids). In the recent recession, the E-condo developers have had to resort to various kinds of "advertising gimmicks" to attract customers to what would have been premium properties in a non-recessionary period.[**EG, WG**]

In one sitting of Parliament, PAP MPs called for more help for residents in the recessionary year of 1998, one MP asked the government to help first-time buyer by freeing the Central Provident Fund (CPF) constraints on the 20% deposit required for private property purchases. Another PAP MP (Kreta Ayer-Tanglin GRC) argued that the government could reduce the cash payment by reducing the quantum by 50% to ten per cent in order to meet the "aspirations of young professionals… If the Government does this, it will not only win the hearts and minds of young professionals so that they will sink their roots in Singapore, but it will also help breathe some life into the property market." However, the National Development Minister replied:

"I must reiterate what Dr. Richard Hu said, that is, that Singaporeans should purchase private property only if they can afford it. It is not advisable for banks to lend or for buyers to borrow beyond what is financially prudent for them, especially at this time of economic uncertainty." The minister noted that the 80 per cent financial limit on mortgage loans in Singapore was higher relative to the 70 per cent limit in Hongkong. "If young Singaporeans cannot afford the 20 per cent cash outlay, then they should start off with the HDB flat and upgrade to private property when they can better afford it. Alternatively, they can apply for the executive condominiums, where they will be given a $40,000 CPF housing grant if they are first-time purchasers".

In Singapore, the state controls all land development and parcels out undeveloped land to tenders in public bidding sessions, with the amount of land parcelled-out based on a concerted, but arbitrary estimation of the impact of supply on public, private, and industrial properties. While the actual amount of space per family unit, ranging from three, four, five, and executive apartment units (approximately $105m^2$ to $180m^2$) are minuscule when compared to land-rich nation-states like Australia and Canada, the effective aesthetic rationalisation of liveable social and community space: public walkways, neighbourhood gardens, parks, and landscaped lake-gardens for larger Group Representation Constituencies like Ang Mo Kio, and the now obsolete Cheng San GRC. An overall relative comparison with neighbouring urban centres and regional cities indicates that the State has performed well in the area of housing and property development for a population of 4 million on an island smaller than Lake Taupo, a fresh water crater lake north of Waiouru in the North Island of New Zealand.

The Elderly

Old people make up a significant proportion of the Singapore population. These citizens, now aged 65 and above, were the backbone of Singapore's two major phases of industrialisation. The proper treatment of elderly Singaporeans is of ethical importance and reflects the due social compensation for the parts they played in the three decades that built

Singapore. Rather than a romanticisation of the aged but a moral position in which state and society demonstrates its care for the people who themselves have made and continue to make known and unknown sacrifices. There are several on-going privileges for the elderly and their families in the state's policy-oriented strategy towards elderly Singaporeans that range from discounted travel on public transport services, pension services for former civil servants, "granny HDB flats", extended family HDB flats, and government grants for subsidised public housing for working Singaporeans who choose to live within a specific distance from their parents' HDB flat. The Singapore nation-state is one of few countries that have adopted such proactive policies towards the elderly. However, the problems that are faced in this developed country are not much different from those of other developed urban centres around the world. Furthermore, the government legislated the *Maintenance of Parents Act (1995)* that provides for the legal status of parents and children with regard to maintenance of the former. This piece of legislation illustrates the nature of the PAP government's politics of anticipation in terms of the resolution of problems that will arise in Singapore's future. The third reading of this Bill invalidates the belief that an Asian city-nation-state like Singapore possesses a culturally filial population. This is clearly not the case, workers in the global modernity of today are more likely than not to behave in a manner that is similar to other centres of urban and economic growth, and the family structure will adapt to the changing environment.[IG]

Singapore's social engineering policies were introduced to adapt to the changing dynamics of global capital movements, and internally, in order to maximise the productivity of all Singaporeans, and workers in Singapore across all sectors and ages. This represents the commodification of the family and of family ties to the extent that the entire stratum remains tenable and stable as long as long as, "commodities cater to more than a desire for instant gratification" (Brennan, 2000:21). Part of the fear is the rapidly ageing population in Singapore soon to be Asia's second highest. As Chan argues, "The formal sources of support, i.e. CPF account funds, by the elderly for living expenses are not widespread, primarily because not all the elderly were covered by the CPF during their working years. This is especially true for the female elderly, but this situation will change for the better as future cohorts retire. It remains to be seen, however, the extent to which today's Singaporeans plan for tomorrow's old age financial security, or whether the belief that children will provide support will continue to dominate. Over all, Singapore's elderly seem to be intimately connected with their families, either by living together with them or via intergenerational transfers with non-coresident children. An examination of the types of transfers that occur within the households reveal that the elderly are active participants in household activities. The elderly also provide transfers to children within the household, in the form of help with housework, child care, financial assistance, or consulting on family decisions and providing advice".[4] This invokes a certain prioritisation among Singaporeans *vis-à-vis* familial households, family structure, parents, culture and ethnicity that leave little difference from other developed urban centres in modernity.[FV]

Can Singapore Avoid the Horror?

Since the Republic's independence, there were two main breaks in the annual economic growth of modern Singapore: the 1985-6 "cost-induced" economic recession, and the 1998-9, "externally-created", "domestically-internalised" recession. The economic solution for the 1985-6 recession was a cut in the Central Provident Fund (CPF) rate by 15%. A similar solution to reduce the wage cost profile by another CPF cut is being touted as the solution by the Committee on Singapore's Competitiveness (CSC) chaired by the former Minister of Manpower. Several National University economists who choose to remain unnamed forecast negative economic growth for the next two years, 2003 – 2005, but recovery thereafter.

There are several explanations of Singapore's current economic problems that support the Faustian foundational fantasy of horror

---

[4] Angelique Chan, "An Overview of the Living Arrangements and the Social Support Exchanges of Older Singaporeans," *Asia-Pacific Population Journal* (1997), 12(4): 48-49.

resurrected by Brennan: the falling value of domestic exports, the high cost of labour relative to Singapore's regional neighbours, the "overvalued" Singapore dollar, the faltering Japanese financial economy, and to a lesser extent, the uncertain political situation in Malaysia and especially in Indonesia. The immediate impact of the 1998-9 recession on the domestic economy has been the fall in the value of private and public property, cautious lending practices by the big four banks, decrease in domestic spending in the retail and service sectors, a contraction in state for property and industrial development, and an increase in financial mergers seen in the case of Keppel Bank and Tat Lee Bank, and the merger of the Post Office Savings Bank (POSB) with the Development Bank of Singapore (DBS).[5] [FV] The Committee's solution suggests a S$10 billion package that includes a cut to 10% from the present 20% in Employers' CPF contribution; reduction in wage costs by 15% by cutting CPF and flexible wages; reducing the levy on foreign workers by S$50-S$100 for skilled and unskilled labour in the two most important sectors — manufacturing and service industries; cuts in income tax or extend rebates for corporate and personal taxes; extension of the 55% rebate for property tax; extending the suspension period for share transactions; reduce customs duties in line with the move to Electronic Road Pricing (ERP); and reduce telecommunications, electricity, and port charges, while a committee of experts known collectively as the National Wages Council (NWC) supported the idea of the wage cut and suggested cutting wages by 3-5%.[6] Because the current recession has been externally induced, it would be impossible for Singapore to negotiate its way out of a globally-induced recession that was catalysed by the September 11, 2001 terrorist attack in New York City, against a leading bastion of global capitalism.

---

[5] See *The Report of the Committee on Singapore's Competitiveness* (Singapore: Government of Singapore, 1998).
[6] See the *Straits Times*, November 13, 1998, p. 1.

An Exhausting Modernity

Part of the foundational fantasy of Brennan's Faustian image of horror in *Exhausting Modernity* is in the actual fulfilment of economic horror during the looming global recession. Such economic recessions provide images of the horrors of job losses through retrenchment, merger, acquisition, and the liquidation of business units daily through the media and in hardcopy in the newspapers for those of us who still can afford to read newspapers in the morning. There is no longer any background to these events because no previous solution will work, new ones will have to be reinvented and implemented through the regular policy structures and their attendant feedback mechanisms. The horror fantasy is one "which accords certain attributes to the subject, and dispossesses the other of them as and by the process that makes the other into an object, that surrounds (as Heidegger might say) an absent background against which it is present" (Brennan, 2000:36).

Governing Singapore's western modernity involves the formulation, implementation, and evaluation of institutions of power that influence, mediate, and modify the politics, education, and family structure in Singapore, 1965-1998. In the recessionary year of 1998, the former Minister for Finance announced off-budget measures that illustrated the importance of education to the Singapore Cabinet. This involves a total of $282 million, including $22 million for improvements in polytechnic CAD-CAM facilities, $22 million for NTU's computer upgrading programme, $30 million for new IT equipment for secondary schools still under construction. The HDB will receive $31 million for infrastructural development of roads and drains.[7] The interlocking mechanism of state, businesses, and unions continue to play a major factor in determining the shape and nature of the family structure in Singapore. Ultimately, the fact remains that the minimum number of intergenerational transfers between parent(s)-and-child(ren) relationships is bi-directional (Chan, 1996).

---

[7] See Richard Hu (Minister of Finance) *Budget Statement*. Parliament of Singapore (February 28, 1998); and *Off-Budget Measures*, Parliament of Singapore (August 1, 1998).

Summary

This chapter has not discussed many other important areas of research such as the impact of migration, the position of minority communities, the ethnic management strategy, the position of Singaporean women, and two generations of PAP political leadership, and the position of the opposition. However, the political leadership of the postcolonial state established comprehensive and integrated structures of political, military, social, and economic governance in order to control the uncertain modernity that Singapore faced in the first three decades of its development. Through this comprehensive and integrated approach, Singapore politics, education, elderly, and economics will continue to prosper in the fear of engaging the foundational fantasy of economic horror. And in order to sustain this belief in the foundational fantasy of horror, more economic management strategies of hope and rationalization will continue to be included under future PAP governments as long as the people continue to believe in the legitimacy of the modernist governance and in the hope of advancement and progress, and avoid the horrors of the non-occurrence against an empty background.

Note

The arguments made in this chapter were discussed at four main conferences between 1993-2000, viz., "On Decompression Theory" *Proceedings, Fakulti Sains dan Politik (FISIP) Universitas Indonesia*, 1993; *The International Association for Asian Studies*, organized by the International Convention of Asia Scholars, "Development, Democracy, and Political Regimes", Saturday, 27 June, 1998; "Thinking Longitudinally: Issues in the Design and Analysis of Panel Data", an international conference organized by the Centre for Advanced Study and the NUS Department of Sociology, Singapore, YWCA, 24-26 February, 2000; and the "Politics Panels I & II" Conference on Families in Japan and Southeast Asia, Centre for Advanced Studies. Singapore, October 4-6, 2000.

References

Brennan, Theresa. 2000. *Exhausting Modernity*. London and New York: Routledge University Press.

Chan, Angelique "How Do Parents and Children Help One Another? Socioeconomic Determinants of Intergenerational Transfers in Peninsular Malaysia," *Journal of Population*, 1996, **2**(1): 43-82.

Chan, Angelique. "An Overview of the Living Arrangements and the Social Support Exchanges of Older Singaporeans," *Asia-Pacific Population Journal*, 1997, **12**(4): 48-49.

Lau, Albert. 1998. *A Moment of Anguish: Singapore in Malaysia and the Politics of Disengagement*. Singapore: Times Academic Press.

Lee, Kuan Yew. 1998. *The Singapore Story: Memoirs of Lee Kuan Yew*. Singapore: Singapore Press Holdings, Times Editions.

Lee Kuan Yew. 2000. *From Third World to First: The Singapore Story – 1965-2000 – Memoirs of Lee Kuan Yew*. Singapore: Singapore Press Holdings, Times Editions.

Parliament of Singapore. 1998a. "Undesirable Publications Act," (Second Reading), *Singapore Parliamentary Reports*. Singapore.

Parliament of Singapore. 1998b. "Films Act," *Singapore Parliamentary Reports*. Singapore.

Parliament of Singapore. 1998. Speech by R. Sinnakaruppan *Singapore Parliamentary Reports* (March), Singapore.

Pierre, J. 1998. "Public-Private Partnerships and Urban Governance." In *Partnership in Urban Governance: European and American Experiences* (J. Pierre, ed). New York: St. Martin's Press.

Runciman, D. 2000. "Is the State a Corporation?" *Government and Opposition*, 35(1): 90-104.

Stoker, G. 1995. "The Comparative Study of Urban Regimes." *In Urban and Regional Policy* (Jon Pierre, ed.). Aldershot, Hants: E. Elgar.

Wolman, H. and M. Goldsmith. 1992. *Urban Politics and Policy. A Comparative Approach.* Oxford: Blackwell Publishers.

Yeo, Kim Wah, and Lau, Albert. 1991. "From Colonialism to Independence, 1945-1965', in Ernest Chew, and Edwin Lee. (eds.) *A History of Singapore.* Singapore, Oxford and New York: Oxford University Press.

Narrative & Public Space

...they are packed so that they look like huge formless masses...
Chekov

Part of the neurosis of living in a metropolis arises out of a detachment from emotions of hunger, joy, pain, and the will to live.[1] The habitable urban space breeds anomie, atomization, and a contrite inability to cope with elasticized choices that offer temporary, but Teflon-like relief from the pressure of the juggernaut of modernity driven by a neoliberal, redistributive system of public justice without side-constraints, and air-bags that don't always work in the right place at the right time. Bereft of control, we spin into rationalizations that convince ourselves we were right into starting a collection of American or Japanese or Taiwanese baseball cards in the late

---

[1] See William E. Connolly's arguments in, "The Will, Capital Punishment, and Cultural War", paper presented at the APSA 1998 Meeting, Boston, MA.

1960s and early 1970s because their fading faces are worth hundreds if not thousands of dollars. This chapter is motivated by the many miniscule components of a global capitalist hierarchy marked by poor alternatives, conflicting advice (of economists, financiers, rent-seekers, and media moguls), and falsifying ideologies. These components form an anarchical political paradox, called the "United" Nations; a parody that lies in the international structure's fallen, perhaps subversive, objective: "to ensure peace among nations". This has since taken on an additional portfolio, an international forum for legitimizing economic sanctions, and the declaration of war for those who do not share new world ideology-isms of liberty, democracy, and justice through transnational capital persuasions.

Narrative and public space encounters modernity through a series of approaches that try to shed light and understanding on the problems associated with a fragile life, and the disgruntled contortions of postmodern movements of architecture and other forms of consumption in the West, floating gently across Africa, Asia, and the Far East through invisible electronic emissions. A confluence of these electrical impulses is Singapore, a nodal point of Asian consumerism, jealously and painstakingly guarded by a proficient team of super-skilled technocrats, bent on productivity, teamwork, and corporate functionalism. The wealth by any calculation is enormous:

> Recently, Lee Hsien Loong quoted $60 billion as the total amount by which the 600,000 HDB [Housing Development Board] flats have appreciated, since HDB first sold them. I thought $60 billion was too low so I checked with HDB. HDB calculated that just over the last ten years, the total capital appreciation of HDB flats has been $133 billion, i.e. on average, each household has become wealthier by $200,000. That is how much wealth Singaporeans have gained, as a result of government policies and Singapore's success.[2] [FV/IG/EG]

---

[2] Goh Chok Tong, "Prime Minister's National Day Rally Speech," August 18, 1996, 16; see also Don Slater, "Affluence & Disorder", in Daniel Miller, *Consumption: Critical Concepts in the Social Sciences,* vol. I, *Theory and Issues in the Study of Consumption,* pp. 57-67.

A great degree of willingness to live, in Singapore as well as other nodal points of capitalist consumption, may be equated with a willingness to work towards material object(s) that mark our point of having arrived at a certain status in life — the foreign car, the "gold" credit card, the Rolex watch, the Endowed or Chaired Professorship — are markers that ensure that capitalism does not run out of style. Neil Postman continues to remain confident that we are all more likely than not to amuse ourselves to death but fails to raise the question of which toys can continually satisfy? The situation has not gone entirely out of control, and we have not been entertained to death, even though we are constantly bombarded by entertainment programs, unnecessary details in the news about families with hexes, overpaid crooks, underpaid teachers, and nameless foreigners dying at the hands of faceless others. These narratives of life and death are the subject that appears to prescribe the narratives that rule our lives, that mediate our minds, that serve to censure and proclaim reality with equanimity, we control and discipline our actions and reactions to suit the expectations of modern narratives of power. These narratives, with or without peanuts, within or without "objective-subjective" histories, become politicized by the power underlying its surface structure: the more powerful the story-teller, the more powerful the story as it gains ascendancy over the millennia as seen in this quote from *The Malay Annals*:

> When they arrived at *Tanjong Bemban*, the Prince went ashore for sport. The princess and all the wives of the noblemen and the wealthy had fun collecting seashells. The princess then sat under a screw pine before the wives of all the nobles. She was overjoyed to see her maids amusing themselves, each in their own way. Some collected snails, while others busied themselves gathering seashells, crabs, mollusks, certain kinds of leaves, corals and seaweed. All the maids were very happy. There were also some of them who picked up flowers to wear in their hair, each in their own manner. There were some who

> ran in a race and in their excitement and joy, tripped and fell to the ground.³

The process of collecting items, previously held as worthless, unnamed objects, over time is at the heart of the system of filling-in empty, bored spaces. In the previous story, there is a clear hierarchy of power that is engendered in terms of the playing out of boredom for the mutual benefit of power holders and their dependants. Similarly, in engaging the political realities of large modern concerns, space is set aside for annual dinner and dances, sporting events, and voyeuristic team events on the television in the spirit of bonding, camaraderie, and fulfillment. But what is being fulfilled has its weaknesses, and pitfalls. In engaging the political reality of modern life, in our haste to fill the empty modern spaces with appropriate activities, events, and inventions, many seem to fall in excitement, violating themselves, but continue to be insulated from pain and agony by ubiquitous ignorance, generous apathy, and consoling bliss.

> After sometime, *Singapura* was attacked by swordfish which jumped to the shores killing many people as a result. If the victim's chest was attacked, the fish would pierce right through him while if the neck and waist were hurt, he would be pierced to the other side. The people could no longer stand on the beaches for many had died.⁴

The eventual rise of the garrison state and its attendant mentality, would continue deep into the late modern period. People would continue to die on the beaches of Singapore during war-time, perhaps being unable to accept any more pain, and in their non-acceptance of modern swordfish, they sought other ways of escape, like Kundera's twirling, effortless, ring-dance, in *The Book of Laughter and Forgetting* ([1978] 1996) that the dancers used to breakout of their modern convictions rising steadily higher and higher up into the air. At the very top, we only find a greater collection of things.

---

³ Edwin Thumboo et al. "Excerpts from Sejarah Melayu" in *The Fiction of Singapore* (Singapore: Unipress, 1990), p. 25.
⁴ Thumboo, *ibid.*, p. 29.

Morality has yet to be finally judged or decided as there is no final edition. We are continuously seeking and re-envisioning new ways to understand and engage a complex and unfair modernity. The pressure surrounds like the ancient swordfish of *Singapura*. Everywhere is a fragile modern, anywhere is the business of living and surviving the competition, and the pressures of filling private spaces with business and pleasure:

> A-Da's coffee shop was located near the end of Jalan Mati. In past years, business had been quite good because A-Da's adopted daughter, A-Ju, attracted many male customers. But since A-Ju married one of the customers last year, business had slowed tremendously. A-Da was about to close down the shop when she [herself] got married to an old customer who used to visit the brothels here...A-Da was the eldest in the batch when A-Feng was a prostitute...like the call of the crow in the night after the storm.[5]

Many male customers who had purchasing power that would ensure the continuity of a patriarchal fiduciary system, one which under girds the modern period as we know it today. [WG] Our knowledge is of course made up of signs and symbols that seem to suggest a certain permanence and fortitude. But these artifacts of the modern are misleading as they are elusive. Yet, life in modernity appears to be more about negotiating the signs and symbols that construct our world, than about simple temporal perceptions of human consciousness. The elite discourse of Descartes, Kant, and Habermas represent optimistic variations on progressive philosophical consciousness that began, without any degree of certainty, in 1596 with Cartesian causality. The technological *tour de force* we know as "progression" or alternatively, "advancement", may be reduced to its epistemological roots within Western discourse entrenched and fortified by 16th, 17th, and 18th century colonialism. The stains and continuities of 17th

---

[5] Zhang Jinyan, "The Dishonourable History of A-Feng", in Thumboo, et al., *ibid.*, pp. 266-272.

century *realpolitik* of Hobbesian political science, Kantian anti-transcendental metaphysical challenges[6], eudemonism, and a spirited Hegelian absolutism similarly influenced Enlightenment narratives of despair with a man-made god who had become increasingly dehumanized by this early form of testing for evidence. Consequently, the (mixed) oral and written traditions, their attendant signs and symbols, and the advancement through the early modern period were three themes sold vicariously by the Church and the State through the belligerent masses for the sake of attaining a civilized life, a break with the past was merely the code for a bridge to the future:

> Doctrines of equality, liberty, faith in human intelligence (once allowed the benefits of education), and universal reason abounded ... Enlightenment thought, of course, internalized a whole host of difficult problems and possessed not a few troublesome contradictions. [**FH**] To begin with, the question of the relation between the means and ends was not omnipresent, while the goals themselves could never be specified precisely except in terms of some utopian plan that often looked oppressive to some as it looked emancipatory to others.[7]

The Janus-ied philosophical ironies of modern "emancipation" and "universalism" influenced Feuerbach, enunciated Marx's resounding critique of the former, and elicited creative responses from the multi-disciplinary schools that would follow, the *Institute for Social Research* being one. This in turn provoked a counter-Enlightenment movement by three generations of critical theorists from Adorno, Horkheimer, Marcuse, Benjamin, and Fromm to Neumann, Pollock, and inadvertently, Habermas.[8]

---

[6] See "The Unavoidability of Conflicts," in John Kekes, *The Morality of Pluralism* (Princeton: Princeton University Press, 1993), pp. 53-75.

[7] David Harvey, *The Condition of Postmodernity* (Oxford: Basil Blackwell, 1990), pp. 13-15.

[8] For a comprehensive discussion of the development of the Frankfurt School, see Rolf Wiggerhaus, *The Frankfurt School* (Cambridge: The MIT Press [1986], 1995); see also, Stephen Eric Bronner, and Douglas Mackey Kellner (eds.), *Critical Theory and Society: A Reader* (London: Routledge, 1989).

Looking close, one finds that this short-list name names that hardly scratch the surface of the modern. In a cosmological nutshell, that which appeared centuries ago to Aquinas became muddied-up and murky by the time of Kierkegaard. The modern approximation of truth had reinvented itself through increasing complexity and scientific verbiage. The dispensation of truth as justice through blind, and even mystical faith in human intelligence compounded by a universal logic and ubiquitous reasoning hardened the modern resolution to solve the problems that it created in the first place. The reinvention of truth through objectivism, empiricism, and positivism would frame a modernity characterized by systems of development, progression, linearity, improvement, scientism, replication, continuity, systematization, calculation, categorization, cartographization, anthropology, urban planning, population studies, and entire vocabularies that sought projection, perfection, purity, and purification.

While modernity refers to a frame of political time, modernism is quite different as it lays the templates of power that hold up, and keep down, modern civilization. Within progressive circles of the social and political sciences, these templates of power are seen in terms of institutional, hierarchical, and structural coercion. Modernism, like other –*isms*, invites a reconsideration of a set of political ideals, often operationalized at the expense of the impoverished, the marginal, the perverse, the minor, the obtuse, diverse and abnormal. The "normality" of Western-motivated colonial projects in Southeast Asia were rapidly supplanted by Eastern, Japanese militarism. Western colonial "peace" was rapidly replaced by Eastern imperial "co-prosperity"; one form of normality imposed on another in a matter of days, the people having to adjust their livelihood accordingly, changing their engagement of modernity as the power circumstances presented themselves:

> The god of peace did not stay for long in Indonesia. A violent civil war erupted. During the daytime, the fully armed Japanese military swaggered around the city, patrolling. The Indonesian mayor, the Dutch mayor and the Commander of the British Forces attended to their respective areas of duty. In the day, the

Indonesians traded in the black market with the Dutch soldiers, joked and shared some of life's secrets with them. However, at night, both sides fired at each other with machine guns.[FH] Street fighting happened every night in the city of *Medan*.[9]

The hierarchical power arrangements of occupation forces represented a war-time modernity that appeared on the larger operational maps of "Theatre Southeast Asia" as being solely under Japanese Imperial Army. Yet, upon closer inspection, the terrain revealed a paradoxical, nightmarish, Hobbesian state of nature — Malayan People's Anti-Japanese Army (MPAJA) activities in Malaya, Muslim freedom fighters in Borneo, and the Philippine islands, Javanese *laskar* units in Indonesia, and elements of Allied special forces strewn throughout the archipelago — that would dominate Southeast Asian modernity for the rest of the war. The "god of peace" was a metaphorical aspiration for the return, ironically, of Western colonial normality, that would eventually pass into the hands of Malay, Chinese, Indian, Eurasian, and Javanese nationalists in the late 1940s, 1950s, and 1960s.

Modernism suppresses difference, and the diversity of real choices. In its benign, soft-spoken version, modernism appears to tolerate certain forms of difference (like constructive criticism), and various attempts to moderate state-centered indiscretions through discussion, debate, and sympathy in that public space of civil society reserved for interest articulation we know as the polity where feedback and creative energy is generated and released.[10] At worse, modernism is about measurement, control, expulsion, deletion, censorship, and management of results. It is about the execution of the public space, and the annihilation of diversity. At its worst, it disappears laughter and leaves silence in its place, because silence is control. Modernism's gratuitous and systematic degradation of human being places

---

[9] Wei Beihua, "Bridges" in Thumboo et al., *ibid.*, p. 338.
[10] See for example, Sonny Yap, "Let Us Put Safety Factor Back on the Public Agenda," *The Straits Times*, November 5, 2001; see also, "Views in Straits Times Forum Page Help Foster Civil Society," *The Straits Times*, December 8, 2001.

Narrative and Public Space 123

in its stable, ideology, propaganda, essentialism, and universalism. Modernism seeks to ensure that everything remains stable, normal, and a gradual fine-tuning of human life and civilization from macro and micro-perspectives:

> [A]fter the new year, the landlady received a letter form the Income Tax Collection Department stating that she had to make a report on her rental income. This made the old lady very upset as she depended on the money to survive. After deducting everybody's PUB [Public Utilities Board] expenses, the balance was already minimal. If that were to be taxed, she would be plunged into hardship. However, the Income Tax Collection Department would act by law.[FV/WG] They would not try to understand her plight. The landlady requested me to fill in the forms for her. Sometime later, the Income Tax Collection Department wrote to each tenant to check on the information given by her. Luckily, the landlady did not understand the figure. So, everything was fine.[11]

The micro-management of public policies by bureaucracies testifies to the coercive nature of state institutions, ensuring objective, unbiased, non-emotional implementation for the "benefit of the greater good", as a result of representative government. In engaging modernity, the old lady was consumed by an administrative machinery that she could not and did not understand. In seeking various ways of commodious living within rules and regulations of public and private spaces, there are things that we need to ignore, and items that we are better left not knowing. Extrapolating this fragment of the modern to larger concerns, we acknowledge that bureaucracies within systems of government are themselves premised on particular belief systems that enable state and society to function. Sooner or later, the smarter ones realize that we are all functionaries of state and society, limited at worst to the extent of our own lay views of the world, and

---

[11] Li Rulin, "The New Aristocrat" in Thumboo, et al., *ibid.*, p. 464.

at best, the intellectual spaces created by theorists thinking ahead of, and, before us.

Accordingly, the inter/nation/al reproduction of public space qua Lefebvre[12] becomes rapidly contextualized by modernism within the metanarratives of modernity. Additionally, the conceit that modernism represents is similarly enunciated, affirmed in the systematic attrition and degradation of the very aesthetics created within its own domain. Words like "productivity", "efficacy", "progress", and "efficiency" are symptomatic of an increasingly commodified reality devoid of passion, pleasure, and performativity; desire and difference; tradition and transformativity; emotion and ecstasy. Nothing is built to last, all is replaceable with the same quantum of satisfaction for each unit consumed at the margin. Modernism is ambivalent because of its occasional atavism.[13] It effectuates the loss of meaning as it empties out meaning (after Lash and Urry) resulting in a museum-like nostalgia, and the optimistic quest for a better age, holding out for betterment and improvement, pleasing all but those it marginalizes on its way forward. For writers like Pauline Rosenau, there is a clear dichotomy, a singular tension between modern/and/postmodern. In *Postmodernism and the Social Sciences* (1992), she narrowly defines the space between modern conviction and postmodern re-arrangement:

> Post-modernists re-arrange the whole social science enterprise. Those of a modern conviction seek to isolate elements, specify relationships, and formulate a synthesis; post-modernists do the opposite.[14]

Rosenau suggests that postmodernists amalgamate elements, generalize relationships, and create disturbing anti-theses. Not quite. "Doing the

---

[12] Henri Lefebvre, *The Reproduction of Space* (Oxford: Basil Blackwell, [1973] 1991).

[13] Although Bauman may not agree entirely with such a comment, his "method" of engaging modern ambivalence is nonetheless instructive. See Zygmunt Bauman, *Modernity and Ambivalence* (Oxford: Polity Press, 1991).

[14] Pauline Marie Rosenau, *Postmodernism and the Social Sciences: Insights, Inroads, and Intrusions* (Durham: Duke University Press, 1992), p. 8.

opposite" is a necessary but not sufficient condition for evoking an oppositional politics, and "speaking truth to power".[15] More often than not, speaking out against coercion, involves more effort, without any more meaning or any less thought. Rosenau's position on modernity, though cursory and intrusive, suffers the fate of all those who attempt to engage the postmodern: it raises the postmodern fear, as we shall see later, a fear that abounds in both thinking and non-thinking persons.

Returning to Lefebvre, we acknowledge the notion of modern public space as a formal indictment of the structure of political narratives that construct civilization.[16] These public spaces exist — as Marshall Berman's sparkling story of Brasilia in *All That Is Solid Melts Into Air* (1982) — continuously, at the surface of human civilization, characterizing and transforming modernity through a shifting (sometimes enabling, sometimes disabling) series of postmodern shapes, ideas, values, traditions, and beliefs that languish, and signify contrasting collages and aesthetics inspired by Salvador Dali, Georg Simmel, Stanley Fish, (the later) Clifford Geertz, Bruno Latour, Graham Parkes, Salmon Rushdie, and Giger.

But what can be made of the public spaces that construct Singapore, Kuala Lumpur, Ho Chih Min City, Bangkok, Manila, Shanghai, Hongkong, Seoul, Tokyo, and Taipeh? How are these living, breathing, dying, and decaying spaces different from New York, Chicago, Philadelphia, Los Angeles, San Francisco, London, Bern, Oslo, Frankfurt, Rotterdam, Gdansk, Seattle, Lisbon, Madrid, Quebec, Brussels, Vienna, Johannesburg, Montreal, Gstaad, or Las Vegas? The stories presented thus far are examples that in fact could have happened in a place other than Southeast Asia. Consider the following segment in a book edited by Thumboo *et al.*:

---

[15] Aaron Wildavsky, *Speaking Truth to Power: The Art and Craft of Policy Analysis* (Boston: Little, Brown, and Company, 1979). Compare this with Manning Marable's recently produced *Speaking Truth to Power: Essays on Race, Resistance, and Radicalism* (Boulder: Westview Press, 1996) for two divergent approaches to similar political problems within the modern North American liberal democratic tradition.

[16] Fredric Jameson, *Postmodernism, or The Cultural Logic of Late Capitalism* (Durham: Duke University Press, 1991), pp. 235-259.

> A luxurious apartment, Mercedes Benz, a diamond-studded Rolex worth twenty thousand dollars ... apparel imported directly from Paris.[FV/EG] All these belonged to an unmarried girl who was not even thirty-two.[17]

Notions of success in the late modern period are modeled on material acquisitions, the attainment and hoarding of consumables that formulate measures of success, that construct ideas of self-worth, social status and dignity. But simultaneously, there is a certain sadness, a certain opportunity cost that cannot be measured in terms of goods and services, in economic standards of living, in expressions of the quality of life, "If this was a society that weighed a person according to his wealth and power, then was she considered a successful person? But again, what did this all mean to her? She may be able to deceive others, but she could never deceive herself. She was not happy and had never been. An inactive loneliness had always enveloped her, and she did not even know where she was heading."[18] Somehow, the idea of success in late modernity is equated with happiness. Yet it appears as deception, a suspension of the primary belief systems, and social support systems that make reality real. But modernity has not provided the light, it has faltered on its projections of certitude, grounded in an achievement society determined by the high culture, reserved for the elite minority and the power holders.

It is worthwhile, I think, to conceive of the prevailing three hundred and fifty years of (Asian and Western) modernism, a modernism in which most people were generally afforded only glimpses of high culture — through stable, unchanging, subservient, and decentered positions — unable to participate in the private and exclusive preserves (and perversions) of the elite to a point where such submission and subordination was not only accepted as the right way for those who were lowly born but also that it was the only way society could function effectively with limited social, occupational, cultural, and political mobility. High society otherwise known

---

[17] Zhang Xina, "Lights Along Orchard Road" in Thumboo et al., *ibid.*, p. 586.
[18] *Ibid.*

as high culture was marked for the select few, mediated primarily by class and ethnicity (as uncovered by postcolonial scholars in the racialized discourse of Portuguese, Spanish, Dutch, British, German, and Japanese colonialism and militarism) would momentarily permit passage for a select few to rejuvenate and sustain the critical mass needed for maintaining the "cultural elite". The political osmosis that empowered the elite to determine the signs and symbols that constructed the cultural aesthetic, that which was seen as artful and beautiful and would be a celebration of the civilized life.

However, with the increasing development of the modern period into the 19th and 20th centuries, the geometrical progression of industry, commerce, capitalist finance, and technology, advancing through centuries of colonialism resulted in the rise of a global political economy fostered within a so-called liberal, free-market in tension with the now defunct centrally planned economics of the Warsaw Pact and Comecon. The rise of industrial capital and the transformation of the global political economy through transnational capital flows catalyzed the deconstruction of elite culture after the second world war in the postcolonial and formerly colonial states. Music, art, and entertainment, formerly produced and provided for the upper classes were now made available for mass consumption. Adorno and Horkheimer's thesis on the culture industry in the 1930s and 1940s provided partial explanations of such cultural devolution. The stage was now set for the rise of postmodernism. Nietzsche, Sartre, Dostoevsky, Kierkegaard, Wittgenstein, Bakunin, and French social theory provided the intellectual putsch toward postmodern deconstruction of modernism and modernity over the last two centuries. Yet, like the single unmarried girl, marked with possessions of modern wealth, we are all uncertain, all not knowing where we are heading, and whether we are actually heading any where as Harvey writes,

> There are some who would have us return to classicism and others who seek to tread the path of the moderns. From the standpoint of the latter, every age is judged to "attain the

fullness of its time, not by being but by becoming." I could not agree more.[19]

Although Harvey's view is (sometimes) offered among graduate courses in political theory, and among some social and political theorists, the dualism of his argument above — between classicism and modernism — weakens the movement towards postmodern sensitivities. Harvey's romantic, narratival attachment to the classical-modern divide in the last four lines of *The Condition of Postmodernity* (1990) suggests a certain desperation and neglect within the frame of late modernity, an optimistic cultural theorist attempting to reconcile modernism within the circular cloister of the modern. This interplay contrasts with the clear modernist contrivances exposed by the names we have named — Lefebvre, Latour, Berman, Postman, Bauman, and others that were not mentioned like Derrida, Foucault, Rorty, and Kariel. The agreement between Harvey's postmodern take on the condition of *modernity* runs parallel to the political narratives of Goh and Lee. Goh's recalculation emphasizes a certain modern disaffection with pure statement and ironically gains political capital out of Lee's rhetorical "objectivism". Harvey's re-conceptualization of the modern period is a larger parchment of modern reality while the two Singapore politicians are engaged in a narrow and limiting debate on the contours of modern Singapore.[FV] Neither the political actors or the cultural theorist (as actor) are sufficiently critical to debunk the formative processes that under-gird the modern, nor can all three be blamed for maintaining modernism, they know no other system or structure. But Harvey has the edge because he has taken time to sit back and reflect on 20th century modernism in a way that would be suicidal to astute politicians like Goh and Lee. Harvey employs variations on (symptomatically post-) modern explanations sustained by textual, spatial, and ethnographic evidence in the post-Enlightenment period. Yet his encouragement to "keep on keeping on" ironically supports the political rhetoric of Goh, Lee, and virtually every

---

[19] Harvey, *ibid.*, p. 359; see also Pierre Bourdieu, "The Aristocracy of Culture", in *Consumption: Critical Concepts in the Social Sciences*, vol. I, *Theory and Issues in the Study of Consumption*, pp. 239-245.

other powerful modern political story-teller who is alive, decaying, or mummified. One tentative conclusion would be that no real or imaginary distinctions exist between modern or postmodern story-tellers with the caveat that the former are easier to penetrate. In encountering modernity, one encounters meaningful connections between modern fragility, and postmodern fragments, in terms of style rather than substance.

All this continues to be done in spite of interpretative collations by modern theorists such as Bradbury and McFarlane.[20] We see postmodern political theories intrepidly marked by diversity, color, depth, superficiality, laughter, resistance, deviance, abnormality, superimposition, perversity, extremity, conflict, sensitivity, persuasion, mixture, contradiction, collision, and consensus — part of an infinite grammar — while unequally and simultaneously repressing postmodern political diatribes. Postmodern political theories tend to gravitate towards decentered, multi-centered worldviews entrenched within Western political discourse. The language of course is the language of former colonizers, primarily French and English. But these *"lingua franca"* do not belong to the colonial masters any longer and have not for a long time, thus making it no longer ironic for Asian political leaders protesting and denouncing the evils of "Western values" and their influence on "Asian morality, customs, and traditions".

By the late 1960s and early 1970s, a rapid post-modernization of political thought was under full swing, a divergence of styles, languages, colors, vocabularies in the humanities, the social sciences, and now, in the post Cold War era, the physical, natural, and biological sciences (already weakened by the lack of funding from de-mobilized military machinery and shrinking military budgets). The intellectual concourse offered various shades of Western European post-structuralism (Lyotard), and North American de-constructionism (Rorty's philosophical pragmatism for one, Connolly's challenge to Death in an other). Not surprisingly, Noel O'Sullivan observed:

---

[20] Malcolm Bradbury, and James McFarlane, (eds.), *Modernism: A Guide to European Literature, 1890-1930* (London: Penguin, [1976] 1991).

> Postmodernism has lit a massive bonfire, comparable to the bonfires lit by the sophists in the ancient world; by Lucretius in the Hellenistic period; by St. Augustine at the beginning of the medieval period; by Pascal and Human in the more recent centuries; by Nietzsche in the last century...What, then, has lit the contemporary postmodern bonfire?[IG] The short answer is comprehensive dissatisfaction with the western humanist tradition, in the optimistic secular form it has assumed in the past two or three centuries. That tradition, or the postmodern interpretation of it, is now in an advanced state of intellectual disintegration.[21]

The postmodern onslaught has not entirely resulted in the disintegration of Western humanism, but it has certainly raised serious contradictions within the latter's meta-narratives. O'Sullivan's observation may be extended to the social and political sciences. Political thought, for example, as the fundamental set of philosophies that under-girds the social sciences, is being gradually engulfed and weakened from within by new and modulated critiques. These postmodern criticisms emerge at the surface, and exist in between the cracks and spaces of public and private discourse, have increasingly deconstructed and laid waste to modern texts.[IG]

There are of course many other such wasted texts/in/time but since postmodernism has no definite "time period", inasmuch as there are no eternal truths, we can only return to a desire for a certain seductive mediocrity as Nietzsche reminds us, "There are truths which are recognized best by mediocre minds because they are most suited to them, there are truths which possess charm and seductive powers only for mediocre spirits ... I name Darwin, John Stuart Mill, and Herbert Spenser".[22] O'Sullivan's bonfire, naturally, is not shared by modern philosophers and theorists for three main reasons: it de-centers the importance of research interests that

---

[21] Noel O'Sullivan, "The Philosophy of Postmodernism," *Political Studies* (1993), (41): 22.

[22] Aphorism no. 253, Friedrich Nietzsche, "People and Fatherlands," in *Beyond Good and Evil: Prelude to a Philosophy of the Future* (London: Penguin Classics, [1886] 1973), p. 165.

have consumed entire lives; it questions the validity of the entire corpus of traditional scholarship built gradually over the years; and, it threatens to undermine the entire political economy of the western tradition. The postmodern challenge is more than mere dissatisfaction or disaffection with traditional scholarship, ironically, it represents a total and consuming rejection, and disavowal of things that matter most to the political, social, and cultural elite, and the ethics by which they govern their lives. As Stallybrass and White note in the Politics and Poetics of Transgression (1986) note, "what may be socially peripheral, may be symbolically central".[23] The peripheral location of postmodernism therefore represents a unique disclosure of the ineptitude and fallacies that modern philosophies appear to uphold and cherish so dearly. These encounters with the paradoxes of center-periphery relations, and the political narratives that construct them, make-up the fragile modern.[FV]

The Fragile Modern

The modern conviction for mapping out certainty is defined in the postmodern Other, with edges and boundaries that are neither neat, nor smooth, nor well-defined; an Other than defies singularity of purpose, uniformity of thought, centrality of power. Hence, there is a discontinuous lack of permanent fixity within Anglo-French postmodern genealogies, for example, encountering modernity, as we encounter death, with a happy pessimism, and a morbid optimism. Leading us to two conceptual problems within the epistemology.

The first problem is as follows: if postmodern convictions centre on a constituent analyses of the grids that structure the modern world, how can political theory make sense of the relationships between such convictions, and the larger ideas of modernity, and modernism? How can we effectively reconcile a modern encounter with a postmodern retreat, modern universalism with postmodern multiplicity? While these questions demand a

---

[23] Peter Stallybrass and Allon White, *The Politics and Poetics of Transgression* (Ithaca: Cornell University Press, 1986), p. 23.

larger, perhaps more permanent endeavor, one possible direction that theorists may take is offered by Nestor Garcia Canclini in his recently translated *Hybrid Cultures: Strategies for Entering and Leaving Modernity* (1996). The book offers a "nuance" epistemological counterweight that attempts to reconcile popular culture with a "subaltern/hegemonic [and] traditional/modern" bifurcation of the popular consciousness.[24] The book, one of several designed to deconstruct a hybrid modernity appears to offer a way-out (if only temporarily) and a way-in to understanding postmodern constituency analyses that involve style over substance, form over function, diversity over dictatorialism. For Canclini, modernism is, "the means by which the elites take charge of the intersection of the different historical temporalities and try to elaborate a global project within them."[25] He offers counter-modern strategies that serve to buffer the 'thinking individual' in the wake of global modernism by using different vantage points as a reminder that the consequences of global uniformity is not something original or unique but a simulacra of sorts, one never successfully leaves the prison of modernity except through the ritual of death, and death rites.[26] **[FH, FV]**

A second problem appearing before political and cultural theorists concerned with anecdotal evidence, analogous political narratives, and the fragility of the modern, is the idea of popular culture, and the epistemological privileging of scholarship in favor of such cultures that emerge out of major North American and European cities. New York, London, Paris, and Los Angeles represent sites where popular culture emerges through tele-connected syndication in the larger political economy of the production of worthless goods and services for the benefit of the

---

[24] Nestor Garcia Canclini, *Hybrid Cultures: Strategies for Entering and Leaving Modernity*, (Minneapolis: University of Minnesota Press, 1996), p. 8.

[25] *Ibid.*, p. 46.

[26] While dying, death, and decay are acts that are often successfully executed, we recall that within the technocism of the 20th century, one actually needs to be certified "dead" by a "qualified" physician, before ever being accepted as officially deceased, a spin on not having lived, or not ever having been dead enough to pretend to be alive. I thank Henry S. Kariel for this comment.

bored, the decaying, and the dead. Goods that are produced for satisfying the immediacy of the moment. Understandably, the stories that make-up popular culture are stories of Big City-politics, consumerism, and society. Not surprisingly, postmodern critiques tend to be heavily concentrated in and around these Western urban centers, the commodified (rather than being co-modified) nodes on the web of a vastly expanding capitalist globe, that form dense nexus across the artifacts of modernity, the producers, the consumers, and the sleepless financial markets.[FV] "They" define "us": our habits, our accents, our retreat into the ethnic-self, the search for ethnic food, the pretence of living a cultured, and sophisticated life. Our aspirations continue to be their achievements ten, fifteen, or twenty years hence. Such an idea of improvement is brilliantly captured in Chekov's cheeky political narratives like *Marriage in Ten or Fifteen Years* (1885), and in the quotation that follows, *The Jailer Jailed* (1885):

> Have you ever noticed how donkeys are loaded? Generally, the poor beasts are piled up with everything one can think of, regardless of bulk or quantity: kitchen paraphernalia, beds, barrels, sacks with infants in them; they are packed so that they look like huge formless masses, and even the tips of their hoofs are scarcely visible.[27]

We need not look far to see how Africans, Asians, and Pacific people have been for the past four to five centuries, "scarcely visible". In this, the so-called postcolonial age, the modern age of universal equality, tempered with righteousness, and international programs on hygiene, health, and environmental concerns, the majority seem hardly better off. Like Chekov's formless masses, the virtual absence of postmodern theoretical work in Africa, Asia, and the Pacific (with respect to their citations and sites in the major capitals of the West) are symptomatic of a larger problem of cultural ambivalence, an incongruity arising out of the cultural logic of late

---

[27] Anton Chekov, *Selected Stories* (New York: New American Library, [1885] 1982), p. 121.

capitalism.²⁸ Even commentators like Jameson (apart from his book, *The Political Unconscious: Narrative as a Socially Symbolic Act*, 1981), marginalizes as it under-develops the non-Western, African, Asian, and Pacific native *Other*. Work on Africa, Asia, and the Pacific continues to rest broadly and rely primarily on Orientalist and Postorientalist scholarship, and increasingly, on the narrow backs of "indigenous", Western-educated, African, Asian, and Pacific academics working in great and lesser Western metropolitan universities. These women and men speak with great promise and strong conviction at various academic debates but are ironically detached from the abject squalor, and physiological deprivation of the people and places they write about. Their people, and their places.²⁹ The conceit and largesse of Orientalist projections and non-Western scholars located within the metropolises of modernity reflect the burgeoning divide and divisiveness of a fragile, modern project. There is no freedom from anywhere, as seen in Noel O'Sullivan reading of another Foucauldian archetype, "the modern dream of freedom is thus an illusion, and every attempt to defend it merely reinforces the triumphant discourse of power". ³⁰

But Jameson's political narrative is encouraging. We see a story ranging from Riviera's famous *Man at the Crossroads*, Rankus, Manning, and Lathams's *AlieNATION*, to Le Corbusier's obscure *Unite d'Habitation*. The significance here lies in the idea that the artifacts of modernity represented in his book appear to rise effortlessly out of an "established" Western architectural mosaic. This is fine, but not fine enough to provide a substitute for capturing and explaining Asian narratival experiences of modernity, a pastiche that has up till recently been described primarily in exotic,

---

²⁸ Jameson, *ibid.*, p. 64.

²⁹ I thank Jorge Fernandes for this thought. I would point to the work of Arjun Appadurai as representing one of the few consistent exceptions, as seen in "Number in the Colonial Imagination" in *Orientalism and the Postcolonial Predicament*, ed. by Carol Breckenridge and Peter Van der Veer (Philadelphia: University of Pennsylvania Press, 1993); "The Heart of Whiteness" *Public Culture*, (1993), 5(3): 796-807; and, *Modernity at Large: Cultural Dimensions of Globalization* (Minneapolis: University of Minnesota Press, 1996).

³⁰ O'Sullivan, *ibid.*, p. 24.

nativized, colors of subordinated, subsumed, and substituted cultures of Africa, Asia, and the Pacific.

Asia generates an abundance of cultural, social, political, and economic (positive and negative) space in the capitalist disjuncture of Singapore *et cetera*. There is a need for a deeper, further, and faster ethnographical exposé of the departments, levels, bureaus, forms, ministries, formations, channels, institutions, and margins that control and mediate politicized spaces. While the state — as the primary institutionalized public space — appears outwardly as secure, and confident, its people, may lack the confidence, remain uncertain, and irresolute about the oxymoron of modernity: that the modern desire for simplicity, simplification, efficiency, and ease, merely leads to greater complication, frustration, angst, inefficiency, and counter-productivity. Yet the prison of the modern is one that defies escapades, except into its own depths. Studies in the light of Kundera's unbearable lightness of living politicized narratives that hold up public space, are analogous to Chekov's over-burdened donkey, its weight being literally applicable to Africa, Asia, and the Pacific:

> "Here's my cell," the old man said, as he bent down to enter a lower-ceilinged room, which because of its proximity to the kitchen, was insufferably stifling.[31]

The postmodern fear, of course, is the same fear that keeps modernism in the driver's seat, a fear that is worse than death because it is a fear of possessing that which cannot be possessed:

> In the postmodern condition, however, the world into which people are born "is no longer seen as having been decreed by fate but as an agglomerate of possibilities".**[IG]** Everything is therefore constantly questioned, everything is provisional, and every individual is haunted by the great postmodern fear,

---

[31] Chekov, *ibid.*, p. 121.

which is the fear of having missed out on what might have been.[32]

Postmodernism then, and the modern ghosts that haunt its provisional domain, keeps deconstructing and reconstructing its variegated relationships with modernism, if only to survive for the moment.

Narratival Frames

The political narratives that hold up and frame modernity suggest a bleak and pessimistic picture of the life we call reality. The reality of the modern age is a fragile one, made up of disparaging sets of uncertain elements.

> But our aim is not to expunge the differences between the ethnic groups. Each community contributing to its own unique characteristics and strengths to our society. If Chinese Singaporeans lose their Chinese cultural heritage, or Malay Singaporeans discard their traditional customs and Islamic values, we become a much weaker society. We must create unity in diversity.[33]

Lee's intention is hard to fault. Hard to a fault. One does not have to look very far to see that Asian political narratives are not so dissimilar from those of Western ones, the differences are more apparent than real. The nature of political narratives, stories of the state, and the society it claims to represent, appear to take on the following character: ideological, dogmatic, author-centered (there state as author), paternalistic, factual, conservative (the wisdom of the ages), anticipatory, convincing, metaphorical, idealistic, sensitive, insensitive, rationalistic, objective, value-free, dualism, managed, orchestrated, complex, simple, stupendous, uniform, tension-filled, marginalizing, overt.[IG] At some level, the theorist must admit that

---

[32] O'Sullivan, *ibid.*, p. 24.
[33] Lee, *ibid.*, p. 29.

political narratives expressed as national ideology are themselves projections of national concerns and insecurities. The fear of being unable to theorize about the ability to survive, or the anticipation of future problems leads to a kind of preventive action that is seen to forestall, prevent, curtail, or circumvent the unknown. Political narratives then, play an important part in all states, and all state-society relations; in the building of political credibility; in the fostering of political ties within and without multiethnic societies; in the production of a myriad of relations that enable the construction and maintenance of a civil society; and, in locating individual and group insecurities in some plausible past in order to anchor the social, political, and cultural belief systems. But the propinquity of the narratival form towards the creation of social justice also enables it to lean the other way — a singularistic and parochial belief in an immutable, non-debatable story, backed by the coercive elements of the state, will have consequences for the meaning of the *public good*, and the text of the nation, in the long run.

For the political theorist, the hermeneutics of narrativization is at best an approximation of epistemological patterns thrown up by the pastiche of post-modernity: in the national *races*, the competition is no more merciful. Like Hegel's problem of the unfinished text, Chekov's political stories, Jameson's form of the narrative, Canclini's revolving-door, O'Sullivan's philosophical concern for the postmodern project, Lee's objective history, and Goh's vision, our fragile modernity represents individually-wrapped, and succinct reminders of the *temporary*, the *fragile*, the *fluid*, and the *marginal*, as we seek understanding, desire instant gratification, demand quick-fix solutions, expect overt attention and anticipate meaningful recognition in encountering modernity. Like the tripping and falling maidens of ancient Singapore, Postman's entertainment-fetish society, Goh and Lee's political rhetoric, the monotonous chanting of angry Youth, and Chekov's huge, packed, and formless masses, the conceit of the late modern period is a reflection of an inescapable incarceration presented to us in birth as we struggle to engage a fragile modernity, not by prolonging life, but by forestalling the *will to death*, in our move towards understanding narrative spaces that occupy the public mind as seen in the real estate public narrative installment below:

> In a bleak appraisal of the market...office rentals for the full year had fallen 15.7 per cent and would continue to sink over the next 12 months. The export-driven Singapore economy has been one of the hardest hit in Asia by the global slowdown forcing an across-the-board downsizing of businesses. But while the economy contracted 5.6 per cent in the third quarter, the flow-on impact on the property market has been much more severe. In Raffles Place, the heart of the central business district, average rentals fell 12.6 per cent in the fourth quarter from S$7.55 (US$4.10) per square foot to S$6.60...Jones Lang LaSalle said the market would remain soft in the coming months. It was the second gloomy property report in two days, after the company produced figures on Wednesday showing mortgagee sales hit record numbers this year amid Singapore's worst downturn since statehood in 1965.[34]

It is the market again that has emerged as the primary site of mRf where the forces of modernity, represented by financial interests, statistical estimates, the property market, and the pressures from the global "slowdown" in this example, contend and clash with the forces of resistance that are represented in citizen and domiciled foreign mortgages claiming a stake in Singapore. These real estate narratives exist in the public domain and keep hope alive for those who are optimistic believers in the central value of modernity as "being modern". Being modern translates into divesting one's financial portfolio into various low and high risk activities in the economy.[**FV, EG**] The readers recognize the words and phrases that make up the contingent decisions that are made in the space of privacy. Yet it becomes exceedingly clear in this and in other examples that the increasing influence of the public arena over the private arena even works when and during an economic

---

[34] "Singapore Office Rentals Plummet", AFP December 27, Thursday, 2001.

slowdown, where ironically, the public narratives being circulated by the media ought to be less believable becomes increasingly (more) believable. The extent of this belief is seen in the acquiescent acceptance by the general public of announcements such as the one where, "More than 20,000 doctors, nurses and non-medical workers employed in the public health-care sector will have their bonuses cut this year because of the recession...A *SingHealth* spokesman said that while there was no need to retrench people, it was necessary to make adjustments and introduce measures that would ensure staff welfare while still providing affordable health care. For most of the 20,000 employees affected, it will mean a shrunken year-end bonus".[35] These public spaces exist contiguously with their narratives serving to support the structures of the public domain through a shifting, sometimes enabling, sometimes disabling series of political shapes, ideas, values, traditions, and beliefs.[**FV/WG, IG**]

---

[35] H. T. Liang, "Bonuses Cut for 20,000 Public Health-Care Staff," Nov 30, *The Straits Times*, 2001.

References

Appadurai, Arjun. 1993. "Number in the Colonial Imagination" in C. Breckenridge and P. Van de Beer (eds.) *Orientalism and the Postcolonial Predicament.* Philadelphia: University of Pennsylvania.

Appadurai, Arjun. 1993. "The Heart of Whiteness", *Public Culture,* 5(3): 796-807.

Appadurai, Arjun. 1996. *Modernity at Large: Cultural Dimensions of Globalization.* Minneapolis: University of Minnesota Press.

Bauman, Zygmunt. 1991. *Modernity and Ambivalence.* Oxford: Polity Press.

Bradbury, Malcolm and McFarlane, James. eds. 1991. *Modernism: A Guide to European Literature, 1890-1930.* London: Penguin.

Bronner, Stephen Eric and Kellner, Douglas Mackey. eds. 1989. *Critical Theory and Society: A Reader.* London: Routledge.

Canclini, Nestor Garcia. 1996. *Hybrid Cultures: Strategies for Entering and Leaving Modernity.* Minneapolis: University of Minnesota Press.

Chekov, Anton. 1982. *Selected Stories.* New York: New American Library.

Connolly, William E. 1991. *Identity/Difference: Democratic Negotiations of Political Paradox.* Ithaca: Cornell University Press.

Connolly, William E. 1992. "The Irony of Interpretation," in Daniel W. Conway and John E. Seery. (eds.) *The Politics of Irony: Essays in Self-betrayal.* New York: St. Martin's Press.

Connolly, William E. 1998. "The Will, Capital Punishment, and Cultural War." Paper presented at the American Political Science Association meeting. Boston, Massachusetts.

Harvey, David. 1990. *The Condition of Postmodernity.* Oxford: Basil Blackwell.

Jameson, Fredric. 1991. *Postmodernism, or The Cultural Logic of Late Capitalism.* Durham: Duke University Press.

Kateb, George. 1992. *The Inner Ocean: Individualism and Democratic Culture.* Ithaca: Cornell University Press.

Kekes, John. 1993. *The Morality of Pluralism.* Princeton: Princeton University Press.

Lefebvre, Henri. 1991. *The Production of Space*. Oxford: Basil Blackwell.

Manning, Marable. 1996. *Speaking Truth to Power: Essays on Race, Resistance, and Radicalism*. Boulder, Colorado: Westview Press.

Miller, Daniel, ed. 2001. *Consumption: Critical Concepts in the Social Sciences*, vol. I, *Theory and Issues in the Study of Consumption*. London & New York: Routledge.

Nietzsche, Friedrich. 1973. *Beyond Good and Evil: Prelude to a Philosophy of the Future*. Translated by R. J Hollingdale. London: Penguin Classics.

O'Sullivan, Noel. 1993. "The Philosophy of Postmodernism"' in *Political Studies*, **41**: 21-42.

Rosenau, Pauline Marie. 1992. *Postmodernism and the Social Sciences: Insights, Inroads, and Intrusion*. Durham: Duke University Press.

Stallybrass, Peter and White, Allon. 1986. *The Politics and Poetics of Transgression*. Ithaca: Cornell University Press.

Thumboo, Edwin, *et al.* 1990. *The Fiction of Singapore*. Singapore: Unipress.

Wiggerhaus, Rolf. 1995. *The Frankfurt School*. Cambridge: MIT Press.

Wildavsky, Aaron. 1979. *Speaking Truth to Power: The Art and Craft of Policy Analysis*. Boston: Little, Brown, and Company.

PART II
MALAYSIA

Consuming Malaysia

> I would like to point out that under current economic conditions where growth will come from domestic sources, bank financing is crucial to lubricate the economy. Banks must, therefore, ensure that credit is appropriately channeled to stimulate consumption and investment.
>
> Mahathir Mohamad
> *Speech, 22nd Annual Association Dinner of the Association of Merchant Banks in Malaysia, October 2001*

An interpretation of consumption in Malaysia might be achieved if we consider Michel Foucault's notion of discursive formations as a way of understanding and employing the mRf. By this I specifically refer to the way in which Foucault uses a multiple unity of discourses of the different types of "consumption" or hypotheses of "consumption" that Foucault favors in *The Archeology of Knowledge and the Discourse of Language* (1972) that carry alternative poses confidently asserting the value of past over the present. On such reassertion occurs with the philosophical problem on public and private space. In Richard Rorty's introduction to

Contingency, Irony, and Solidarity (1989), he suggests that Plato's attempt to fuse "public and private" space had similar considerations as follows:

(1) an attempt to answer, "Why is it in one's interest to be just?"; and,
(2) Christianity's claim that "perfect self-realization can be attained through service to others".

I argue in this chapter that Rorty's quote initiates a series of arguments that may be examined and analyzed in the consumption patterns of late modernity in Malaysia. Rorty resurrects Plato's argument so that he can contextualize it in terms of a didactic shift away from classical prescriptions of reality to the disempowering theories in theology and metaphysics. Yet the problem in late modernity — the experience of global and technological transformation today — is that the liberalizing influences of a heavily Teutonic historicism on the parochial nature of religious dogmatism, theological prescription, and metaphysical speculation that dominated the pre-enlightenment period. I argue that the nature of consumption in late modernity goes beyond the explications of the classical foundationalists and German historicists. Neither are the views of the liberal historicist Jurgen Habermas in *The Structural Transformation of the Public Sphere* (1989) overtly valuable for understanding consumption in Malaysia. Habermas views the public sphere as one that resonates best within countries predisposed to a strong tradition of civil society activity, and one where the idea of a public opinion is created in terms of the public discussion of ideas that are teleological in the sense of being directed towards the securing of a common good such as virtue, governance, or, as in the case of this book's focus, "consumption". Habermas also argues that civil society issues into a public site of commerce, thereby returning the reader to the platonic conundrum of a fusion of public and private space. The mRf on the other hand uses five concepts to illustrate the patterns of economic consumption in Malaysia. This overview is premised on the following:

(a) Malaysia is a multi-ethnic, multi-cultural, and multi-religious country;

(b) There is a gendered division of labor along traditional and religious lines; and,

(c) Malaysia's pro-consumption, consumer-driven approach to resolving the recessionary pressures in the 1997-98, and the 2001-02 recession.

These three premises suggest that the idea of late modernity in Malaysia appears to be much less about the collapse of public and private spaces within democratizing civil societies and more about the importance of state-led, state-defined, and quasi-state determinism. On the other hand, a possible neoMarxist view — one neither held by this writer nor used in this book — would be one where such a collapse of both public into private and private into public is the result of the withering away of the state after the conflation of class structures previously stratified but eventually and inevitably weakened and emaciated by internal class contradictions, inherent class antagonism, and driven by both the longitudinal and historical exploitation of working class surplus value by a capitalist, bourgeois elite against the backdrop of a powerfully rising consciousness of worker demanding justice. Yet such a neoMarxist thesis would be very quickly invalidated on account of evidence such as the impact of voting patterns, popular support, and quality of life arguments and other "democratizing agents" in Malaysia.

Narratives & Discursive Formations

An alternative interpretation to consumption in the late modernity of Malaysia is through a derivative of the Foucauldian discursive formation seen in the mRf. Brown's work-gender thesis [**WG**] will be covered in a third narrative below. In the M/R argument, only four of the five concepts are potentially discernible in the two illustrations below with regards to Connolly's exclusionary/inclusionary goods [**IG/EG**], Brennan's foundational fantasy of (economic) horror [**FH**], White's vulnerable consumer [**VP**], and the important centering of Vattimo's modern value [**FV**] (rational economic solutions for irrational economic problems) are

148 Modernity and Consumption

illustrated in the pro-consumption impetus of the Malaysian government and its consumption stories:

> Malaysia's engines of growth over the past decade — electronics and manufacturing [**EG**] — stuttering in the wake of the global recession...Almost 60 per cent of respondents surveyed recently by recruitment website JobStreet.com felt it would be difficult to get a job — the lowest level since the survey began after the 1997 Asian crisis [**FV**]. For optimism and confidence, fast forward to the sales launch of two-storey link houses in the middle-class suburb of Subang Jaya, where 1,800 people are on tenterhooks [**VP/FH**]...Robust sales at selected property developments and a 25-per-cent jump in motor-vehicle sales over last year are driving the government to believe that it can keep the economy from slipping into a recession by getting Malaysians to spend...Increased consumer spending will tell retailers, restaurants and hotels to raise their inventory from wholesalers...Wholesalers will buy more from manufacturers, who in turn, will raise production levels [**EG/FV**]. More jobs will be created and economic growth rates will increase. Malaysia's economy contracted by 1.3 per cent in the third quarter [of 2001], worse than analysts' forecasts of a 0.5-per-cent contraction. Dr Zainal Aznam Yusof, a National Economic Action Council member, thinks there are mildly encouraging signs. He noted that private consumption grew at a slightly faster rate of 2.1 per cent in the third quarter, compared with 1.6 per cent in the second quarter. But checks show that although car sales are up, retail outlets, entertainment outlets and eateries all report slower-than-usual business. At a seafood restaurant in the middle-class suburb of Bangsar, business is down 20 per cent [**VP**]. At the Kuala Lumpur International Airport, shop tenants are asking for a sharp cut in rental charges...In a recent report, Goldman Sachs said it believed that the next six months would confirm that Malaysia's recession this time would be deeper than that of

Malaysia's recession this time would be deeper than that of 1998, when 83,000 people lost jobs [FH/VP]. It pointed out that the 1997/98 period represented a pause in the export boom, while today's exports were contracting significantly. But what about the consumption story? Goldman Sachs' take: It believes the consumption story will dissipate over the next six months as the growth of new jobs slows sharply, affecting household income and inflation.[1]

The consumption story is often used as part of a larger strategy to boost domestic consumption within a subject-participatory political culture that consistently returns overwhelmingly results for the incumbent Barisan Nasional (BN) or National Front (NF) a coalition of ethnic-based, communally-rooted political parties led by the United Malays National Organization (UMNO). Even BN-coalition partner parties led by the long-standing, highly respected, and widely popular team made up of the chief minister, Yang Amat Berhormat Datuk Patinggi Tan Sri (Dr) Haji Abdul Taib Mahmud, and the deputy chief minister, Yang Berhormat Tan Sri Datuk Amar Dr. George Chan Hong Nam in Sarawak's state elections in September 2001 — that have proven over the past two decades to be supportive of the central government's policies in KL under Mahathir — have garnered incredibly high voter turnouts with the highest number of seats secured by the SUPP. Given the recent results from the polls, Sarawakians are comfortable with the past five years of goods and services delivered to them under Taib's leadership at the state level and Datuk Seri Dr Mahathir Mohammed's national leadership despite the two recessions and the surprising and startling case of former deputy prime minister, Dato' Seri Anwar Ibrahim. One could thus argue that there exists a basket of goods and services that contribute to a national "political good". The

---

[1] *The Straits Times*, Dec 4, 2001. See Brendan Pereira, "KL's Spend Policy" *The Straits Times*, December 4, 2001; and Reme Mohammed, "Hard Times in Malaysia...and Money Lenders", *The Straits Times*, December 4, 2001. See also, P. Ramasamy, "Schools Echo Malaysia's Ethic Politics", *The Straits Times*, December 21, 2001, p. 29.

collective political good is itself contingent on the electoral and constituency performance of the Members of Parliament.

The collective political good is a form of inclusionary good (to use Connolly's term) with cosmopolitan beginnings and complex plural endings that are characterized by plurality and depth rather than singularity and surface. The collective political good therefore has a tendency to vary positively with current levels of governance, and changes in consumer tastes with regards to the kinds of intangible services and tangible goods available within the basket. The collective political good is itself limited to and dependent upon the kinds of goods that fall within its collective. If indeed the idea of a Malaysian collective political good exists, and the assumption here is that it does indeed, it would be reasonable to argue that the exchange and consumption of the collective political good occurs primarily in the public sphere. The situation breeds the rise of a kind of public or national morality in which the collective political good and its consumers determine through civil associations and through state and quasi-state enterprises the nature of its public morality. If indeed this argument is accepted, then the resultant morality becomes an ethical product over time that eventually pressures citizens to conform, and the marginalization of public space to the extent the private space becomes conditional, ephemeral, and decrepit. The private has ironically become contingent on the public. Therefore, and as we shall see, decisions made by consumers on consumer goods and services no longer represent the conscious choices of private, interest-seeking, wealth-maximizing individuals but rather symbolize "social status", "public prescription", "public morality", and "public constructions" as *illustrated in the current strategy that emphasizes* domestic spending. The connection across national public space between Johore and Singapore is seen in the continual consumption patterns that impact on one another:

> ...the spillover effect of the economic crunch in Singapore ...on retailers, restaurant owners and poultry farmers in the southern Malaysian state [**VP/FH**]. Not to mention how the layoffs are affecting the estimated 40,000 people who cross the Causeway daily to earn a living in the Republic [**FH**]. The

state executive councilor told *The Straits Times*: 'When Singapore is doing well, Singaporeans come here in big numbers and spend more money. Everyone does well. The petrol stations, seafood restaurants and shopping complexes. 'When Singapore is down, most seafood restaurants suffer a 30 per cent drop in business.'...'Our retail sector in Johor Baru traditionally depends on foreigners, especially Singaporeans...Chamber of commerce statistics indicate that, on average, 1.2 million Singaporeans cross the Causeway every month. Since Sept 11, that number has fallen to 900,000 a month...Hypermarkets such as *Carrefour* [and other supermarkets] have opened in the past few years to cater for Singaporean shoppers who cross the Causeway regularly to take advantage of their stronger dollar...Human Resources Ministry statistics indicate that nearly 8,000 people in the state have lost their jobs [**FH/VP**]. Johor's is the second highest total after Penang. Many of those affected are Malaysians from other states who, until recently, were working in Singapore.[2]

The consumption story in Malaysia's late modernity and the idea of story-telling in Malaysia on a wide-ranging and daily basis is a crucial mode of expressing, transforming, and passing on culture to the next generation. The story-teller within each individual reclaims textual experiences that are familiar and ambiguous, with familiarity and ambiguity going back into modern Malaysian history.

Historical Narratives

The history of political and economic differences in Malaysia provides an interpretive language for examining consumption. Between 1955 to 1995 the Federation of Malaysia illustrated the struggles between and among

---

[2] *The Straits Times*, Dec 4, 2001.

oppositional forms of political, cultural and economic dominance for the sake of consumer wealth, and the right to consume the country's bourgeoning wealth. The historical social formations of Chinese, Buddhist, Hindu and Islamic culture pre-existed the Western European colonization of Southeast Asia by the Portuguese, the Dutch, and the British, who were all congenitally consumerist in orientation.

The British colonial period was noted for its conspicuous role in shaping and designing Malayan consumer modernity (modernization based on consumers interacting between local and foreign markets). The separation of ethnic communities in accordance with occupational specialization and a "work ethic" that resulted in the breeding of suspicion, hate and enmity between and among the various ethnic communities over economic goods. However, the colonial state structure, bent on ensuring the efficacy of its Southeast Asian colony, provided the overarching frame of authority that prevented widespread ethnic violence and chaos.

The post-1945 era proved to be the unquestionable major political disjunction that saw the demise of British colonialism and the rise of Malay control over politics while the Chinese continued to dominate in commerce, and became known as advocates and practitioners of a consumer modernity that distinguished them from the non-Chinese residents of Malaya. The massive ethnic, social and religious distinctions caused by the association of wealth and economic class with poverty and race were kept in a fragile balance by the English colonial state structure through the police, military and volunteer units.

The idea of Malay nationalism was less that of an overt putsch by "resistance from the ground" and more of a simple transfer of political power from one set of elites to another in 1957, the year of "internal self-government". The recipient "multiethnic" elite class comprised the Malay Royal Houses, wealthy tin and rubber merchants and Western-trained Malay intellectuals. Unlike the equally decadent Dutch and French enterprises in the Orient that refused to relinquish their Southeast Asian colonial possessions, the British preferred a process of gradual political transformation. This was important for two reasons, firstly, that it would emplace an entire strata of English-trained leaders who were (they thought) sufficiently imbued with the right type of Western ideals for government and would hence be more amenable to the retreating Empire. The smooth transfer of power from a foreign set of elites to a local set of elites justified the existence of another frame, a diplomatic device, seen in the British "Commonwealth". Secondly, the gradual transition of power provided a ready-made market in the people of the Third World, people who were assumed by the former to be effectively socialized into thinking that British-made goods were of the highest quality and desirable goods for tropical use. The British "legacy" also resulted in the uneven and underdevelopment of her colony. British Malaya had repeatedly raped the land, *inter alia*, for tin and rubber. Single crops of rubber and other tropicalized produce were exhausting the mineral balance of the soil. Malaysia became the world's largest tin-producing country and was then subjected to fluctuations in the global price mechanism: over-producing when there was a glut and under-producing when there was none. These products had to compete with laboratory-based alternatives derived from the "First World's" petro-chemical industries.

Thus the entire British plan of retreat to the East of the Suez canal was in effect a last ditch attempt to save their embattled empire from total and complete disintegration with a certain degree of style and distinction that would ensure British firms with medium to long term profits as they had enjoyed in the past. The British colonial state in Malaya was patriarchal as it was paternalistic, serving as the moral, social and political guide and mentor for the new state.

The rise of the Malay state since 1955 — as the agent of political order and social change — has resulted in material wealth for many Malaysians of all ethnic groups, bumiputra and non-bumiputra alike. Over the forty year period, the state created conditions that suited its niche in the economic reality of a commodified global economy. In order to sustain such economic conditions and establish links with(in) the international processes of cultural, linguistic, and social commodification, the state had to ensure that there was political stability. Hence, the (re)structuring of order in modern post-colonies, as Arjun Appadurai observes, is about drawing on the:

classificatory and disciplinary apparatuses that they inherited from colonial rulers and that in the postcolonial context have substantial inflammatory effects.[3]

The effects of the colonial inheritance was to discipline and punish labor. The new state manipulated the struggles of labor by deliberately de-linking its class consciousness from its political consciousness. It emaciated labor by correlating and then linking the surplus value of their productive effort (or productivity) to wages and salaries. In order to reconcile global and local capitalist demands for lower wages with the problem of worker demands, the interventionist state, as the intervening variable, reconstructed plausible social and economic narratives that would ensure its political survival.

The race riots of 1969 while serving as the opportunity for the formation of Malay ethnocratism were also an indicator of future problems in state-society relations. The Malay ethnocrats had "no other choice" but to rise to the occasion in order to reassert their political and economic rights *vis-à-vis* the non-Malay communities and to prevent the outbreak of further ethnic violence throughout the Federation. The ethnocrats could not envision any other kind of politics in their multiethnic society.

While many Malay Malaysians benefited from the affirmative action policies, since 1970 under the NEP (Kamal, 1988), and now under the NDP, resulting in a large Malay middle class, there are many Malays whose lives have not changed much since the institution of ethnocratism. The non-Malay bumiputra — the Dayak, Iban, Orang Asli and Orang Laut, to name a few — while Constitutional inheritors of specific rights that accrue to indigenous people of the Federation are just beginning to receive basic physiological amenities. Political tokenism best describes their situation, a situation in which they are mere cultural tokens or trinkets of Malay ethnocratism awaiting exploitation by the tourist and mass consumption

---

[3] Arjun Appadurai, *Modernity at Large: Cultural Dimensions of Globalization* (Minnesota: University of Minnesota Press, 1996), p. 146.

industries. The Melaka-Eurasians are an example of a fringe community that is beholden to the Malay state. Their economic, social and political survival is marginal to the capitalist success of Malaysia and the objective of becoming a developed nation and entering the First World by the year 2020. Although many Chinese Malaysians have benefited from Malaysia's economic success, their cultural and political narratives reflect a showcase of "trade-offs" to Malay ethnocratism. Political apathy and a preference for wealth-creation have resulted in a rather contradictory existence: they continue to be economically powerful but are politically weak. Their political affiliations are a reflection of a fragmented political awareness and disenchantment with an irreconcilable oppositional cultural and political Malay hegemony. The Chinese are torn between making "authentic" claims to Malaysian citizenship and citizenhood, and fighting for social and political equity. These are not necessarily one and the same event. Claims of authenticity require subscription to the politico-cultural ethos of Bangsa Malaysia and the implicit acceptance of the cultural norms of Bahasa Melayu. After forty years, there is still no Chinese university, no clear site for the expression of intellectual interrogatives of the Malay state. The alternative route leads the Chinese to a direct confrontation with the Special Rights of the Malays, a Constitutional imperative (Kamal, 1988).

Unfortunately, the Malay state continues to periodically imprison leaders of the legitimate opposition; legitimate leaders, primarily Chinese, who have been returned to political office by the same electoral machinery that has kept the Malay ethnocrats in place. The past forty years have in effect seen an encroachment of Chinese business, culture and art. The Chinese are also reproducing at a rate that is less than the population replacement level. After a few more decades, the Chinese will become, like the Indians and Melaka-Eurasians, a fringe community on the outskirts of the Malay state.

Thus while Malaysia has, for all intents and purposes, done an excellent job of preventing overt ethnic violence between and among its multiethnic population, and securing relative economic wealth for many citizens, the grid of power that holds up Malaysian modernity, a late modernity that is mediated by the Malay state.

Work-Gender Narratives

Malaysia — a vivid nexus of culture, politics, and religious differences discernible at different levels in other cosmopolitan, democratizing societies in late modernity — is deeply embedded with gender biases and prejudices that form an extensive surface structure within the patriarchal discursive formations of its patterns of consumption. Work-gender narratives of women in Malaysia and Singapore are often organized into specific cases, studies that are divided along biologically reduced lines and entrenched in the social imaginary via the powerful media instruments of advertising and marketing through television, radio, the internet, and street level consumption. The social imaginary often segments women and minorities together, the one collapsing into the other, while simultaneously representing other "difficult" and "abnormal" categories in lepers, the mentally-deranged, lunatics, psychotics, gays, lesbians, queers, transsexuals, transvestites, prostitutes, the physically and mentally-challenged, and other human beings all lumped together into a Pandora's box that many would prefer unopened lest its opening renders normal society unable to function in the face of abnormality.[4] The intention of moderns and those who subscribe to the late modern ethos of modernity are those who expect and demand a normal and nominal understanding about the world in a believable "truth-knowledge-fact" equation that develops within the social imaginary with a vocabulary of symbols that are simple and easy to consume, and comfortable to live by. Work-gender narratives focus on the margins of social intercourse, the liminal interstices between and among weird, sensational and semi-fictional fillers of newspaper reports and tabloids. The work-gender distinction makes normal people feel "uncomfortable", as we have seen earlier in Chapter 2, establishes the tenuous position that women who move into the public arena from the private one are in turn expected to fill the void of "their traditional responsibility" even though they might be contributing significantly to the family income through work in the public arena. However, the modern

---

[4] Antonio L Rappa, "Imprisoning the Other", *Peace Review*, 1998, 11 (1):157-160.

value of advancement and progress and improvement and development means that all resources will ultimately have to be channeled towards the workplace in order for individuals, families and entire societies to survive late modernity. While women make up half the world's population, it becomes puzzling when wonders why they earn less than ten percent of the world's income and own even less of the world's assets. This phenomenon has attracted the attention, finances, professional specialization, and effort of intellectuals, journalists, film-makers, marketing and advertising types, politicians, and social, cultural, and political activists. One can safely say that women today have more avenues to voice their opinions and beliefs as women and as citizens. While there are structural and legal regulations and laws in place that make women equal to men, the differences are seen in the ways in which societies treat women. The consumption patterns of women workers and women homemakers are closely watched and monitored by advertising and marketing agencies seeking to further the sale of goods and services. Marketing and advertising executives are the late modern pushers of advanced forms of capitalism across the globe. The world of marketing and advertising are two jointly secure worlds that possess huge instrumental resources for the management and promotion of the commodification of gender, and of men and women. This is very well analyzed in Susan Bordo's *Unbearable Weight: Feminism, Western Culture, and the Body* (Berkeley: University of California Press, 1993); and her chapter, "Material Girl: The Effacements of Postmodern Culture", in Donn Welton's (ed.), *Body and Flesh: A Philosophical Reader* (Cambridge, Mass.: Blackwell Publishers, 1998). The modern value of consumption is often seen in the political rhetoric involving welcoming women into the public sphere for work. In early December 2001, for example, MCA president Datuk Seri Dr. Ling Liong Sik stated ironically after launching the Wanita MCA's exhibition, "It is a time where we need Malaysians to spend more locally to stimulate the economy and to save on foreign exchange...Love Malaysia, Buy Malaysia Campaign" and claims that such a campaign worked in the past, and that "women play an important role in consumer spending and would help the government in its efforts to boost the economy".[5] The "Buy Malaysia, Love Malaysia" campaign as a political and economic strategy to resolve the problem with the 2000-2002 recession reflects the economic strategy of buying and purchasing goods and services (on one hand) with the political strategy that is itself an expression of love for the nation [FV] (on the other). The launching of the political campaign by the MCA president, who happens to be a man, at a Wanita MCA exhibition is revealing in three main ways. Firstly, in order to appeal to the consumers, one has to appeal to women possibly because of a belief that women love to go shopping to "de-stress" and for "self-motivation": women are perhaps perceived to be the major consumers in Malaysia. Secondly, the politico-economic strategy of consuming domestic goods and saving foreign exchange implies that a certain responsibility lies with women who are expected in many instances to manage household duties. And thirdly, the "Buy Malaysia, Love Malaysia" campaign fuses masculine and feminine "qualities"; the masculine qualities are seen in the idea of the Nation, the Fatherland, and enshrined perhaps in the revolving constitutional monarchy where the Sultan or Agung — always a male — is the Head of State and the embodiment of the modern Malaysian nation. But the idea of consumption at the retail and "domestic" or householder level is a feminine quality, where women are in charge of household management and where there are clear indications that such management logically requires weekly if not daily purchases at the local markets. The expression of love for the nation is itself an expression of a feminine quality for a masculine quality: women's common subordination and love for her nation embodied in the Agung. Therefore in the public realm (where most buying and selling or consumption takes place) becomes a convenient site for the mixing of masculine and feminine traits to the extent that work-gender narratives become reduced to fleeting, vague, and conflated images of class, gender, and ethnic inequalities. The work-gender contradiction is further

---

[5] *Wanita MCA* is the Women's Wing of the Malaysian Chinese Association. *The Star Online*, Sunday, December 2, 2001.

complexified by parliamentarians who during the Budget debate raise what are considered "women's issues" in the following narrative:

> The topic of love and marriage surfaced during the debate on the Budget, with two women DAP MPs raising the problems faced by Malaysian women who married foreign men (ST).[6]

There continues to be a distinction made between marriages to foreign men and local men. From the local perspective, the idea of women marrying foreigners is often considered taboo, or at least frowned upon by the cultural gatekeepers of traditional societies while the reverse appears less polemical. This is partly because the preservation of tradition appears codified in legalism where patriarchal lineage is preserved and matrilineal ties are not. The foreign woman who marries a local man takes on the last name or surname of the man and his father, and his father's father. Foreign men who marry local women on the other hand enter into a different economic relationship in which the woman "loses" her father's name and takes on her husband's one. While this is not unique to Asia, and while there are those who desire hyphenated versions of last names, most women take on their husband's names in marriage. This itself contributes to the root imbalance between genders and results in the problem of "equal" treatment versus the "equitable" treatment of women within the work-gender ethic. Not surprisingly,

> Both Batu Gajah [Member of Parliament] MP Fong Po Kuan and Seputeh MP Teresa Kok said women who married foreign men faced various restrictions that were not imposed on Malaysian men who had foreign wives.[7]

Additionally, there is a patriarchal motif that exists in the background where women continue to be seen as the weaker sex and men the stronger

---

[6] Democratic Action Party. The DAP is an opposition party primarily based in the west Malaysian peninsular but with branches in the east Malaysian states of Sabah and Sarawak. See "Paradox laws on marriage to foreigners", *The Star Online*, December 4, 2001. See also, Hwa Mei Shen, "Men's role in ending violence" *The Star Online*, December 4, 2001

[7] "Paradox laws on marriage to foreigners", *The Star Online*, December 4, 2001.

one. Such biological reductionism permeates and percolates deep into the engendered psyche:

> However, Datuk Mohamad Aziz (BN–Sri Gading) cut in to say that such laws were meant to protect Malaysian women. "Besides, the men here are great too," he quipped. Fong, however, was indignant, saying that Mohamad's views reflected an archaic thinking that women need "protection."[8]

The concerns of the gender-neutral journalist appearing within the MPs' discourse during the Budget debate does not change or alter the fact that these issues are often trivialized to the point where they are no longer perceived by the public as being significantly legitimate despite having the M/R argument illustrated again:

> Kok said that women's choices should not just be confined to local men only, when Malaysian men ended up marrying their foreign maids. Then, several backbenchers were heard teasing them that they could go ahead to marry whoever they wanted. Women Affairs and Family Development Minister Datuk Shahrizat Abdul Jalil said today's men should rise to the challenge of knowing what women want from them. "I think the women now are not merely looking for a life partner who is compatible, but also someone of quality," she said. She noted a practice now where women married men who were younger than them.[9]

While it is considered "normal" for men to marry younger women, the consumption practice of women marrying younger men on the other hand however is considered a "phenomenon". The work-gender contradiction has resulted in more spaces opening up in public and private, more avenues for women to explore, more alternatives for women to consider, and more channels for women to develop than at any other time in the history of

---

[8] *Ibid.*

[9] "Paradox laws on marriage to foreigners", *The Star Online*, December 4, 2001.

human civilization. What appears clearly in support of the work-gender contradiction is that women now not only work in the same places as men but also compete for similar positions thereby increasing their occupational and social mobility. Modernity has resulted in the weakening of the traditional strangleholds that men have had over women, and the displacement of conventions previously held predominantly by males. Malaysian women have left home for the marketplace to increase family income and for self-actualization, the satiation of curiosity, education and more ideal and abstract motivations such as gender equality, rights discourse, and quality of life arguments. At another end of the spectrum are cases that tend or at least appear to be unfounded or based on spurious allegations committed under the cover of Parliamentary privilege:

> At one point, PAS MP Mohamad Sabu rose from his seat to ask if Malaysia would face similar problems similar to that in Singapore where South Russian men were imported for their single women.[10]

Here is a media report about an Opposition Malaysian MP making a statement not only about a foreign country but also about single women in a foreign country. The work-gender contradiction, while creating more spaces for women in late modernity also demarcates these new sites as public points of complaint and resistance in the language of masculinity. However, the recessionary pressures in Malaysia and the rest of the world, perhaps with the exception of some countries have resulted in the marginalization of women in terms of actual occupations. This is itself an extension of the modern Faustian foundational fantasy of horror writ large. Women make up at least 50% of the population and have since 1957 been gradually entering the workplace. Women have not displaced men's jobs, and have tended to occupy lower levels within the workplace structure. The work-gender contradiction that leaves the household and family structures partially vacant are now being re-filled by women who are often the first to lose their

---

[10] "Paradox laws on marriage to foreigners", *The Star Online*, December 4, 2001.

low-level jobs. According to the Human Resources Minister Datuk Dr. Fong Chan Onn said most of the women who lost their jobs were from the electronics sector where women made up 53% of the 34,502 workers laid-off since January 2001. At the national level, the Malaysian Deputy Prime Minister Datuk Seri Abdullah Badawi noted that 86.7% of the 34,502 retrenched workers were Malaysians.[11]

Export-led Consumption Narratives

Export-led consumption for Malaysia's population of 21.8 million generates large amounts of revenue for domestic consumption in terms of primarily exclusionary, environment depleting goods and services.[12] The country has potentially 82 trillion cubic feet of natural gas reserves seen in the Malaysia-Thailand Joint Development Area (JDA) in the Gulf of Thailand that is jointly-run by the Malaysia-Thailand Joint Authority (MTJA). The 1999 agreement between the Petroleum Authority of Thailand and the Malaysian oil and gas company, Petronas (Petroleum Nasional) to develop a network of gas pipelines has resulted in resistance from local inhabitants in these parts, another illustration that supports the modernity/resistance model. Malaysia with a total land area that exceeds 127,300 square miles and is slightly larger than the US state of New Mexico exports over 300,000 barrels of oil per day. Crude oil production fluctuates between 660,000 bbl/d and 730,000 bbl/d for the past five years since 1997. Petronas (Petroleum Nasional) has invested in exploration and production in Syria, Turkmenistan, Iran, Pakistan, China, Vietnam, Burma, Algeria, Libya, Tunisia, the Sudan, and Angola. Overseas operations now make up nearly one-third of Petronas revenue. In 2000, Malaysia exported the majority of its oil to markets in Japan, Thailand, South Korea, and Singapore. Since the Asian financial crisis of 1997-98, official government reports indicate that

---

[11] Wani Mutthiah, "Women most affected by lay offs", *The Star Online*, December 4, 2001.

[12] *The Straits Times, New Straits Times, Information Malaysia*, official government reports, *Dow Jones*, the *Economic Intelligence Unit, AsiaWeek*, and various other regional economic and business sources.

Malaysia experienced a 7.5% decline in real gross domestic product (GDP) in 1998, real GDP growth of 5.6% in 1999 and 7.5% in 2000. However, the weak export sector is likely to significantly reduce real GDP growth in 2001. A major restructuring of the Malaysian central bank, *Bank Negara*, and the banking sector as a whole has tended towards greater stability in the wake of the case of former Deputy Prime Minister and Minister for Finance, Dato' Seri Anwar Ibrahim, the 1997-1998 recession, and the 2000-2003 recession. Mergers and acquisitions continue to be the signal choice of this sector in 2001-2002 in a country where a fixed exchange rate between the ringgit and the U.S. dollar exists. This capital control, the brainchild of Datuk Seri Dr Mahathir Mohammed in September 1998, cut-off a large exeunt of liquidity in the short to medium terms. However, a relaxation of these controls, once thought likely, have become increasingly unlikely since September 11, 2001. Malaysia also accounts for about 17% of total world Liquefied Natural Gas (LNG) exports in 1999-2000 and is likely to Bintulu LNG complex in Sarawak. The Bintulu facility is designed to be the largest LNG liquefaction center in the world with a total capacity of 23 million metric tons per annum with operations scheduled for late 2004. Apart from some exports to the United States, LNG exports to Singapore total 150 million cubic feet per day.

Summary

This chapter provided an overview of Malaysia in late modernity to convey a sense of the egregious nature of the Malay-dominant state. The future of private space in Malaysia is largely contingent on the public nature of Malay state ethnocratism. The chapter analyzed the structures of the nature of the Malay public through a critique of the authoritarian structures and the resistance to these structures in terms of the ancestral claim, the political economy of inequality, the pure ethnocracy, the state as the definer of tradition and religion, sites of resistance and technology. The narratives of Malaysian life over the past forty years are not only an explicit illustration of the Malaysian world view but also occupy implicit cultural and political spaces within the larger frame of the world capitalist economy. Statal narratives in the Malaysian case are largely interventionist in nature, seeking to imbue a specific Malay ethos in cultural, economic and political spaces.

At the start of this chapter we saw how the Rortyan initiative covered a series of important theoretical paradigms in the history of ideas which were then employed as the conceptual starting point of the modernity/resistance argument and the overview of Malaysian politics that followed. Rorty's insistence on the weaknesses of the platonic worldview in terms of the fusion of the "public" and "private", and the disempowerment of theology and metaphysics led to the later belief that public and private space was potentially if not conceptually separable. Such a separation posits another kind of puzzle in late modernity. Unlike Habermas' *Transformation of the Public Sphere* (1991) where the public interest appears optimal in countries with a strong tradition of civil society action, and where public opinion is created in a self-directed manner towards securing common utilitarian goals. However, for all the benefits and advantages of the ethical teleology contained inside it, the Habermasian motif is not congruent with the modernity/resistance argument on the public-controlling private sphere. Under M/R public and private spaces are reconceptualized vis-à-vis the value of being modern, the foundational fantasy of horror, consumer vulnerability, exclusionary/inclusionary goods, and the work-gender thesis. These five concepts within the mRf argument help conceptually arrange and illustrate the overall pattern of consumption in Malaysia's late modernity based on:

(a) the multi-ethnic, multi-cultural, and "multi-religious" Malaysian culture;
(b) the gendered division of labor along traditional and religious lines; and,
(c) the state's pro-consumption, consumer-driven approach to resolving the recessionary pressures in the 1997-98, and the 2001-02 recession.

Therefore, consumption in Malaysia's late modernity is a confluence of several narratives that have evolved over time into a quasi-hegemonic social formation based on the importance of exchange-value of capital over the use-value of utilitarianism. In criticizing any cultural hegemony, the political analyst re-imagines the logos as replicating the form of the ethnic self with partial fragments of "knowledge" that supports the period that appears at the end of a life sentence.

References

Appadurai, Arjun. 1996. *Modernity at Large: Cultural Dimensions of Globalization.* Minneapolis: University of Minnesota Press.

Bordo, Susan. 1993. *Unbearable Weight: Feminism, Western Culture and the Body.* Berkeley: University of California Press.

Bordo, Susan. 1998. "Material Girl: The Effacements of Postmodern Culture", in D. Welton, *Body and Flesh: A Postmodern Reader.* Cambridge, Mass: Blackwell Publishers.

Foucault, Michel. 1972. *The Archeology of Knowledge and the Discourse on Language.* New York: Pantheon Books.

Habermas, Jeurgen. 1989. *The Structural Transformation of the Public Sphere: An Inquiry into a Category of Bourgeois Society.* Cambridge, MA: MIT Press.

Kamal, S. 1988. *The New Economic Policy After 1990.* Kuala Lumpur: Malaysian Institute of Economic Research.

Karni, R. S.. 1980. *Bibliography of Malaysia & Singapore.* Kuala Lumpur: Penerbit Universiti Malaya.

Lee, Kuan Yew. 1962. *The Battle for Merger.* Printed at the Government Printing Office, Singapore

Lee, Kuan Yew. 1965. *The Battle for a Malaysian Malaysia.* Ministry of Culture, Singapore.

Mahathir Mohamed. 1998. *The Way Forward.* London: Weidenfeld & Nicolson.

Rappa, Antonio L. 1999. "Imprisoning the Other," *Peace Review,* **11**(1):157-160.

Rappa, Antonio L. 2000, "Surviving the Politics of Late Modernity: The Eurasian Fringe Community" *Southeast Asian Journal of Social Sciences,* (2000), 28, 2, 153-180.

Rorty, Richard. 1989. *Contingency, Irony and Solidarity.* Cambridge: Cambridge University Press.

Family & Education

This chapter examines the traditional family structure and the modern educational structure in Malaysia and provides the basic demographic breakdown in terms of the various social, cultural, economic, and political dimensions of Malaysia in late modernity. This chapter analyzes the "traditional" impediments to consumption in Malaysia, and the slippages that accrue to the M/R argument with reference to the family and education. The value of positivist theoretical conceptualizations, methodology, survey instruments, and publications arising out of the two main data bases on Malaysian family life, the first Malaysian Family Life Survey (MFLS1) and the second Malaysian Family Life Survey (MFLS2) are used to illustrate the implications of such survey data on discursive formations in the public sphere. The chapter shows how longitudinal data-gathering methods have resulted in the reification of the status quo and the construction of a public imagination that depedestalizes private spaces of personality, subjectivity, and irrationality, for, and in place of rational community, objective research, and accurate measurement.

The chapter also explains the nature of consumption in the family and education in Malaysia in terms of the five concepts of the foundational value of modernity, the foundational fantasy of horror, the notion of education as an exclusionary as opposed to an inclusionary good; the vulnerability of the consumer in late modernity; and the work-gender contradiction. If the family is considered the realm of the private, and the educational system considered the realm of the public, to what extent do both dimensions of Malaysian modernity impact on each other? Is it clear that there is some degree of fusion of the public and private spheres or is there a clearly defined boundary between the two? Could a third position be possible where there is a significant domination of one sphere over and into the other, and if so, what kinds of evidence provide support for this claim?

The Context in Malaysia

The Malaysia State has both constitutional options, general regulatory provisions, and government gazettes in addition to its current housing and rural development programs. There has also been a diversification of the kinds of associations in Malaysian civil society that are concerned with family issues. This is becoming increasingly important for State planning authorities such as the Prime Minister's Department (PMD) because the total population for all Malaysians in the year 2000 was 21,793,293 with 50.27% (10,956,005) males, and 49.73% (10,837,288) females (based on the public data available from the US Census Bureau, International Data Base). By the year 2010, the total population will be approximately 26,143,972 with 50.3% (13,149,494) males and 49.7% (12,994,478) females or an approximate net increase of 19.96 % increase over a ten year period. By the end of the year 2020, the total number of Malaysians would be 30,740,277 with 15,461,927 males and 15,278,350 females. This is politically significant for two reasons (1) the incumbent Barisan Nasional (National Front) or BN led by the United Malays National Organization (UMNO) will not be overly burdened by imbalances in gender or a horrifying Malthusian-like increase in population size; (2) as a result of population increases over the next 20 years, the UMNO-led BN will need to manage its growing population in terms of providing the kinds of resource infrastructure and physiological infrastructure along the strategies that have worked in the past such as the NEP and NDP. Thus, this second political significance stresses the importance of the "modern" as the centralizing value of successful population management writ large and the State policies, programs and regulations on the family and education in the context of Malaysia. Therefore, in order to maintain its current rate of economic success that is built and founded on the fundamental value of being "modern", much more resources have to be placed aside to account for the growing population. By the year 2020, when *Wawasan 2020* (Vision 2020) is meant to have run its course, Malaysia's population will still be relatively young.[1] This means that Malaysia's dependency ratio will not be as high as neighboring countries, e.g., Singapore's dependency ratio will be 10:1 by the year 2030.[2] The dependency ratio in Malaysia is likely to be much lower than that of Singapore, in a sense, making it easier for economic development, family development and educational progress with a relatively younger and larger population base.

One clearly written and analyzed positivist backdrop to family and education in Malaysia comes in the form of the work of James P. Smith's report on *Income and Growth in Malaysia* (1983) which critically analyses the impact of economic change on male Malaysian workers' natural life-

---

[1] *Wawasan 2020* or *Vision 2020* in English is a teleological metaphor that represents an end objective and a process of achieving that aim through an economic strategy that has clear — in fact, perfect–vision, hence the use of the number 2020 as a convenient benchmark. What is also interesting is that the current top political leadership will be octogenarians and older in 2020, very likely to be out of political office, while one cannot rule out that the political map of Malaysia will not be significantly different.

[2] For Singapore, the *Inter-Ministerial Committee on Aging Report* (1999) indicates that the old age dependency ratio is usually defined as the number of persons aged 65+ per 100 persons of working age (15-64). In 1999, the old age dependency ratio was 10.4/100, in other words, 1 elderly person was supported by 10 working aged persons. In 2030, the old dependency ratio increases to 29.5/100, i.e., 1 elderly person will be supported by only 3 working aged persons. I wish to thank Angelique Chan for this reminder.

170 Modernity and Consumption

cycles, wages and occupations since 1945, although Malaysia was established as an independent, UN-recognized state in 1963 under the Federation of Malaysia concept. The primary data source for Smith's research is MFLS1. In establishing the nature of these life-narratives in quantifiable and measurable terms, Smith goes on to describe the Malaysian labor markets during the relevant periodization for these cohorts of male Malaysian workers, and then concludes with deductions through a statistical analysis of market determinants and what I interpret as the complex interdependence of social life-narratives.[3] James' believable life-narratives that quantify income and wages in Malaysia over an important period of its growth and economic development reflects an important quantitative calculation of modern economic consumption of Malaysian male cohorts that are digitized masses, apparently devoid of personality, tradition, religion, culture, and ethnicity. They appear as formless cogs in an ever enlarging wheel of development and the knowledge gained about them may be used to calculate their life-span, understand their present, past, and perhaps future occupational motifs, plan for unforeseen circumstances, and predict worker productivity and calculate productive value of the workers over time and space. The foundational fantasy of horror in this instance would be the inability to calculate precisely, and to locate the individual profiles of these male or female Malaysian workers, their position within the life-cycle, their occupational and wage structure, their class and social benefits, and their internal migratory patterns. An inability to calculate, emplace, and predict worker profiles within the foundational fantasy of horror would find its modern equivalent in structural economic failure and systemic economic breakdown. This has not happened in Malaysia despite the economic downturns and recessionary pressures of 1973, 1989, 1998, and 2001, but certainly provides the driving force behind the rational, modern calculus of disaster avoidance in the context of familial life, quality

---

[3] James P. Smith, *Income and Growth in Malaysia*, R-2941-AID, RAND, 1983. See also, Smith, James P., *Malaysia's Growth Challenges Some Tenets of Development Theory*, RAND, Policy Brief, CP-65, July 1984.

of life expectancy, education seen in the quantitative literature on family structure, ethnicity, intergenerational support, and parental roles.[4]

Family and the Social Imaginary

The social imaginary represents a set of partial images captured by women and men in their daily tasks which they believe to be true. The partial images are the result of the information and informational access explosion that came about after the communications revolution in the early to mid–1970s with the personal
computer. What is interesting about these social images is that they are built on fragments of public images that are created when digitized individual citizens come in contact. The resounding acceptance of modernity's enumerative and statistical vocabulary often reify the status quo making it a kind of three dimensional mathematical prison from which no one escapes. The ability to organize enumerated data where there is the transfer of individual, personal, stylistic and personal identity of private space to one that is formless, seamless, digitized, and devoid of the person in the public sphere is a characteristic of life in late modernity, and indeed, familial life in Malaysia. The intention seen above is to replicate such measures of modernity, developed for developed countries, to other "less" developed

---

[4] Julie DaVanzo, February, "Living Arrangements of Older Malaysians — Who Co-resides With Their Adult Children?," *Demography* (1994), 31,1; Karen Leppel, "The Relationships Among Child Quality, Family Structure, and the Value of the Mother's Time", Ph.D. dissertation, Princeton University, 1980; see also, Nancy Yinger, "Women's Economic Contribution, Relative Income, and Fertility Decision Making in Malaysia", Ph.D. dissertation, John's Hopkins University, 1984; Angelique Chan, "Family Function, Ethnicity, and Modernization: The Case of Peninsular Malaysia", B.A. thesis, Reed College, 1989; Antonio L. Rappa, "Ethnocratism: The Case for Malaysia", Ph.D. dissertation, University of Hawai`i at Manoa, 1997; Angelique Chan and A. Lillard, and Robert J. Willis, "Intergenerational Educational Mobility: Effects of Family and State in Malaysia," *Journal of Human Resources*, (1994), 29, 4, 41; and Angelique Chan, "How Do Parents and Children Help One Another- Socioeconomic Determinants of Intergenerational Transfers in Peninsular Malaysia," *Journal of Population*, 1996, 2(1): 43-82.

172 Modernity and Consumption

countries. Of course, the seemingly unambiguous economic developmental state path that Malaysia has undertaken has resulted in a shift over the past four decades from a British postcolonial backwater to a less developed country, and then to a newly industrializing one. The consumption of familial relationships through the instrument of survey research is about garnering the "retrospective life history surveys and time use surveys" of Malaysian family life in late modernity to that of other countries. This template provides confidence and familiarity of prescription to the extent that all other places become meaningful only when they appear to exhibit the similar patterns of familial life that are substantiated by public policies based on empirical research and the rules of evidence.

MFLS

The first of these surveys by RAND were initiated primarily by Julie DaVanzo and her associate researchers who developed survey instruments in the mid-to-late 1970s to research how the Malaysian (and by implication, global) economic factors impinge and influence birth-spacing, the size of the Malaysian family by ethnicity in order to deduce specific conclusions that were useful to policy-makers and for public policy programming on fertility issues. MFLS1 was followed up by MFLS2 a decade later in 1988-1989. MFLS2 included an interview bank of a new cohort of women aged 15-49 in 1988. An interesting observation made by the later survey by Sine and Peterson indicated that "fetal mortality events appear to have been underreported, as is the case in most retrospective surveys. Exact birthweights were reported for over 90 percent of births to MF22 respondents; the distribution of these birthweights follows the expected pattern. Contraceptive data compared well to similar data from other sources. Trends and patterns in breastfeeding were as expected, though a strong digit preference in duration reporting was noted".[5] According to the

---

[5] Jeffrey Sine, Christine E. Peterson, *The Second Malaysian Family Life Survey: Quality of Retrospective Data for the New Sample*, MR-110-NICHD, RAND, 1993.

summary of the initial report, the three major conclusions drawn from MFLS1 by the demographers were:

(1) the survey's successful completion and organization of data show that similar surveys can be conducted in other less developed countries;
(2) retrospective life history surveys and time use surveys — the most innovative parts of the survey — can produce reliable data that support detailed statistical analyses of family behavior in less developed countries; and,
(3) the analyses yield empirical evidence about the roles of particular community factors and public programs in contributing to changes indicated by the data.[6]

The summary of the Field and Technical Report "describes the study sample and the surveying and fieldwork procedures used to collect the project data. The authors are research directors of Survey Research Malaysia, a private survey firm based in Kuala Lumpur, which handled the data collection phase of the project. Malaysia is described and summary given of respondent and household selection and checking and coding procedures".[7]

Analysis of Family

What can be deduced about MFLS1 in terms of the five concepts of the mRf vis-à-vis family in the Malaysian context? The following section summarizes the five concepts in support of the mRf:

(1)   [FV] The fundamental value from the MFLS1 survey researchers' points of view and from the Malaysian citizen-respondents' points of view

---

[6] William P. Butz, Julie S. DaVanzo, *The Malaysian Family Life Survey: Summary Report*, R-2351-AID, RAND, 1978.

[7] R. Jones, N. Spoelstra, *The Malaysian Family Life Survey: Appendix C, Field and Technical Report*, R-2351/3-AID, RAND, 1978.

center on the important characteristics of what it means to be "modern" given the way in which MFLS1 was implemented and conducted in 1978.

(2) [**EG/IG**] It is difficult to estimate which parts of Malaysian family life constitute exclusionary goods except for conspicuous consumption that indicates how the consumption of these goods in the familial setting decreases the private (individual) value while simultaneously increasing the costs to private consumers. It appears that the need to develop large housing areas for familial settlement and for familial activities in the public sphere are the clearest examples of exhibiting direct social costs to the detriment of the Malaysian environment while increasing total public debt and burden.

(3) [**FH**] The foundational Faustian fantasy of horror in the ways in which Malaysian consumers of family and education involve the fear of economic failure, and correlate success with economic productivity — where there occurs a centering on the foundational value of the "modern". In Malaysia, MLFS1 represents the Malaysian consumers' familial data. The fantasy forsakes (interpersonal familial) time (occurring in private spaces) for (economic) power and (political) control of public spaces.

(4) [**VP**] In order for the family to survive in late modernity, Malaysian consumers can expect to be as vulnerable to public consumers (as those in the modern western countries are) to global, regional, and local pressures in the need to consume (and very often, goods and services that are not really needed by the consumer). Greater awareness of the conventionality of western modernity's certitude cannot be left un-interrogated: domestic public space is not invulnerable and is similarly challengeable and contestable in the Malaysian family in late modernity.

(5) [**WG**] Something is lost when women leave their families in the private, familial spaces of tradition for the public, neutral spaces of the public; while something is gained in the shift from private to public space. The thing that is lost in terms of the work-gender contradiction is that women appear to have greater control over their lives, yet the social expectation is for them to perform biologically reductionist roles upon returning to the household sphere. The conceit present here is that men are

not expected and not burdened by these social expectations of filling the displaced space. Women are thus torn apart between social expectations and private demands. Increasingly, women are resisting both the social public and private tradition but end up being caught in between thereby satisfying the foundational fantasy of horror in their social imaginary. The following section deals with increasingly important forms of familial representation by the public.

Family Planning in Malaysia

The introduction and use-value of family planning may be historically traced to pre-War colonial Malaya in which the British colonial state supported the seminal work of Sanger and Howe in late 1920s Southeast Asia. The initial work of the Family Planning Association of the Federation of Malaya and the Family Planning Association of Malaysia continues to be represented in Malaysia's late modernity in terms of providing opportunities for women that are not immediately available and where traditional resistance to family-planning methods are strongly-held beliefs especially in rural Malaysia and provide (1) pap smear screening and breast examination; (2) infertility tests and gynecological problems; (3) menopausal treatment; (4) sexual and reproductive health counseling.

Analysis of Family Planning

The analysis of the family in Malaysia's late modernity may be interpreted along the five concepts within the mRf frame as follows:

(1)   [FV] The fundamental value derived from the activities of family planners tend to center on the important characteristics of being "modern", that is to day, to reject traditional forms of subjective, illogical, unplanned familial actions and activities within the family to modern forms of logical, scientific, planned familial patterns that are organized round public lectures and public education supported by state and civil society organizations. This

contributes to our re-questioning of public space determining private familial space. The evidence and scientific data is overwhelming to the extent that it becomes virtually impossible for women to resist what has become a public determinism of "women's" issues. Women are unable to plan for themselves so they need other women and men acting in the public arena to plan, educate and organize their familial lives.

(2) **[EG/IG]** It becomes increasingly clear that the consumption of exclusionary goods such as family planning arranging living arrangements in Malaysia also exhibits an ambiguous dimension. Because on one hand there is the exclusion of private and traditional practice but the inclusion of modern, scientific, and organized modes of ensuring that familial life in terms of (1) pap smear screening and breast examination; (2) infertility tests and gynecological problems; (3) menopausal treatment; (4) sexual and reproductive health counseling have produced positive benefits for women, children and indirectly for men too. However, it is not so much that modernity provides solutions but more importantly, that modernity provides the solutions to problems created by modernity in the first place. This is illustrated in the need for examinations, tests, and treatments which are derivative of the kind of environmental degradation that is being experienced because of the other aspects and powerful dimension of the juggernaut of modernity.

(3) **[FH]** The foundational Faustian fantasy of horror forsakes (interpersonal familial) time (occurring in private spaces) that could be used to seek traditional modes of medical and para-medical situations for (family planning and public policy) empowerment emanating from the control of public spaces by the experts in the field and in the laboratory. The question of resistance to modernity is recaptured by a distraction and ironic engagement in the political economy of pharmaceuticals that supports much of medical research and training and upon which money family planning as a science needs to depend upon for survival. The organizational survival of family planning is an objective that ought not cloud issues of public health and familial needs yet can practitioners and critics tell the difference

between organizational goals and organizational strategies for survival? The differences are not as clear as the bureaucrats would have the public believe.

(4) [VP] This leads into the nature of consumer vulnerability as public consumers of goods and services produced by family planners and family planning organizations that are built on modern western models. Consumer vulnerability undermines the possibilities for challenging the conventional ethos of western modernity's scientific and logical certainty, although there are spaces that can and ought to be interrogated: for example, where it becomes public that organizational strategies for survival do not fit customer-client satisfaction and the slippages are clearly displayed and promoted ironically by the same media vehicles at some stage promoted and highlighted the modern value of the organization itself.

(5) [WG] The modern conceit present in family planning involves an aggregation of partially consumed, partially digested understanding(s) of the scientific vocabulary used by population demographers and family planners in their contributions to the social imaginary. Women are therefore consumed as digits of data, their families are consumed by the public as familial cases and digits. The enumerated familial digits produced by the demographic study of these families contribute to a larger project — and there is always a larger one — of modernity. The work-gender contradiction in terms of family planning is a powerful resource for modern State planners and economic managers who formulate, implement and periodically evaluate policy programs on how to get more people into the workforce and how women might be tapped in ways that they have previously never been tapped before. Women in Malaysia are the vastly untapped potential economic resource that economic planners and family planners will need to shackle in order to achieve *Wawasan 2020*. Malaysian women in the 21st century are unlikely to remain an unproductive economic resource if the next economic and developmental transformation is to effectively take place in a timely manner and according to schedule. While resistance is likely in terms of a return to religious and traditional roles in the home environment, the pressures of globalization on Malaysian economy are likely to force women into the workplace to supplement if not make significant contributions to

family income if only to survive a highly punitive modernity that is callous, seamless, and devoid of passion.

Education

The Malaysian education system is founded on an advanced, integrated system of primary, secondary, post-secondary, colleges, and universities under the rubric of the National Education System. At the primary school level there are two main types of schools: national and national-type schools. At these schools, Malay language (officially known as Bahasa Malaysia) is the medium of instruction and English is a compulsory subject, and Malaysian students have a choice of studying Islam or Moral Education. There are also national-type schools where Tamil and Chinese are the instructional medium, and Bahasa Malaysia and English are made compulsory subjects, although students can choose to study either Islam and Moral Education (ME). The implication here is that most Malays and Muslims are expected to study Islam while ME is for non-Muslims, as opposed to the formal teaching of other world religions such as Judaism, Hinduism, and Christianity. The national-type schools themselves are the net outgrowth of the former vernacular schools that were created in the earlier part of the 20th century, some in the 19th century, by local educationists Not surprisingly, the important conceptual aspects of modernity — basic science is also taught at the primary school level. The system becomes interesting at the secondary school level where there are four main school types. Academic-type schools provide humanities-based, and science-based curricula, and other subjects of a general, vocational and technical nature. There area also Religious Secondary Schools in Malaysia that offer compulsory courses in Arabic language, the *Tassawur*, the *Qu'ran*, the *Sunnah*, and the *Syariah* or Islamic law; while the Technical Secondary Schools, and the Vocational Secondary Schools add alternative choices for students at this level. There are two major forms of public assessment: involving continuous assessment and common public examinations. Since 1963, the education system in Malaysia has centered on three basic pillars: (1) language policy and the importance of Bahasa Melayu (Malay Language); (2) science and technology for economic development; and (3) national development. Language policy has continually evolved, and has to evolve continuously in a kind of tousle between the traditional grounding effect of Bahasa Melayu and the modern developmental effort of English language as the language of modernity, and the language of development. Science and technology have been at the forefront of subjects taught at primary, and secondary schools and at universities and colleges around the country. The introduction of science and technology has not been made compulsory within the education system therefore students have a choice of subjects in terms of their own performance at publicly-held examinations where the grade achieved generally determines the place in the next stage of the educational process. This is because there currently is a quota system that privileges Malay and other bumiputra communities over non-bumiputra ones. This quota system has been in place since the implementation of the 1970 NEP in order to eradicate poverty and the association of ethnic identity with occupation within a political system of quasi-ethnic authoritarianism known as ethnocratism. The Malaysian state has undergone three major transformations since its inception in 1963 as the Federation of Malaysia, Sabah, Sarawak, and Singapore under *Tunku* Abdul Rahman Alhaj. By the mid 1970s and under the Tun Razak, the second prime minister of Malaysia, the pro-bumiputra education policy was underway not in an overt manner in terms of policy pronouncements and legalese but in terms of the implementation of the spirit of the NEP. *Allahyarham* Tun Hussein Onn, the third prime minister who took his oath of office on January 15, 1976, appointed Datuk Seri Dr. Mahathir Mohamad as education minister, and eventually as deputy prime minister. Datuk Seri Dr. Mahathir Mohamad succeeded Tun Hussein Onn as *perdana menteri* in 1981. A continuation of the stringent language, science and technology, and nationalism policies of the early decades continued to be refined and was rejuvenated in terms of the NDP which seeks a similar set of policy objectives. The only aberration was the sudden sacking of Datuk Seri Anwar Ibrahim the heir apparent to Mahathir because of sodomy and allegations of contravention of the Official

Secrets Act in his former capacity as deputy prime minister of the Federation. Interestingly enough the emphasis by the Malaysian ethnocratist state supported by its state ethnocrats on education policy can be seen in terms of the appointment of the education minister which was always considered an important if not crucial stepping stone to the office of the prime minister itself. The state ethnocrats are those civil servants chosen out of ethnic identity as a prerequisite rather than ability or merit. For a significant proportion of the postcolonial state history of Malaysia after the initial announcements and program implementation of the NEP in 1970-1971, non-bumiputra Malaysians found it an uphill task to secure places in the Malaysian Civil Service (MCS) because of the racial quota. While this quota has since been lifted, there continues to be a degree of bureaucratic lethargy in terms of the admission of non-bumiputra Malaysians into the MCS. The following problems and arguments continue to dog Malaysian civil servants bent on service improvement: (1) are sufficient numbers of capable non-bumiputra Malaysians graduating from the Malaysian universities given the fact that the universities and colleges themselves were subject to a similar racial quota system in the past? (2) are there sufficient numbers of capable non-bumiputra students who are offered jobs in the public sector or would these jobs be primarily reserved for bumiputra Malaysians because of security or other arrangements? (3) Malaysia is a constitutional monarchy where those with royal blood have favored access to certain symbolic, ceremonial, and politically influential privileges; where the MCS exists as a possible route for many Malaysians to rise to the rank of a top level bureaucrat; where one might enter the political process by way of the communally-based political party system in any of the states; and where one might become a very powerful and influential business person because of the relative strength, or relative non-weakness, of the Malaysian economy even in the recessionary period of 2001-2002. Yet it is very difficult for a non-bumiputra, with the exception of a few non-bumiputra politicians such the current Chief Minister of Penang State, to reach the top political office in Malaysia in as much as it has been impossible for a woman or a person of color to become a US president since 1776. (4) The education service has had to grapple with the problem of many Malay bumiputra who opt for non-science and non-technical subjects. What does this fact say about the chosen bumiputra ethnic group in accepting or in challenging or in resisting the pressures to conform to a modernity that is designed on the vocabularies of science and technology in order to fulfill the promise and prospects of progress and development and a "higher standard of living"? (5) What does it say about an education system in late modernity where the profession of a particular religious belief is the sine qua non for important public office? Could one assume that this represents at some level the marginalization of about half the population on religious grounds? Interestingly, and in terms of the "facts" of history, the current system has resulted in a predominantly peaceful situation of multiracialism where the Malays have endeavored through the State to capture a larger proportion of the traditional Chinese share of economic power. There have been few and relatively minor "riots" based on ethnic inequalities and the presence of non-bumiputra in Malaysia appear to support rather than supplant critics who make such claims. The citizens of Malaysia for the most part, the non-bumiputra who have been to a certain extent "discriminated" by the NEP and NDP appear not to have voted with their feet. This is in effect a kind of resistance to modernity. Datuk Seri Dr. Mahathir himself has much to share in the peaceful development of the country. He has achieved much over the two decades that he has been prime minister. He has battled the Malaysian monarchy, weakened the traditional power of the courts, and streamlined the legal system to a more efficient one. He has cleaned-up the MCS to make it one of the most efficient and least corrupt civil services in Asia and the world; and he has often stated publicly that Malay bumiputra cannot rely on racial quotas and other forms of affirmative action, or ethnic safety nets to secure a future place in Malaysian society. (6) He has improved the position of women in traditional society and created more avenues for women than any previous prime minister of Malaysia. Part of the reason for Mahathir Mohamad's drive towards economic advancement for men and women is his own "soft-spot" for "academia":

> Meiji University has worked very hard to become one of Japan's leading Urban Universities. This is truly remarkable. I

have always had this soft spot for academia as I was once a Minister of Education. Education is one of the most important resources any country must have to develop rapidly. In fact education, especially at the university level is a significant prerequisite for the growth and resilience of the economy. Universities must therefore continue to excel in the pursuit of knowledge. Universities have a key role to play [in] the country's needs of a professional pool of talent.[8]

The Malaysian education system has proven itself to be sensitive to changes in the regional and global markets by advancing curricula that preclude old-fashioned methods of pedagogy for the use of cutting edge information technology throughout the education system with the use of the internet, video conferencing, and the widespread use of PC-based technology that is tied to the larger and resource rich Multimedia SuperCorridor (MSC). The MSC was designed to be the technological software and technological hardware backbone of the new economy in Malaysia. Training and re-training continue to play a significant role in the nature of education in Malaysia primarily because the new cabinet leaders that the prime minister has brought in are driven and technologically-savvy, technocrat-turned-politicians who have adopted what they perceive as radical changes to the education system beginning with relevant political legislation. If there is any marker of modernity that the Malaysian prime minister will be remembered for it will be the strength of the political will to develop and manage the new education system as seen for example in the Education Act (1996); National Council on Higher Education Institutions Act (1996); the Private Higher Educational Institutions Act (1996); National Accreditation Board Act (1996); the Universities and University Colleges (Amendment) Act (1996) and the National Higher Education Fund Board Act (1997) that have been

---

[8] Dato Seri Dr Mahathir Mohamad, "Speech on the Conferment of an Honorary Doctorate", Meiji University, June 8, 2001. Note that there is a distinction between the honorific titles, "Dato'" and "Datuk"; however, media and official government reports use both honorific titles for the current prime minister.

designed to accommodate the pressures of late modernity on the Federation of Malaysia.

Analysis of Education

(1) **[FV]** The fundamental value derived from the activities of educationists and education planners centers on the important characteristic of being "modern", that rejects traditional forms of subjective, illogical, irrational, and simplistic educational methods and introduces logical, scientific, organized, and highly complex educational strategies with pedagogical skills that are innately tied to technology and technological development and the progress associated with development, achievement and advancement in civilization as seen in the MSC as a marker of social progress. It is difficult to resist this drive to remain modern because the masses do not possess that option, for them, opting out is equivalent to disengaging with modernity and not to engage with modernity is the end of survival within our cosmology of a three dimensional world view. The social imagery of the public thus becomes the primary form of articulating modern self-worth, and modern self-esteem. The public determines the educational activities of modern private space to the extent that there can no longer be autonomous private space.

(2) **[EG/IG]** The educational good is perhaps one of the best examples of an inclusionary good as long as the good represents the right kind of education. The problem for political theorists resides in determining the nature of the "good" itself. The educational good is inclusionary to the extent of satisfying the following criteria in Malaysia: (1) it cannot lead to further environmental and social degradation; (2) the educational good cannot privilege one class or group or community over others in terms of the allocation of educational resources; (3) the educational good cannot unevenly redistribute the educational resources towards political goals; (4) the educational inclusionary good in Malaysia offers reasonably similar access to educational structures for all citizens; (5) a genuine inclusionary good will not discriminate against its clients or clientele by way of social

status, ethnicity, language or religion. Given these five criteria, it becomes somewhat idealistic to speak of the Malaysian education system as primarily an inclusionary good. The subjects taught at the primary schools and at the universities often place a high emphasis and priority on science and technology. This means that the graduates of the political socialization process are most likely themselves to become consumers of the very architecture that they are trained to uphold; this situation makes consumption in Malaysia in terms of such a categorical process a done deal or a self-fulfilling public prophecy. Modernity provides the kind of educational solutions to workplace problems that were created by the educational process itself. Such "fulfillment" is seen in the continuing need to upgrade, develop, examine, test, and generate educational technologies and vocabularies that fit national interests and public goals. If a fiction is repeated sufficiently, and often enough, as the great philosopher once said, the fiction becomes reality, stories become truth, and truth becomes knowledge. This does not imply that the educational world in Malaysia's late modernity is built on a fictitious set of inclusionary and exclusionary goods and services. Rather, the claim here is that the serious treatment of modern public goods like education makes it difficult, indeed virtually impossible to tell the real educational value from less valuable educational narratives.[9] The contradiction is seen in the ways in which the State endeavors to ensure that the ethnocrats, in the example below, the teachers themselves, remain within the educational structures for the right reasons and with the right benefits:

> The Cabinet has approved the setting up of a RM1 billion fund which will enable 300,000 teachers to apply for car loans....announced by Education Minister Tan Sri Musa Mohamad following an agreement between the Government

---

[9] All we seem to have are some hints, signs, and flashes of postmodern encounters of late modernity, challenging, resisting, defying but fading-in and fading-out like weak and strong radio signals. See for example, Leslie Lau, "Abdullah Wants Probe into Segregation of Indian Students: Complaints by Parents Reveal that it is Actually More Common than Earlier thought", *The Straits Times*, December 18, 2001, A7.

and Bank Simpanan Nasional and Bumiputra-Commerce Bank Berhad with each bank contributing RM500 million. Interest rate for the loan remains at four per cent and the present eligibility conditions are unchanged....Citing the situation in 1997, Musa said the ministry approved 1,350 applications for car loan involving RM40.1 million. In 1998, 1,342 applications for RM39.3 million worth of loans were approved and 2,133 applications involving RM64.1 million in 1999....[In the year 2000] 3,118 applications worth RM93.9 million were approved....[and in 2001 approvals were given to] 2,828 applications for RM113 million....this new scheme is needed to ensure more teachers could benefit from the car loan scheme....vastly benefit teachers, especially those who are serving in rural areas and have yet to own a car.... In an immediate reaction, National Union of the Teaching Profession secretary-general Datuk N. Siva Subramaniam welcomed the move but urged the Government to ensure that the loan facility was extended to all teachers.[10]

While the car loan scheme will certainly facilitate difficult road travel for teachers living and working in the rural areas, especially to and from the primary and secondary schools, it will also generate new income for the automobile makers and distributors, and increase the demand and consumption for such exclusionary goods. The political announcement and the subsequent response from the teachers' union to have these loans extended to all teachers is a real possibility, and a sign of late modernity in Malaysia where the vicious circle of consumption continues to propagate itself in ways never thought possible previously. This makes, for example, resistance from student groups in terms of protests, sit-ins, challenges to the University administration, and letters to local newspapers about student loans and tuition fees a virtual impossibility:

---

[10] P. Sharmini, "RM1 billion revolving fund to provide car loans for teachers", *The New Straits Times*, December 1, 2001.

> In a letter to the *New Straits Times* Mohamed Abdul Latiff, the Chief Executive Officer of the National Higher Education Fund Corporation [NHEFC] rejected an earlier student-letter's claim on November 20, that the USM students in Penang did not receive their student loans. Latiff argued that a total sum of RM33.7 million has been remitted to the Bumiputra-Commerce Bank Berhad to be paid out to 9,604 students at the USM main campus in Penang and 402 at the Kubang Kerian campus ... However, this depends on the availability of the students' data as provided by the university to determine whether or not students are continuing with their studies. The corporation will not make payments to students who fail in their studies. An understanding has been reached between the corporation and all institutions of higher learning, public or private, that the students' data should be disclosed before funds are disbursed.[11]

Students are therefore expected to take their public education seriously and perform to the public standards set by their educational institution under the NHEFC loan scheme. From the students' perspective, the possibility of resisting the exclusionary pressures of the educational good are generally weak because the political economy of education is highly systematized and deeply embedded within the social and psychological structures rooted in Malaysia's late modernity.

(3) [**FH**] The foundational Faustian fantasy of horror forsakes traditional educational time (in private space) for modern educational technology, science, and pedagogy based on local and foreign teaching expertise and professionalism within the public sphere processes of the primary, secondary, college, and university institutions. The question of resistance to modernity in education arises out of the marginalized space currently occupied by religious schools primarily found in rural areas, and in the national-type vernacular schools of the Tamil and Chinese variety. In order

---

[11] Letter to *The New Straits Times*, December 1, 2001.

to resist the changes in late modernity, these religious and vernacular schools have to resort to three main strategies: (1) adaptation; (2) assimilation; and (3) retreat. The religious schools employ strategies that appeal to the religious fervor, and conviction of their students and their families. Modern modes of education are limited to the use of paraphernalia that do not encroach or intrude on the religious rites and practices. The success of these religious schools is seen in their continual development in terms of the *madrasah*-type educational programs and the support of religious-leaning state governments such as those found in Kuala Trengganu and Kota Bahru. The vernacular schools on the other hand have been co-opted into the "establishment" via the National Education System. This process of quasi-assimilation allows for the co-existence of traditional language on one hand and modern State control on the other. The net result of such co-existence often leads to an erosion of traditional ties for modern ones such as the emphasis on national allegiances rather than local bonds. The horror narrative is repeated in terms of political rhetoric that illustrate and caution against remaining backward and unable to adapt to changes in the world system. The horror story is one where the educational system becomes dysynchronous with the global developments in international public spaces.

(4) [VP] The vulnerability of the student as a consumer of the educational good and as a consumer of educational facilities is seen in the changes to the curricula often a result of changes in State political elites who want to steer the system one way or another. The student is vulnerable because she or he becomes almost entirely dependent on teachers and their pedagogical strategies who are themselves directed by bureaucrats and other administrators in the MCS and within the schools, colleges, and universities themselves. The public space is filled with rules and regulations that are consequences of changes in technology, changes in expectations, changes in the supply and demand of ideas at the global level, and changes in the political economy of educational goods and services. It becomes ironic that these publicly determined goods and services increase the costs of education at an increasing rate, while consumers become increasingly vulnerable as

they persist in the belief that higher education equals greater economic success. In order to protect the principals as consumers and producers of the education good itself, the State has to periodically decide to reward those who support the system:

> The Government will create 30,000 posts for the promotions of school principals, headmasters and senior assistants from both the primary and secondary schools over the next 12 months. Education Minister Tan Sri Musa Mohamad said the promotion exercise involved funds mounting more than RM300 million...the Ministry will emphasize...strengthening the management aspects at all schools...involving 23,955 principals, headmasters, senior assistants...The ministry hopes with the creations of more upgraded posts for principals and headmasters, the quality and leadership at the schools will correspondingly improve...Musa said the move to upgrade schools and creations of new posts for school administrators were part of the ministry's efforts to give recognition to the teaching career in general.[12]

They are willing to sacrifice and pay more in the present for the possibility of a future certainty that may or may not be achieved. The private space is itself an extension of the foundational fantasy of horror where conversations, arguments, celebrations, births, deaths and festivities often center on the school calendar. The public space of the school determines the familial private space of the family. Public education has all but extinguished private ways of tutoring and learning because of the lack of time, and the speeding up of the rate of information production within the world economy.

---

[12] Nik Imran Abdullah, "30,000 promotions for principals, HMs, senior assistants Exercise will cost education Ministry RM300 million in nxt 12 months", *The New Straits Times*, December 1, 2001; see also, P. Ramasamy, "Schools Echo Malaysia's Ethic Politics", *The Straits Times*, December 21, 2001, p. 29.

(5) [WG] The modern conceit present in education in Malaysia's late modernity represents an aggregate of partially consumed, partially digested interpretations of the scientific, technical, and technological vocabularies employed by the political elite, educational technologists, teachers, counselors, senior students, and citizens working in the political economy of education where the dominant top tier roles are played by men, and where women occupy supporting roles. Women and women students are digits of data, cases used by the educational political economy for the benefit of the larger economy and for economic development. The question of the work-gender contradiction for education in Malaysia's late modernity is seen in the higher proportion of women present in teaching jobs. This represents an imbalance in the distribution of the gendered workplace as women continue to occupy the majority of jobs at the low and middle sections of the educational spectrum. Women have been displaced from the traditional, private spheres of the home environment where "private" and "domestic" work is perceived as economically unrewarding; the contradiction arises again when the social imaginary generates the expectation for women to continue to be responsible for tasks at home as well as in the workplace environment of the public sphere. The Malaysian prime minister has been seriously aware of the global difficulties that women face in the work and the home environment:

> ...basic facts about the situation of women in the world today. Women earn one tenth of the world's income, own less that one tenth of the world's property though they grow half of the world's food and form nearly half of the world's labor force. Two thirds of the world's illiterate are women. While progress has been made in terms of women's access to education, women still comprise two-thirds of people who cannot read or write. Women still represent 60 percent of more than one billion adults who have no access to basic education. Girls constitute the majority of the 130 million children with no access to primary school; worldwide, girls currently attend school 55 percent as much as boys do. Only 10 percent of

parliamentary seats and six percent of cabinet positions are occupied by women.[13]

The Malaysian prime minister has been at the forefront of developing Malaysian women as a crucial worker category and as a productive resource for the Malaysian labor market in late modernity. Malaysia's political, social, and cultural system in late modernity continues to be characterized by male control of the primary positions of power and main wage-earning capacity in the public realm while women hold important, but only secondary, non-wage-earning positions in the private spaces of the family and domestic arena. Late modernity is marked by collective forces that convince, inveigle, entice, deceive, and mislead women out of the private spaces and into the public ones; these collective forces ironically pressure society to recognize women as a long-ignored, as politically potent voices, and as economically-relevant yet primarily untapped human resource for the country's economic development. Women enter the labor market and into a variety of positions where some form of wage or nominal allowance is provided for services that take them away from traditional, unpaid, and, low status, under-recognized roles. Yet the very contradiction of the work-gender thesis is that the vacuum created by the exeunt from the classic "traditional, unpaid, and, low status, under-recognized roles" needs to be filled because the unpaid and under-recognized work is the fabric of society. Once this fabric is torn or begins to fray, it is difficult to repair. This may be seen in the statistics on the increasing age at which women are likely to get married; the longer hours they are away from their family home during the work-day; the number of children a woman is willing to have in a single marriage; the rates of divorce among younger women and men married over the past five to ten years; the willingness among older married women to divorce their husbands; the disenfranchisement that women feel with traditional duties fulfilled by their mother's generation; and, the desire among women to perform and occupy social, political, and economic positions played by men.

---

[13] Mahathir Mohamad, speech titled, "Malaysian Women: Challenges Towards the Next Millennium", Intan Bukit Kiara, Kuala Lumpur, September 28, 1996.

These questions are directly related to the nature of the consumption patterns, the futility and the hopelessness created by modernity and the need for intrinsically worthless goods and services as markers of social achievement, as much as the "contemporary structure of economic domination in the global city is based on increasingly remotes nodalities of power and authority".[14]

Summary

Something is lost and something is gained for every item sold and for every item that is purchased in terms of the level of pleasure and fulfillment derived at the point of consumption. This makes the issue of consumption a political one because of items for sale and purchase are time-based and have a limited spatiality (shelf-life). This chapter illustrated and analyzed the family and education — as important components of the process of consumption — in Malaysia's late modernity in terms of the "modern" as the central value in modernity; the foundational fantasy of horror; the notion of education as an exclusionary as opposed to an inclusionary good; the vulnerability of the consumer in late modernity; and the work-gender contradiction. The family is a vital part of the private realm, and the educational system is often considered as being part of the public realm. Both public and private may appear to have influenced each other as seen in the illustrations of political rhetoric and public policy, but each instance appears to suggest a stronger directional influence from the public into the private realm. Rather than a clear boundary existing between the public and private, it appears significant that Malaysian public space has become the primary agent of change and transformation in the private sphere. That the initial hypothesis that there was fusion between public and private was in effect the encroachment of the public into the private to the extent that the former and the latter appear to have collapsed into each other. The family and education are themselves consumption goods and services; items for

---

[14] Michael J. Shapiro, *Reading the Postmodern Polity*, p. 98.

sale and purchase; commodified things to be ranked-ordered; products to be differentiated; and all with a certain level of satisfaction to be derived but only with a limited amount of gratification and a narrow margin for guaranteed satisfaction whether they be car loans, promotions of letters to the local press. The competition for material wealth drives the competitors to levels of behavior never thought possible previously. This is seen in the recent spate of anti-social behavior among teenagers and adult Malaysian alike (Zahn-Waxller, Cummings, and Iannotti, 1986) and social correlations with low self-esteem and low levels of self-confidence (Campbell, 1998). The main conclusion one can make from the analyses of the MFLS and the policies surrounding family and education in Malaysia's late modernity is that the public sphere has become increasingly potent in the private domain. Consumption is the solution that will dissolve the recessionary pressures, and represents the salve of economic development as seen in Datuk Seri Dr. Mahathir Mohamad's pronouncement that "under current economic conditions where growth will come from domestic sources, bank financing is crucial to lubricate the economy. Banks must, therefore, ensure that credit is appropriately channeled to stimulate consumption and investment".[15] Malaysian leaders especially in the post-Mahathir era must take cognizance of the fact that while material achievement is crucial, it is not a sufficient condition for achieving these intangible goals of the public good of education and the private one of the family.

---

[15] Dato Seri Mahathir Mohamad, speech at the 22nd Annual Dinner of the Association of Merchant Banks in Malaysia, Shangri-la Hotel, KL, 12 October, 2001.

References

Brown, Peter. 1994. *Restoring the Public Trust: A Fresh Vision for Progressive Government in America.* Beacon Press, Boston.

Butz, William P., DaVanzo, Julie S. "The Malaysian Family Life Survey: Summary Report", *RAND*, 1978; **R-2351-AID**.

Carrier, James G. 1982. "Knowledge, Meaning, and Social Inequality in Kenneth Burke." *American Journal of Sociology*, **88**(1): 43-61.

Carroll, Terrance G. 1984. "Secularization and States of Modernity." *World Politics*, **36**(3): 362-382.

Chan, Angelique and Lillard, A. and Willis, Robert J. 1994. "Intergenerational Educational Mobility: Effects of Family and State in Malaysia," *The Journal of Human Resources*, **29**(4).

DaVanzo, Julie (1994) "Living Arrangements of Older Malaysians – Who Coresides with their Adult Children?", in *Demography*, **31**(1).

De Man, Paul. 1986. *The Resistance to Theory*. Minneapolis: University of Minnesota Press.

DeHoog, Ruth H. David Lowery, William E. Lyons. 1990. "Citizen Satisfaction with Local Governance: A Test of Individual, Jurisdictional, and City-Specific Explanations." *The Journal of Politics*, **52**(3): 807-837.

DeLuca, Tom. 1995. *The Two Faces of Political Apathy*. Philadelphia: Temple University Press.

Di Palma, Giusseppe. 1970. *Apathy and Participation: Mass Politics in Western Societies*. New York: Free Press.

Digeser, Peter. 1992. "The Fourth Face of Power", *The Journal of Politics*, **54**(4): 977-1007.

Dore, R. P. 1964. "The Search for Modernity in Asia and Africa: A Review Article." *Pacific Affairs*, **37**(2):161-165.

Gusfield, Joseph R. 1967. "Tradition and Modernity: Misplaced Polarities in the Study of Social Change" *American Journal of Sociology*, **72**(4): 351-362.

Jenkins, Richard. 1996. *Social Identity*. London and New York: Routledge.

Jones, R., Spoelstra, N. 1978. "The Malaysian Family Life Survey: Appendix C, Field and Technical Report", *RAND*; **R-2351/3-AID**.

Katzenstein, Peter J., Keohane, Robert O. and Krasner, Stephen D. (eds.) 1999. *Exploration and Contestation in the Study of World Politics*. Cambridge, Mass: MIT Press.

Shapiro, Michael J. 1992. *Reading the Postmodern Polity: Political Theory as Textual Practice*. Minneapolis and Oxford: University of Minnesota Press.

Sine, Jeffrey, Peterson, Christine E. 1993. "The Second Malaysian Family Life Survey: Quality of Retrospective Data for the New Sample", *RAND*; **MR-110-NICHD**.

Smith, James P. 1983. "Income and Growth in Malaysia". *RAND*; **R-2941-AID**.

Smith, James P. 1984. "Malaysia's Growth Challenges: Some Tenets of Development Theory". *RAND*; **CP-65**.

Woshinsky, Oliver. 1995. *Culture and Politics: An Introduction to Mass and Elite Political Behavior*. Englewood Cliffs, N.J: Prentice Hall.

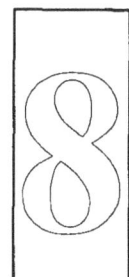

Narrative & Public Space

...the "author-function" is not universal or constant in all discourse. Even within our civilization, the same types of texts have not always required authors; there was a time when those texts which we now call "literary" (stories, folk tales, epics and tragedies) were accepted, circulated and valorised without any questions about the identity of their author. Their anonymity was ignored because their real or supposed age was a sufficient guarantee of their authenticity.

Michel Foucault, *Language, Counter-Memory, Practice* (1977)

The rise of literary criticism to pre-eminence within the high culture of the democracies...has paralleled the rise in the proportion of ironists to metaphysicians among the intellectuals. This has widened the gap between the intellectuals and the public.

Richard Rorty, *Contingency, Irony, and Solidarity* (1989)

"Why indeed is it important to be just?" according to the historicists, this interrogative no longer exists as a valid philosophical question because there are larger questions with more pressing issues such as the extent of narratival space in terms of how political stories represent an extension of the way in which political and non-political figures are "consumed" in Malaysian modernity.

We recall that late modernity in Malaysia is defined as the confluence and coincidence of traditional and modern public and private spheres where coincidental activity, common interests, differences, and similarities germinate, evolve, develop, merge, and disappear. We also know that modernity in this book is primarily concerned with the consumption of goods and services, both tangible and intangible types of goods, that are in themselves agents of change. As an agent of change in modernity, consumption practices themselves transforms the vestiges of tradition into goods and services for sale and purchase in the public sphere. For example, the Malay tradition of celebrating Hari Raya holidays in Malaysia has now come to be associated with fireworks, colored lights, gift-giving, the purchase of new clothes for the family and the individual, and the celebration with music, traditional dances, and sumptuous food. The onset of modernity has resulted in the extension of the range and quality of fireworks, the type of colored lights, the range of gifts, the different types of new clothes. The prices of these goods and services have also risen, and therefore there is something to be said about the kind of modernity we live in terms of the narratives at the market place or in the market square where goods and services made for salubrious traditional festivals and proper rituals are now activities that promote a commodified global reality. This is the hyper-commodification of culture. When the religion of most Malays in Malaysia, Islam, is added to the picture, the consumption pattern becomes a complex mixture of traditional Malay rituals and religious requirements of Islam that are visited with commoditized traditional and religious items, goods and services that have engulfed the transportation, communications, and housing activities related to the pilgrimages to the Holy center of Islam, Mecca. Since the cost of many of these activities have tended to rise over the years, someone and some groups are clearly making a profit. This causes a theoretical tension between the concept of capitalistic interest and the kind of surcharge for services that are allowed under Islamic "business" practices. The tension is further heightened by the difficulties of those Muslims who desire to follow their religion strictly but meanwhile have to keep their own businesses afloat in the "secular" business world, where it becomes important to engage the neoliberal international political economy on a daily basis for economic survival. The kinds of political narrative that exists in Islam and within Malay culture is perhaps the subject matter for another project. However, it does appear that increasing levels of commodification, or as some scholars understand it, commoditization, of cultural and religious practices of Islam, Christianity and other world religions provide opportunities for the rise of cracks and slippages of resistance against modernity. A possible outcome of the frustration of the tensions created out of the process of commodification in late modernity plays out in terms of voter preference and voting behavior. Rather than voting for the incumbent, highly popular, development-minded, and economically successful *Barisan Nasional*, these voters of the Malaysian northeast have over two general elections voted for PAS. The PAS opposition governments in Kelantan and Trengganu are not known for being as "progressive" and "development-oriented" as their successful counterparts in BN are in Kuala Lumpur, and in fact have made it public that they are interested in building an Islamic state in Malaysia which poses a considerable cause for concern to the moderate Muslims throughout the rest of the country, and for the non-Muslims in Malaysia itself. Political Islam in Kelantan and Trengganu continue to represent tropes of a looming political groundswell against modernity and the forces of political, social, and economic change in Malaysia. The consumption of the political good in these Malaysian states are contingent on three main ingredients: (1) the state of relations with the federal government in KL; (2) the nature of religious teachings of the Islamic religious teachers at the local level; and, (3) the state of relations at the grassroots level with non-Kelantan, and non-Trengganu Malaysians.

Another indicator of Malaysian modernity is illustrated in the political rhetoric of its leaders and the countervailing narratives of its citizens. The rhetoric of Malaysian modernity is about how the values and norms of political, social, economic, and religious survival change, coincide, overlap, cancel, and/or are reconciled by the Malaysians themselves and the people with whom they come into contact. We seek to understand Malaysian modernity by looking at its authority and non-authority figures, and the stories and narratives that construct their personalities and their political positions (Bamberg, 1987; Raz, 1990; McCabe and Peterson, 1991).[1]

Consumption patterns in Malaysia may otherwise be defined in terms of sale and purchase of political rhetoric and political narratives between the citizen as consumer, and the state as producer of rhetoric. Politics is therefore another good to be produced for sale and purchase, or auctioned off to the highest bidder. These are the goods that bind the Malaysian state and the Malaysian citizen together through hierarchies of power and discourses of authority [VP]. A hierarchy of power (Anderson, 1993) is exemplified in the Malaysian Civil Service while a discourse of authority (Pye & Pye, 1985) is reflected in the speeches of the highest political leaders of Malaysia (Keyes, Kendall, and Hardacre, 1994).[2]

The Federation of Malaysia is the second largest political formation in the Malay Archipelago. Since independence in 1957, Malaysia has played a significant role in Southeast Asian politics through such political regimes as ASEAN, APEC, and the FPDA. The importance of political history of the country ranges from the "Malayan Emergency" with the MPAJA; the "Malayan Union" controversy; "Konfrontasi" with Sukarno's Indonesia, the rise and demise of ASA, and Maphilindo; the establishment of ASEAN, APEC, ASEM; various territorial claims over the Spratley Islands; the

---

[1] Michael G.W. Bamberg, *The Acquisition of Narratives: Learning to Use Language* (Berlin and New York: Mouton de Gruyter, 1987); Allyssa McCabe and Carole Peterson (eds.) *Developing Narratival Structure* (Hillsdale: L. Erlbaum Associates , 1991).

[2] Elizabeth Anderson, "Rational Choice among Incommensurable Goods" in *Value in Ethics and Economics* (Cambridge: Harvard University Press, 1993), pp. 59-64; Lucian Pye and May W. Pye, *Asian Power and Politics: the Cultural Dimensions of Authority* (Cambridge: Belknap Press, 1985); Joseph Raz (ed.), *Authority* (Oxford: Blackwell, 1990); Charles F. Keyes, Laurel Kendall, Helen Hardacre, *Asian Visions of Authority: Religion and the Modern States of East and Southeast Asia* (Honolulu: University of Hawaii Press, 1994).

"abortive" politics of the EAEC, and the double-claim over the Sabah territory by the Philippines and Malaysia.

Since 1990, Mahathir Mohamed implemented policies to combat the Asian economic crisis, while developing solutions to the regional environmental haze, the Sorros affair, suggestions of anti-Semitism, and the fall of the 32-year old Suharto government. The nature of political narratives in Malaysia involve the disbursement of meaning through hierarchies of power and discourse of authority that establish political and social realities symbolic to state and citizen, while former leaders like Anwar Ibrahim sit uncomfortably in solitary cells pondering their eventual return to politics [VP].

The extent and impact of political narratives on the polity is dependent on prevailing hierarchies of power within its territories: the greater the political power, the stronger the political narrative, the higher the chances of its survival as "fact" and "truth". The chapter explores Foucault's "method" of deconstructing the power hierarchies represented by several speeches of recently ousted Deputy Prime Minister and Minister for Finance, Dato' Seri Anwar Ibrahim who was up till 1997/1998, the clear prodigy and political heir apparent to Mahathir Mohamed. The chapter concludes with several variations on how Foucault approaches the problem of politics, and how some Malaysians encounter and reconcile the latter's demands. Malaysia's population was estimated to be 20.56 million in 1996, comprising 19.65 million Malaysians, and 907,000 foreign nationals, according to the Statistics Department. Of the number, 16.48 million are in Peninsular Malaysia, 2.16 million in Sabah and 1.92 million in Sarawak. The figures showed 59% (12.13 million) are bumiputras, 26% (5.34 million) are Chinese and 8% (1.52 million) are Indians.

> Anwar Ibrahim was born in Penang, Malaysia, on August 10, 1948. He received his secondary education at the Malay College, Kuala Kangsar, an elite school reputed for producing many of the country's leaders in government and business. He graduated from the University of Malaya in 1971 with a degree in Malay Language Studies. While at the university, Anwar

rose to national prominence as a dynamic student activist and vocal spokesman on social, economic and political issues such as rural poverty, wealth distribution and political corruption.[3]

Some sixty years earlier, Max Weber became increasingly concerned with the largesse of Western rationalism and the inevitable iron cage syndrome — rationality as the means and the ends of social imprisonment or social life. For Weber, the modern state, "possesses an administrative and legal order subject to change by legislation, to which the organized activities of the administrative staff, which are also controlled by regulations, are oriented. This system of order claims binding authority, not only over the members of the state, the citizens, most of whom have obtained membership by birth, but also to a very large extent over all action taking place in the area of its jurisdiction. It is thus a compulsory organization with a territorial basis. Furthermore today, the use of force is regarded as legitimate only so far as it is either permitted by the state or prescribed by it. Thus the right of a father to discipline his children is recognized — a survival of the former independent authority of the head of a household, which in the right to use force has sometimes extended to a power of life and death over children and slaves.

The claim of the modern state to monopolize the use of force [VP] is as essential to it as its character of compulsory jurisdiction and of continuous operation".[4] Weber's notions of modern state rationality and society in his Economics and Society manuscripts, conceived sometime in 1913, would influence the direction and tenor of dominant stories, metanarratival flows within the social and political sciences before and after this century's two world wars. Weberian sociology revitalized thinking about "a modernity" associated with the ironic effects of development and progress in the decaying British, French, Portuguese colonies — what Paul Kennedy referred to obliquely in 1988 as imperial over-reach — across Africa, India,

---

[3] Deputy Prime Minister's Office, Malaysia. Edited by the Chief Executive, Information and Management System Unit, PMD.

[4] Max Weber, *Economy and Society: An Outline of Interpretive Sociology* (Berkeley: University of California Press, 1978), p. 56.

Southeast Asia, the Far East and the Pacific Rim. On the French Atlantic seaboard, other thoughtful processes, in the wake of Hitler's Europe, were beginning to take shape, beginning with an assistant of the founder of the phenomenological school, Edmund Husserl, a certain Martin Heidegger. The latter's brief failure as a potential philosopher to the Nazi State when he was rector at the University of Freiburg in 1933, and Hannah Arendt's *Origins of Totalitarianism*, to the resurrection of Left "bankism" in the fall of Vichy France. By the mid-1950s, when Anwar Ibrahim was still in primary school, a new phenomenological force in the shape of Michel Foucault had already begun a self-imposed retreat into dissertation work that developed important excavation of sites of resistance to technological-based, rationalist, structures of social and political power. The Foucauldian "method" began as a means to understanding, a genealogy of beginnings, an uncovering of layers within layers of archaeological epistemes that surround and immerse society's "progress" forward, inward, and backward to the present. However, unlike Weber, Foucault was careful not to entangle himself with the problem of modernity, a problem that puzzled thinkers from Kant, Fichte, and Hegel to Russell, Mannheim, Heidegger, Sartre, De Beauvoir, Lyotard, Deleuze, Adorno, Horkheimer, Baudrillard, Barthes, and Habermas. At about the time that Bauman, Kariel, Postman, Berman and Rorty began considering approaches to the problems of modernity, practical problems that Anwar Ibrahim, the future prime minister of the Federation of Malaysia would have to engaged inasmuch as Mahathir Mohammed, did in 1976 with *Menghapi Cabaran*, coinciding with the deaths of Martin Heidegger and Mao Zedong. Anwar's own narrative continues with his establishment and founding of the Islamic Youth Movement of Malaysia (ABIM), serving for a decade as president from 1972, about the same time that Sheridan Smith's English translation of Foucault's *Archeology of Knowledge and the Discourse on Language*. As President of ABIM, Anwar advocated socio-political reforms and tried to raise public consciousness on civil liberties in Malaysia.[5] ABIM was a religious based organization that

---

[5] Deputy Prime Minister's Office, Malaysia. Edited by the Chief Executive, Information and Management System Unit, PMD.

put pressure on the government of the Federation to devote time and energy to their special interests. Characteristic to Malaysian politics is the radical position of its top leadership. Mahathir, for example, was considered a "Malay ultra" was imprisoned and had his book banned in the late 1960s and early 1970s. Anwar's radical student movement in the form of ABIM would ultimately lead him to political success resulting in a re-interpretation of those narratives of civil liberties that he used to espouse as a radical student leader. The unearthing of Anwar Ibrahim's political narrative in the modern Malay state runs parallel to Foucault's own way of approaching modernity: one, a radical Asian student leader and devout Muslim, looking forward to political influence in a homophobic country, the other a radical French student, and discrete homosexual, turning backwards to intellectual influence that would result in his work being taught at Oxford and Cambridge in the early 1970s. [IG]

Foucault's Method

Foucault's method differs from ordinary perceptions found in the "social sciences". He was not interested in the atypical research methodology employed by modernist social scientists who possess qualitative and quantitative analyses, both or either involving some degree of participant or non-participant observation, and some pseudo-mathematical arrangement of data. Neither was Foucault's method directly related to Merleau-Pony, Sartre, Ricoeur, or "the unknown Saussure who had been dead fifty years to the cultured public"[6] or a purely poststructural linguistic deconstruction of the means of communication as seen in the work of Jean Jacques Lyotard, Jean Baudrillard, Jean Loup Thébaud, Jacques Derrida, or an early Richard Rorty. Neither is Foucault's method Husserlian-Marxist (phenomenological-Marxism) nor similar to the Marxism of Perry Anderson, Terry Eagleton, or Frederick Jameson. Foucault style differs from the critical theorists, and communitarians like Jurgen Habermas. The result of all these "established"

---

[6] Lawrence Kritzman, ed. *Michel Foucault: Politics, Philosophy, Culture: Interviews and other writings 1977-1984* (New York: Routeledge, 1988), p. 21

methods, and others in the social sciences involve the measurement to the extent of enumerating the subject in question in terms of its locus in political, social, economic, and cultural space; and ultimately, rendering the subject into an objectified, colorless, alienated, atomized being reduced to a thing or entity relative to some configuration of temporal knowledge. Foucault stood out and above these seemingly ordinary styles of intervention and understanding, and continues to present a powerful influence over neoMarxists, liberals, democrats, socialists, communitarians, latter day anarchists, social and political theorists, cultural relativists, feminists, psychoanalysts, and literary scholars who began establishing themselves in the early 1970s as the early interlocutors of Foucault, and with direct, indirect or both kinds of references to Foucault's work. Across the globe on the other side of the world, the 1980s were eventful years for Anwar Ibrahim, Malaysia and Southeast Asian,

> with increased assertion of cultural identity among the youth and pronounced activism directed towards social and economic restructuring. In a country where ethnic and religious divisions run deep, Anwar [continues to be] a firm advocate of solutions to national problems that transcend ethnicity and religion ... he was elected president of the Malaysian Youth Council, a multiethnic, multireligious organization which was instrumental in forging national unity in the wake of racial riots in the late 60's. Anwar's political career started with his election as a Member of Parliament in the 1982 general elections. In the same year, he was elected as the leader of the Youth Wing of UMNO, the largest component party of the ruling National Front coalition. His first Cabinet appointment was as Minister of Culture, Youth and Sports in June 1983. Thereafter he rose through the ranks, taking on the portfolios of Agriculture and Education before being appointed Minister of Finance in March 1991. In 1989 Anwar was elected president of the UNESCO General Conference for a two-year term. His keen interest in culture, education and intellectual development

brought him to be closely associated with various think-tanks and organizations such as he Malaysian Institute for Policy Research and the International Institute of Islamic Thought, of which he was a co-founder. He has also been president of the International Islamic University, Malaysia since 1988. For promoting inter-cultural understanding, Anwar was conferred the Georgetown University, Washington D.C., President's Medal in 1994. In May 1998, he was conferred Doctor of Humane Letters, *honoris causa*, by Ateneo de Manila University. While he was conferred the order of the Knight Grand Cross of Rizal, the highest order of Rizal in August.[7]

Even the existentialist Sartre's support for Mao's people's justice through courts of the people's revolution, as Kritzman reminds us, was for Foucault juridically questionable as it privileged discipline and punitive recourse to legal-rational forms of justice (Kritzman, 1988). Yet in looking at these various methodological styles, we find Foucault traversing across the entire spectrum of structuralism, phenomenology, poststructuralism, hermeneutics, the history of ideas, Marxism, and neoMarxism. What made his style so intellectually seductive? Foucault did not pretend to be anyone or anything special. But this was not modesty, this was a pure interest and concentration of thought, distilled drop by drop, into a deeper understanding and unveiling of the presentations and representations of reality as depicted by devoted historians, historiographers, medicine men, school teachers, policemen, customs officials, philologists, psychoanalysts, psychiatrists, priests, therapists, and politicians. Politicians who use their influence and man-dated offices to carve out spaces of political dominance within the iron cages of the bureaucracy and administrative system, and at the grassroots levels where the quotidian activities are remonstrated in the daily rhetoric of ethnicity, religion, capitalism, language, culture, and custom, fermenting and anchoring themselves, representing the mien of society. Politicians who determine the metanarratival conversation within the state and society.

---

[7] Deputy Prime Minister's Office, Malaysia. Edited by the Chief Executive, Information and Management System Unit, PMD.

Politicians who control the layers of speech, thought, and action, as they orchestrate the march of modernity.

> Since 1991, Anwar has led a group of Southeast Asian intellectuals and businessmen to conferences and meetings to envision the creation of a more cohesive Southeast Asia to be realized by promoting economic prosperity and a vibrant civil society in the region. The group has produced a report title[d] *Towards One Southeast Asia* and is actively promoting understanding among societies through the process of constructive engagement. Dato' Seri Anwar Ibrahim was elected Deputy President of UMNO in November 1993 and was subsequently appointed Deputy Prime Minister of the Federation of Malaysia. After the 1995 general elections, Anwar was re-appointed Deputy Prime Minister, retaining his Finance portfolio. The Deputy Prime Minister is married to Datin Seri Dr. Wan Azizah Wan Ismail. They have five daughters and a son." [8]

In a 1997 speech to the Women's and Youth Wings [WG] of the predominant Malaysian political party, United Malay National Organization (UMNO), Anwar quoted the Holy Qur'an:

> And surely We shall try you with something of fear and hunger, and loss of wealth and lives and crops; but give glad tidings to the steadfast, Who say, when a misfortune striketh them: Lo! We are Allah's and lo! Unto Him we are returning. Such are they on whom are blessings from their Lord, and mercy. Such are the rightly guided. (Al-Baqarah, 155-157) [9]

The invocation of holy scripture gains spiritual and moral credibility for the speaker in a state where more than half the population are Muslim and where the official symbols of the nation — flag, crest, national anthem —

---

[8] *Ibid.*

[9] Anwar Ibrahim, speech at the "Joint Opening of the UMNO Youth and Wanita Assemblies" on September 9th, 1997, in Kuala Lumpur, Malaysia.

bear testimony to Islam. This in itself draws complications for simplistic Weberian categories of traditional, rational-legal, and charismatic leadership. But for Foucault, Anwar's religious invocations signal an entry point for launching a demythologizing exercise against spiritual reigns of power. Religious pronouncements at the head of a political text are moral guides for speaker and what is spoken, denigrating the possibility of political challengers on religious grounds; reminiscent of a medieval preparation for mass organized movements like the "Crusades", re-historicizing a righteous, moral, and holy past. To be rightly guided by an omnipresent being bears upon the futility and fatalism of its followers. Up till the point of his arrest on allegations of sodomy, Anwar represented the epitome of the modern Caliph, perhaps not quite comparable to the Four Rightly Guided Caliphs — yet both a political leader, and a spiritual leader, determined to lead his followers towards the inevitable certainty of the Hereafter, while simultaneously reminding Party stalwarts of the political and social successes that have followed their rightly guided political party, UMNO:

> This year's assembly follows immediately after celebrations to mark the 40th anniversary of Independence. Our country's independence is closely linked with UMNO because it was UMNO which mobilized the Malays and the people as a whole to liberate the nation from the shackles of colonialism. In 40 years, we have built a stable and successful nation, governed under a system of parliamentary democracy, where the people live in freedom from fear and oppression, where they are free to engage in religious practices, enjoy freedom of speech and movement, where all citizens share the responsibility of maintaining harmony, [of] participat[ing] in political life and economic and social development and no one is marginalized.[10]

---

[10] Anwar Ibrahim, Speech at the Joint Opening of the UMNO Youth and Wanita Assemblies on September 9th, 1997, in Kuala Lumpur, Malaysia.

No one is marginalized except those considered marginal, abnormal, divisive, subversive, criminal, and disrespectful [VP]. The forty years that it took to develop Malaysia's success as a multinational did not come without some kind of erosion. One type is seen in the penetration of foreign goods and services deep into the heartland of the Malaysian political economy, in spite of the State Authority's efforts at the maintaining a balance between tradition and modernity, verbalized by Anwar's public rhetoric. When Malaysian modernists are faced with the technical superiority of Western pharmaceutical political economy, traditional safeguards arise out of the Malaysian timber and woodwork. Neither product is really superior, this is merely a representation of an economic battle for markets that has reached deep into the rural villages and threatened the private, space of traditional Malaysian anti-male-impotence methods [VP/EG]:

> A Malaysian medicine man has issued a challenge to Western specialists over treatment of impotence, saying a traditional aphrodisiac was more effective than the Viagra pill. In a letter to the *New Straits Times* yesterday, the man, identified as M. Nor, said Viagra has a 70-per-cent success rate and cost more. "Our local mixture of honey, ginger and telur ayam kampung (eggs of village-reared chicken) with a regular intake of vitamin E should do wonders and save money".[11]

Traditional methods conjured and concocted in rural Malaysia, and forming part of an old, Malay-influenced cultural dynamic within the private spaces of the kampong now has to compete with a product of the international pharmaceutical political economy of public entrepreneurialism. The severity of the situation is seen in the Malaysian Health Ministry reply to a question raised at the Dewan Negara:

> Malaysian men are ranked among the highest users of Viagra pills not because they need it to enhance their sexual activities but for fun, Health Ministry Parliamentary Secretary

---
[11] *The Straits Times, AFP*, and the *New Straits Times*, June 5, 1998.

> S. Sothinathan said today. "However, the ministry has not conducted a study to find out as to why Malaysian men used the pills although they are active without the pill. Although only two per cent of the population were men aged 65 and above, the number of men using viagra were more than that." Although this group may be sexually active without the pill, they still consume it. I have not consumed it, and neither have I reached the age to say why these people consume it," he said to a supplementary question from Datuk Christina Tibok Vanhouten. To another supplementary question by Datuk Ghazi Hasbullah Ramli on whether any comparative study had been conducted on Viagra and local sexual stimulants such as *Tongkat Ali*, Sothinathan said the Institute of Medical Research was conducting a study. "If the local products are found to be more viable, we will commercialize it," he said. He said enough instructions have been printed on the packages to warn people from using the pill without doctors prescription.[12]

People are happy to consume because consumption of goods and services provide temporary relief and instant gratification. Although these effects do not last, and cannot last long, they are increasingly reproducing "sites" in the public arena where some kind of recognizable "passion" or "desire" can inhabit a callous and objectifying system in small creative spaces previously held in private. While the traditional methods of improving the quality of life exist in the local market, officials in Malaysia as in most other states in modernity become increasingly dependent on the language of modernity, the vocabulary of science and medical research institutes to determine the value of a product or service. This situation reflects how important it continues to be modern that the value of being modern is itself celebrated deeply in the psyche of the consumers, producers, and regulators (such as civil servants, administrators, and other bureaucrats) that the use of rationality and logic becomes second nature. These two narratives illustrate how local consumers

---

[12] M. K. Megan, "Malaysian men take Viagra for fun? Health Ministry attributes fun aspect to why consumption is among highest", *The New Straits Times*, 1998.

have themselves become increasingly vulnerable [VP] to foreign dependence based on foreign (read, international) benchmarks of quality assurance and product efficiency. Ironically, the local officials and State authorities are themselves "willing" agents of the technologizing effects of a globalized and late modernity. [EG] The use of neutral and value-free, scientific logic itself promotes a certain aura of authority — a fetishization for science as expertise — that generates truth value from observable "fact". The objective language use therefore decenters the importance of the role of the consumer away from private decision-making to a marginal, perhaps obscured one that becomes increasingly reliant on the power of the State and "official authorities" as interlocutors and agents of change in late modernity. Meanwhile, in another part of Malaysia, a local English daily, *The Star*, reported,

> A lorry attendant escaped the gallows and was instead jailed 12 years by the Federal Court yesterday when a drug trafficking charge he faced was reduced to one of possession. J. Ravi, 35, who was also ordered to be given 10 strokes of the rotan was originally charged with trafficking in 395.3g of ganja at a house in Gombak at 1:30 am on 16 December, 1989. Counsel Karpal Singh told the court that Ravi had accepted an offer to plead guilty to a reduced charge under Section 39A(2) of the Dangerous Drugs Act 1952, which carries a maximum 20 years jail term. The offer was made by the prosecution due to a feeble chemist report ... Karpal Singh, in mitigating, had urged the court to take into account the fact that Ravi had been remanded for almost eight years since his arrest on 16 December, 1989, and that he was married with three children.[13]

Like Anwar, Ravi is married with children and continues to live life under different circumstances unlike the dead Foucault, whose physical life was on the wane as Anwar's political life appeared ascendant with the crescent of his career and the star of his achievement. Foucault's re-claiming of the

---

[13] *The Star*, 18 November, 1997.

penal system in *Discipline and Punish* — albeit geographically distanced from Malaysia, a country he never visited nor knew — is itself an urgent reminder of the similarities shared between European and Asian punishment systems; a reminder to scholars for the need to investigate and question apropos theoretical explanations of physical reality. How the gradual uncovering and demythologizing of power centers around the world exploit the cracks in society reserved for the spastic, the lunatics, the insane, and the criminally incorrigible [**VP**]. The major problem for the Weberian rationalist is that these drug pushers, drug traffickers, prostitutes, and pimps are model prisoners in prison, but not model citizens in society: that the validity and use-value of the prison system is not only outdated, but invalidated by a self-evident, self-fulfilling epistemology [**EG**]. But these criticisms of Malaysian modernity may be similarly leveled at most Western European countries at some point in their own modern narratives, and political rhetoric in and out of the "Cold War". Truth is functions within the ironic context of human "civilization". "Each society," said Foucault, "has its own regime of truth: that is the types of discourse [**VP**], which it accepts and makes function as true".[14] Hence, Anwar's quotation from the Holy Qur'an is legitimate and truthful in his pronouncements as Deputy Prime Minister inasmuch as Malaysian legalese is acceptable to Ravi's *weltanschauung*, partly because the regime supports its belief, partly because of his own subscription to its tenets, and partly out of the multiplicity of Foucauldian constraints used by postmodern political theorists understand political acquiescence. But the death of Foucault has left us resigned to a cache of printed demonstrations and even admonitions of his (sometimes narcissistic) worldview, reflecting an intellectual in search for understanding but resulting in a pastiche of theoretical re-adjustments to reality or realities that did not always fit. Writers intimately involved in making ethnographic records of Foucault's work themselves find it difficult to place Foucault in a single category (Smith, 1972; Barry, 1985; Kritzman, 1988). This was not because Foucault was an introvert, or an overly private person, but because his mode of thought often simultaneously traversed the

---

[14] Michel Foucault, *Power/Knowledge* (New York: Pantheon, 1980).

peaks of dominant philosophies and the valleys of their dead antecedents, making any singular categorization virtually impossible, hardly leaving space, even after his inaugural College de France lectures in 1970, for the possibilities of intellectual posterity that availed him since the publication of *Madness and Civilization*. Foucault was modest in this way. In stark contrast, the politician often needs to construct texts that deliberately draw attention to the politician rather than the textual evidence. Modern political rhetoric is fraught with connections to a glorious past, or at least some historical truth that makes it possible to go on with the reality of the present, that will not subvert the achievements of successive state policies. UMNO's political supporters, financiers, the political opposition, economic investors, and Malaysians as a whole need to believe in the truth of the system, founded on the politics of "certainty", contextual "legitimacy", and celebrations of national unity. These represent the markers of political, social, cultural, and national confidence — factual, serious, grounded, yet visionary, and brimming with self-confidence, an international prestige — linking economics, history, Islam, and politics all together:

> We celebrate our independence with a confidence bolstered by a sense of pride over our achievements. Our founding fathers could not have imagined their descendants would come this far in such a short time. Neither could they have imagined that Malaysia would achieve such renown and command such respect throughout the world ... Muslim intellectuals — both lay and religious — have a crucial role to play in nurturing, among their co-religionists, a deep understanding of Islam and contemporary realities and in promoting religious values through proper means. We must be moderate and pragmatic, which does not mean sacrificing fundamental principles and beliefs in the name of modernity ... The contemporary thinker Sheikh Yusuf al-Qaradhawi exhorts Muslims to understand well what he calls *fiqh al-awlawiyyat*, that is, the principle of ordering priorities as an approach in resolving issues and the needs of the Muslim community ... Our tradition abhors haste

and enjoins care, prudence and circumspection in the [Malay proverb], it is like drawing a stand of hair from a mass of flour without breaking the hair or disturbing the flour. It is related that the caliph Umar ibni Adbul Aziz was once chided by his son, Abdul Malik: "O Father! Why have you not reformed society and established justice (that is, to correct the weakness of the Umayyad administration before him). By god, I am not afraid to establish justice even if it means being cast into a boiling cauldron. Caliph Umar replied, "My son, do not be hasty. Know you not that the Almighty God criticises drinking in the Quran? It is only with the third mention that wine is prohibited" ... [The Malay] tradition has always placed a high value on thoroughness and abhorred superficiality, as illustrated in a *pantun*:

> If you are going to clear the trees
> Don't forget to bring a plough
> Do not be like a lotus reed
> Its shoot reaches for the sky,
> but its roots do not touch the ground

We must stand shoulder to shoulder in support of our beloved leader, Dato' Seri Dr Mahathir Mohamad, and renew our faith in the dynamism and resilience of our economy.[15]

Anwar's rustic narrative exemplifies an ideological pronouncement, a political reproduction of Malaysian state rationality, premised on hard economic pragmatism, Islamic philosophy, and Malay myth, it reflects the nature of deconstructed truth in the Malaysian state's modernity. Part of this modernity is the continuing control of public morals, as defined in terms of "correctly guided" behavior by citizens and believers alike [FH]. For

---

[15] Anwar Ibrahim, Speech at the Joint Opening of the UMNO Youth and Wanita Assemblies on September 9th, 1997, in Kuala Lumpur, Malaysia.

example, the largest, most established English daily newspaper in Malaysia, the *New Straits Times*, reported that:

> A carpenter, who is serving 15 years in jail for raping his 16-year-old stepdaughter was today sentenced to 18 years' jail and 10 strokes of the rotan by the Sessions Court after he pleaded guilty to raping another stepdaughter. Ramli Ang Abdullah, 47, of Kulim, admitted to raping the 13-year-old girl at No 18E, Kampung Padang Tembak in Kulim about 9 am on July 7, last year. Judge Ghazali Cha ordered the sentence to run concurrently with the 15 years' jail sentence, which he is serving now for raping the older stepdaughter. This was Ramli Ang's third conviction. Deputy public prosecutor Azmi Ariffin told the court that the 13-year-old stepdaughter lodged the police report on July 8 last year. He told the court that the victim's ordeal began in early 1996 when the victim and her mother stayed in Air Itam, Penang. In the incident, Ramli Ang, a Muslim convert, had asked the girl to buy him cigarettes. "When the victim returned from the shop, she was given RM1 by the accused who later asked the girl to go to the bedroom and raped her," Azmi said. The second incident took place in April last year at their new home at Kampung Padang Tembak. Azmi said the victim was alone and was cooking in the kitchen when she was ordered by Ramli Ang to go to the room. When she refused, the accused dragged her into the room and raped her. The girl was repeatedly raped in May 1997 and on July 7, the victim was again raped. Azmi said Ramli Ang was arrested about 1.45 pm on July 7 after the victim's 16-year-old sister lodged a police report that she (the older sister) was raped by the accused on July 6. The victim lodged her report a day later. Azmi urged the court to pass a heavy sentence as the accused did not show any remorse despite being previously jailed for committing the same offence. He said Ramli Ang was jailed seven years and given five strokes of the rotan for raping a

foreign tourist in Air Itam on Feb 20, 1989. Besides being sentenced to 15 years' jail for raping his older stepdaughter, the accused was also ordered to be given 10 strokes of the rotan. In mitigation, Ramli Ang apologised to the court and expressed regret for his action. He pleaded for a lenient sentence and asked that it run concurrently with his present jail sentence.[16]

This narrative indicates three things about the power or effect of Anwar's power over the political, social, and moral realms in Malaysian modernity. Firstly, it is clear that not everyone subscribes to his utopian pleas, and that the dream of a dynamic and resilient economy based on moral recommendations by the State, is not readily and cannot be readily accepted by one and all. Ramli Ang's "documentary" is not extraordinary. In fact, his incestuous serial paedophilism reflects the strident similarity between Malaysia and the rest of the world, regardless of race, language or religion. Secondly, this illustrates the cracks that are already apparent in Malaysian society regardless of the State's ideological propositions or its quaint attempts at reifying state policies at the grassroots through mosque, minaret, and bureaucracy. Thirdly, Ramli Ang Abdullah represents arrested abnormality, a citizen caught by a public, reported in public, and rightfully removed of his public (and obviously private) rights [FV] as public as Foucault's reading of the Nietzschean challenge to the "supremacy" of the metanarratival myth addressed in *Beyond Good and Evil*, and the *Twilight of the Idols*. In confronting the monumental pressures of modernity, the fissures that emerge slowly between the dysfunctional cross-over between modern and traditional, old, and new, fact, and fiction, religious and secular are representations and markers of the modern onslaught driven by the greed of un-moderated capitalism that deem the verisimilitudes of ideology, nationalism, religion, and the State as farcical, comic, and passé.

A recent report in the Sunday Tribune, an old English daily reflects the severity of a certain twist in "moral capital". Federal funds are dispensed

---

[16] *New Straits Times*, February 1988.

throughout the Federation of Malaysia to monitor illicit activities by Muslims by a kind of public-defining private "religious police" [**WG**]:

> The Islamic Religious Affairs Department is monitoring closely the activities of transvestites (*pondans*) and even considering taking action against those suspected of being involved in immoral activities ... The officer said that the department here would be following the steps taken by their ... counterpart[s] on similar matters ... Meanwhile it is reported that these transvestites charge their clients between RM30 to RM50 for their services. Some of them are even categorized as high class, and are only available by reservation through the telephone. Their charges are as high as RM500 per customer. If one is to drive around the town at night, they can be seen openly soliciting with clients at their base located at the Beautiful Jade Centre.[17] [**FH**]

The power of Foucault's orthodoxy lies in an original, authentic, veritable, and aesthetically-pleasurizing, non-subscription to post-Enlightenment, even and including post-Nietzschean methodological orthodoxies. He preferred to question the metanarratives that characterize the post-Enlightenment epistemologies of truth. Rather than claim that Foucault had no specific "method" or that he "circumvented" and avoided attempts to pin his style to a single mode of deconstruction, I argue that his "method" in effect employs certain strategies with specific signifying concepts that do not constitute a particular whole. His method is his style, at times effusive, and ebullient, at other times compressed, ambivalent, and precarious. No one can claim that Foucault employed a specific number of set ways of approaching conceptual problems, in fact, he went out of his way to avoid such unifying sequences. The three approaches that are most discernible are: (1) Foucault's stress on demythologizing hierarchies of power through textual, historical and

---

[17] "*Pondans* Activities Closely Monitored," *Sunday Tribune*, 14 June, 1998.

symbolic deconstruction; (2) Foucault's subversion of arguments; and, (3) the analyses of rationality.

The Foucauldian stress on deconstructing the myth of power structures is a useful tool for understanding Anwar's position. Anwar's narratives were chosen because of the powerful hierarchies it represents in Malaysian modernity. There is power in his rhetoric because his words bear consequences for Malaysians, the shaping and construction of their "present", and the development and projection of their "future". This is not to state that there are no other methods of analyzing Malaysian power relations, merely that these power relations are in fact potentially explicable via Foucault's ideas on demythologizing hierarchies of power. Anwar's words have effect but not over the entire spectrum of Malaysian society. There are many — the Malaysian medicine man, Ravi, and the paedophile, Ramli Ang Abdullah, who do not believe, reject or challenge Anwar's authority (as State Authority) and the hierarchy of power that he and his office represents.[18] In Foucault's view, this would be a conceit.

As we have seen, Foucault's method helps exploit the cracks in Anwar's power system: the myth of the political "Caliph", the foundational image of a rational intellectual, the façade of radical student activist, the credibility of having run several government ministries, including agriculture, international trade, and finance; the impression of a wholesome Muslim family, and the credibility of foreign awards. All these contrast starkly with the prevalence of crime, drug smuggling, and whipping within the context of Malaysia's disciplinarianism. Do Malaysians accept Anwar's political narratives because of the force of his intellect, or because of the system of rewards and punishments? Or are they in love with his image, the policies he promotes, or have they been so endemically socialized by ideological nationalism that, as citizens, there can be no other life? We have seen how Anwar's politics also contrasts with Foucault. Foucault's own background, his belief in the normalcy of homosexuality, his circumvention of inexplicable political events, and our concurrent deconstruction of his life as

---

[18] For the official list of all government bureaucracies, positions, and policies, see *Information Malaysia*, 1995.

his method, and the general failure of his life's "method". Foucault, like Anwar could not (and cannot) hope to influence all sectors in society: there will always be the abnormal, illegitimate, erratic, and the obtuse.[19]

Foucault never admitted to being a philosopher, and in fact, made it a point to distance himself from the universalizing, metanarratival arguments of modern philosophy. His method of philosophical inquiry rejects modernist "standards" and challenges it by going the opposition way, by supporting marginal arguments and diffusion of thought over common patterns and logic sequencing. The three Foucauldian strategies excavate the political and cultural past through the analyses of literature and the language of the problematic itself to reveal more information, and to yield greater transparency, even if these multiple, historical narratives would both originate in abstraction and divests no permanence.

Demythologizing Hierarchies of Power

These hierarchies of power appear on the surface as monolithic and omnipotent, but this is part of the successful purveyance of the power-myth itself as seen empirically in Western forms of colonialism in the 18, 19, and 20th centuries; Nazi Germany, Stalin's USSR, Mao's regime in China, Soekarno's Indonesia, and North Korea under the Great Leader, and the Dear Leader. Since the advent of "civilized mankind", and the concentration of power in the form of a person, or council, or assembly or legislation, the coercive state has developed a dualistic character: the ostentatious display of power through public punishment described by Foucault in *Discipline and Punish*. The public display of overt penalties as examples of what would happen to those who do not observe the law seen throughout the Portuguese, Spanish, Dutch, French, and British colonies. The other aspect of this dualistic nature is the public pardoning or the politics of absolution. The idea behind public absolution mitigates the case for the state as merciful,

---

[19] See Michel Foucault, *Power/Knowledge* (New York: Pantheon, 1980).

and forgiving, therefore appealing to mass emotions, but glosses over the majority of those still incarcerated:

> Tawang anak Jamal, 34, was convicted of life imprisonment for armed robbery, but received news that the Head of State Tun Datuk Patinggi Dr Haji Ahmad Zaidi Adruce bin Muhammed Noor granted him clemency on Hari Raya Adilfritri. "I will definitely write a letter to our honourable Head of State to express my heartfelt gratitude," pledged Tawang in front of his lawyer Bong Ah Loi recently. Tawang was then 17 years old when he and two other teenagers, aged 15 and 16, respectively committed armed robbery of cash amounting RM194 and a wrist watch valued RM70 from two men at Mile 181/2, Bukit Song at Miri-Bintulu Road on November 15, 1981. Tawang was carrying one unloaded shotgun belonging to his father, a retired Ranger, whilst committing the offence. The trio were later arrested and charged under section 5 of Fire Arms (Increased Penalties) Act 1971. They were the only ones in the State so far being charged under this section. They pleaded guilty to the charge before the then Sessions Court Judge Joseph Wong on December 28,1981. Each of them was sentenced to life imprisonment and whipped with six strokes of rotan ... Tawang, spent 17 years in the cell at Lambir Prison. He stressed that he would now treasure every moment he has with the parents especially his father. Tawang, who is the second eldest in the family of five children, is currently helping his parents at the farm. He added that he needed some time to adapt himself to the society before getting a job. "Any job will do," he said. Inseng said she and her husband were very happy when an officer from the Prisons Department informed them about their son's release. "The whole family went and waited outside the Lambir Prison to

welcome our son back home," she said. "We thought that we would never see our son again," she said with tears of joy.[20]

The public pardoning of Tawang by the Governor represents the freeing of the incarcerated self form the world of the abnormal and marginal into the world of the "free" and the normal. The process of rehabilitation, is long cruel, and arduous. Apart from canning by rotan carried out in the privacy of the prison — quite different from the France in Foucault's rendition — which is mandatory for some crimes, execution for serious crimes like murder and drug trafficking is by hanging from the gallows until death. A gubernatorial pardon for armed robbers like Tawang is like a public lottery. There are many participants, or contenders, but only one big winner. Punters in a state lottery are not detracted by the low statistical probability of winning. Prisoners under life sentences or on the infamous death row at Pudu have nothing to lose but their lives. Even the most fragile of possibilities of freedom will motivate some kind of hope that all is not lost. "They don't come to Paris any longer for freedom. They come to have a taste of an old traditional culture. They come to France as painters went to Italy in the 17th century to see a dying civilisation".[21] The biggest winner in any lottery, casino or gambling organization is the organization. In the case of the state, a public pardon provides credibility, stature, and legitimacy to the state: the public belief that convicted criminals ought to be committed to prison is buttressed by the "humanity" of releasing a prisoner on "good behavior" for moral, humane, social, and political credit. But of course, public pardoning cannot be done en masse or it may reduce the political stability of the land under the state's jurisdiction. The human face of the state is therefore "stern" but "fair" thus providing or propagating the idea of equal representation and treatment under the law. The ordering of society along legal-rational, Weberian rules helps ensure that there is no collapse of social and political order. Suharto fell from power because he lost political

---

[20] Clarence Ting, "TYT Grants Freedom to Life Prisoner After Spending 17 years in Cell," *Sarawak Tribune*, 12 February, 1998.
[21] Lawrence Kritzman, ed. *Michel Foucault: Politics, Philosophy, Culture: Interviews and other writings 1977-1984* (New York: Routledge, 1988), p. 5.

will after 32 years. Interim president Habibie is not rapidly resolving the problems faced by the people in the street throughout Indonesia. The subject of political, social, economic, religious, and cultural discussion in Indonesia has never been the *masyarakat* or the people: it has always been the leader. The following narrative illustrates the importance of controlling society, what Foucault speaks of in *The Order of Things* which, "asked the price of problematizing and analyzing the speaking subject, the working subject in the living subject. Which is why I attempted to analyze the birth of grammar, general grammar, natural history, and economics. I went on to pose the same kind of question in the case of the criminal and systems of punishment: how to state the truth of oneself, insofar as one might be a criminal subject. I will be doing the same thing with sexuality, only going back much further: how does the subject speak truthfully about itself, inasmuch as it is the subject of sexual pleasure? And at what price?"[22] On July 8, 1996, the *New Straits Times*, a large Malaysian English daily reported:

> Pahang may introduce whipping for various religious offences as allowed under the Islamic Administration and Pahang Malays Customary Enactment 1982 (Amendment 1987). The Pahang state government through its Religious and Education Committee chaired by Datuk Adnan Yaakob and the State Islamic Affairs Department is conducting a study on this matter. Under the enactment, those convicted of illicit sex, immoral activities and deviationist teachings are liable to fines, caning or both. At present, the Syariah Court in Pahang only imposes fines. Although caning is allowed, it has yet to be enforced as the state government is still studying its procedures and implications, Datuk Adnan said. "We cannot rush into doing things as such matters are sensitive and can create controversy. "We have to study, for instance, how caning can

---

[22] Lawrence Kritzman, ed. *Michel Foucault: Politics, Philosophy, Culture: Interviews and other writings 1977-1984* (New York: Routledge, 1988), p. 30.

be carried out, the thickness and the length of the cane," Datuk Adnan said, after giving away Pahang Foundation scholarships to students at the Kuantan municipal council on Saturday. On deviationist teachings in Pahang, Datuk Adnan said that the state government always encouraged the public to attend religious classes so that they would not be influenced or misled easily. "This problem occurs everywhere. That is why the state government always encourages the people to gain a deeper understanding of the religion."[23]

While in early 1997, another English daily, *The Star*, reported the following:

Representatives of parent-teacher associations from 87 government and private schools in Perlis yesterday presented a cane to school principals to symbolize their desire that teachers educate, discipline and if necessary cane their children. "We are confident that the 48,368 primary and secondary schoolchildren in Perlis will be more disciplined from now on and strive to pursue knowledge," said the deputy director of education Sulaiman Ismail. The cane presentation ceremony was attended by more than 2,400 teachers and hundreds of parents, some of them in tears and expressing full hope that teachers would help their children. "We do not want to abuse the students but educate and discipline them into becoming useful citizens and the cane has always been a symbol of instilling discipline," he said. Apart from the cane, some Muslim parents handed over a copy of the Qur'an to the principals in the hope they would also improve their children's spiritual development. Farmer Ahmad Lebai Noh, 64, said he was moved by the parents' realization of the usefulness of the cane which was viewed as an old-fashioned form of

---

[23] "Pahang looking into caning those convicted of religious offences," *New Straits Times*, July 8, 1996.

punishment. "I have always stressed not to spare the cane. The cane disciplined me when I attended Qur'an classes as it had landed many times on my palm. I recall with fond memory my father's words to my teacher — cane him if he is naughty and lazy but don't break his bones or make him blind".[24]

The cane or rotan is a symbol of discipline. The rotan is an Asian cultural symbol of punishment like the Western whip [FH/VP/EG]. These two pieces, and two narratives, indicate the relative strength of social discipline, and reflects the continuity of a tradition of corporeal punishment from one generation of Malay Malaysians to the next. The filtering and socialization of individuals within a corporal society of discipline supports the maintenance of structures of hierarchical power. Yet there are perennial discipline problems, a result of the conceit of human behavior. Ultimately, these structures expose their weaknesses, sometimes through mismanagement and faulty economics as seen in international communism, at other times through political expose, corruption, ethnic cleansing, and capitalism as greed). All structures in modernity constitute some form of hierarchy of power. The more obvious ones are political and economic structures. Increasingly, as John Rajchman pointed out in his 1985 work on Foucault that there is an increasing need to reconcile the power of technologies, to struggle against such domination as technological hierarchies of power continue to mediate, modify, and dominate the environments we inhabit. And then coincide and inhabit traditional corporal hierarchies of power as seen in the story about the Perlis education system and the symbolic metaphor of the "cane" as an instrument of discipline. Foucault was of course not the only one to warn and raise caution about the dangers of control, but his method makes us increasingly aware of the insidious, secretive, concealed, cryptic, and disingenuous ways such power affects not only the present, and conceptions of the past, but also about future generations. Foucault tells us that It is only through the decanonization of power and the interrogation of the penal system — both

---

[24] "Principals Given Cane of Authority," *The Star*, Kuala Lumpur, 9 March, 1997.

public, private, and institutional — that we can gain grater access into the knowledge of ourselves as the subjects of normality as opposed to the others, the objects of our abnormality. [**FV**]

A Subversion of Arguments

Foucault taught us to perceive of power differently. For example, marginalization and repression characterize his power/knowledge modality. Foucault reminds us that repression is constructed out of several complex strategies, including the preservation of knowledge, the maintenance of hierarchies of power, and the use of sexuality as a strategy of repression within the socialization process. But we can only understand *inter alia* repression if we consciously subvert our own stereotypical perceptions. Additionally, we have to undermine our long-standing arguments, question, and re-question our own intellectual positions to further the cause of knowledge. Otherwise, our stagnant repetitive claims will remain with us always. And we may possess the faulty ones, as Foucault ironically reminded us before his own death, "Well, do you think I have worked like that all those years to say the same thing?"[25] Similarly, the idea of repression may be clarified, ironically by the Deputy Inspector General of the Royal Malaysian Police on the problem of "social ills" among youth:

> Deputy Inspector-General of Police Tan Sri Samsuri Arshad said, "we cannot pretend everything is all right because things will only get worse and will work closely with the education authorities and other agencies such as the Community Welfare Department which has the necessary expertise, including counselors, for youth ... Caning should only be administered under certain circumstances such as after investigation has

---

[25] Lawrence Kritzman, ed. *Michel Foucault: Politics, Philosophy, Culture: Interviews and other writings 1977-1984* (New York: Routledge, 1988), p. 14.

been carried out to determine whether the student was involved in any wrongdoing".[26]

Even toward the end of his life, Foucault did not think much about his own work. He was not impressed by his own scholarship, perhaps partly out of modesty, or even for the prospect of popular appeal. But this mode of approaching knowledge enables the intellectual, and the power-seeker to avoid the problems and burdens of previous methods, that ought to be discarded as their purpose has been served. Unlike most academics, Foucault was not interested in furthering the preservation of the foundations of his own career. Unlike the heroes and politicians in Malaysian modernity, Foucault did not pretend to construct theoretical explanations of reality for the benefit of society, the immodest prevention of social ills from destroying the platforms of the powerful. "it's true, that I'm not a really good academic. For me, intellectual work is related to what you can call, aestheticism, meaning transforming yourself. I believe my real problem is this strange relationship between power, knowledge, scholarship, theory, and real history...I know that knowledge can transform us, that truth is not only a way of deciphering the world (and maybe what we call truth doesn't decipher anything) but that if I know the truth I will be changed. And maybe I will be saved. Or maybe I will die but it think that is the same for me."[27] The finality and terminality of his own demise was much closer than he expected. His own death was in effect, his own final subversion. What is clear, however, is the fact that he did probably did it all for one thing, "I hope I'll die of an overdose of pleasure of any kind".[28] This flippancy is a stark contrast to the pragmatic world of Malaysian politicians who possess the technical and managerial skills of a rapidly advancing developmental third world economy. However, in their flight to maintain the levels of economic grow that prudent fiscal, monetary, budgetary, and social policies

---

[26] "Samsuri: Social Ills Can Be Overcome," *The Star*, 12 March, 1997.
[27] Lawrence Kritzman, ed. *Michel Foucault: Politics, Philosophy, Culture: Interviews and other writings 1977-1984* (New York: Routledge, 1988), p. 14.
[28] *Ibid.*, 12.

have provided since the 1970s, Malaysian leaders ought not to forget to subvert their own arguments once in a while, to invalidate, and interrogate their own beliefs, if only to die from an overdose of pleasure.

The Analyses of Rationality

Foucault challenged rationality that leaders like Anwar did not, and ironically, Anwar has paid the price for believing and supporting in the system that has incarcerated him. For political leaders, rational thought is often equated to modern and progressive thought. Rational thought is about making and discovering logical sequences of thought to solve or resolve modern problems. Yet when the Asian currency crisis erupted, the rationality of the early 1990s suddenly evaporated. Malaysian Prime Minister became increasingly vocal about his belief in a foreign conspiracy to destabilize, weaken, and devour the Malaysian *ringgit*, much to the chagrin of many Malaysian political leaders, who believed that he ought to have kept silent about it. However, history will show that Mahathir was right: the speculators that he envisaged, however, did not possess any particular hatred towards third world countries with large debts and weak economies. Rather, these currency speculators have no loyalty to any single nation nor do they work towards the detriment of a particular state. Rather, these currency speculators only owe their allegiance to a neutralist corporate politics of industry.[29] Mahathir's rhetoric that led to Malaysia not accepting IMF bailout plans. The same kind of rhetoric that has saved the country from the economic problems and obstacles posed by IMF regulations in Thailand, Korea, and Indonesia. It is the same kind of blundering non-logical irrationality that Foucault supports at the intellectual level:

> I have tried to analyse forms of rationality: different foundations, different creations, different modifications in which rationalities engender one another, oppose and pursue

---

[29] See for example, Peter J. Katzenstein, *Corporatism and Change: Austria, Switzerland, and the Politics of Industry*, (Ithaca: Cornell University Press, 1984).

> one another...During the 1960s I wanted to begin as much with the phenomenological account (with its foundation and essential project of reason, from which we have shifted away on account of some forgetfulness and to which we must return) as with the Marxist account, or the account of Lukács. A rationality existed, and it was the form *par excellence* of Reason itself, but a certain number of social conditions (capitalism, or rather, the shift from one form of capitalism to another) precipitated this rationality into a crisis, i.e. a forgetting of reason, a fall into the irrational. I tried to take my bearings in relation to these two major models, presented very schematically and unfairly.[30]

The irrationality of capitalism lies within the seductive nature of its fraudulent logic. It is the belief that since capitalism can deliver certain goods, it can solve human problems. This conceit is Foucault's warning: the vacuity of modern capitalism. The different foundations, creations, and modifications of engendered rationalities are in flux, in competition, and act in contrarian ways. The crisis of rationality is the crisis of modern Reason. This is why modern narratives of crime and punishment reported through the mass media cease to shock and confound us; and even if they do possess some shock value, do so only for a short period of time. We have become so alienated from our humanity, atomized within the boundaries of our knowledge, and anaesthetized to the severity of our crimes that we do not perceive of the crimes that are committed in service of preventing crime. The concluding remarks made by any political speaker at any political event are desultorily similar as to have no effect and make no impression. The randomness of our being and the conflation of public and private spaces have made unjustifiable demands on our consciousness as human beings. We have forgotten how to think, act, and behave in a conscionable fashion. Anwar and Foucault never met. Yet their pronouncements are themselves

---

[30] *Ibid.*, p. 29.

reflections of the power of their own influence over the societies in which they inhabit. Anwar will end up as Prime Minister of Malaysia after years of sacrifice, tolerance, and hard work. He too, like Foucault will learn to deconstruct oppositional hierarchies of power, further marginalize the abnormal, weak, and useless digits that look, speak, and talk like us. Anwar will also learn to unlearn his own self, to reject his own past, to subvert his own thoughts that paved the way to the upper most echelons of political power in modern Malaysia.

Summary

Michel Foucault, Anwar Ibrahim, Tawang Anak Jamal, J. Ravi, and Ramli Ang Abdullah could be any Malaysian citizen. They could effectively represent productions of the social imaginary of the "modern", scripts that need to "discipline" and "punish" and be "disciplined" and "punished". Theirs are public-determined, private-regarding scripts that are constitutive of the discursive formations of the ageless texts in Malaysia's late modernity. As Foucault points out in the quote to this chapter, "Their anonymity was ignored because their real or supposed age was a sufficient guarantee of their authenticity".[31] Coincidentally, Weber's iron cage itself reflected the incarcerating influence of a bureaucratized society, that was brandished by the political and intellectual power of (former popular labels) like Anwar and Foucault. The main difference between the two labels is that one demands attention to a political ideology, and the other an intellectual one. The problem is telling them apart because "within our civilization, the same types of texts have not always required authors" (Foucault, 1977). The *Private* has ironically become contingent on the *Public*. Decisions about consumer goods and services no longer represent the conscious choices of private, interest-seeking, wealth-maximizing individuals but instead symbolize "social status", "public prescription", "public morality" and "public constructions" grounded in a foundational fantasy of modernity.

---

[31] Michel Foucault, 1977, *Language, Counter-Memory, Practice*. Ithaca, New York: Cornell University Press, p. 125.

This foundational fantasy of modernist development may become horrifying in the manner that Brennan describes, but not because of the differences in the individual psyche, but because of the differences between the perception of reality seen through variations in the interpretation of the rhetoric and the narratives that we have seen. The differential interpretations along the points of contact are points of resistance between and among the agents of modernity (in Kuala Lumpur, the federal capital of Malaysia) on the one hand, and, the agents of traditionalism (in Kuala Trengganu, the capital city of Trengganu, and Kota Bahru, the capital city of Kelantan) on the other, clearly demonstrates the slippages that arise out of late modernity, and helps us think about the nature of resistance before justice within the public defined, private spaces of our lives. In engaging the international system, specific material goals are public benchmarks of achievement such as the *Putra World Trade Center* in Kuala Lumpur, the Malaysian capital, and in the new federal government offices at *Putrajaya*. These are material celebrations of economic wealth and performance that are public reminders of consumer culture and material achievement in late modernity. Their destruction and fundamental modern vulnerability were played in the horrifying terrorist attack on the World Trade Center's twin towers in New York City on September 9, 2001. The imperfect politics of consumption therefore leads to a continual contestation of ideas (Katzenstein, Keohane, and Krasner, 1999) seen in the NEP in the pre-Mahathir period and the NDP and *Wawasan 2020* during Mahathir's administration. The Malaysian has state assumed the responsibility of providing equal opportunities for bumiputra Malaysians and non-bumiputra Malaysians alike with the modern hope of eradicating both classes of citizenship in the future so that all Malaysian regardless of ethnicity, language, social class, or religion have equal access to the resources that support quality family life and quality education. Yet this is difficult for the KL government because of the fine balance that needs to be and is often needlessly negotiated with the consequences of political strategies and public policies that are based on affirmative action, ethnocratism, ethnic management, and indigenous claims to material aspirations defined by the consuming public. As Malaysian consumers drive towards a bourgeoning high culture, typical of countries at some point in the democratic transition. But as Rorty observes, a rise in the proportion of ironists to metaphysicians has in effect led to a less knowledgeable public and a less knowledgeable academy, ironically, "a widening gap between the public and intellectuals" (Rorty, 1989).

Note

A much earlier version of this project was written presented at the International Convention of Asia Scholars, Leiden, Netherlands, June 25, 1998.

References

Anderson, Elizabeth. 1993. *Value in Ethics and Economics.* Cambridge, Mass.: Harvard University Press.

Anderson, Perry. 1979. *Considerations on Western Marxism.* London: Verso.

Bamberg, Michael G. W. 1987. *The Acquisition of Narratives: Learning to Use Language.* Berlin and New York: Mouton de Gruyter.

Deputy Prime Minister's Office, Malaysia. Information and Management System Unit, PMD.

Foucault, Michel. 1977. *Language, Counter-Memory, Practice.* Ithaca, New York: Cornell University Press.

Foucault, Michel. 1980. *Power/Knowledge.* New York: Pantheon.

Katzenstein, Peter J. 1987. *Corporatism and Change: Austria, Switzerland, and the Politics of Industry.* Ithaca: Cornell University Press.

Keyes, Charles F., Kendall, Laurel and Hardacre, Helen. 1994. *Asian Visions of Authority: Religion and the Modern States of East and Southeast Asia.* Honolulu: University of Hawaii Press.

Kritzman, Lawrence. ed. 1988. *Michel Foucault: Politics, Philosophy, Culture: Interviews and other writings 1977-1984.* New York: Routledge.

Malaysia, Government. 1995. *Information Malaysia.* Kuala Lumpur: Jabatan Penerangan Malaysia.

McCabe, Allyssa and Peterson, Carole (eds.) 1991. *Developing Narratival Structure.* Hillsdale: L. Erlbaum Associates.

Pye, Lucian and Pye, May W. 1985. *Asian Power and Politics: the Cultural Dimensions of Authority.* Cambridge: The Belknap Press.

Raz, Joseph. ed. 1990. *Authority.* Oxford: Blackwell.

Weber, Max. 1978. *Economy and Society: An Outline of Interpretive Sociology.* Berkeley: University of California Press.

Consumption & Its Discontents

> Ironically, a state can serve class interests even when it derives much of its legitimacy from a public condemnation of that class.
>
> Michael J. Shapiro,
> *Reading the Postmodern Polity:*
> *Political Theory as Textual Practice*, 1992

Consumers can't help consuming goods and services without reading the "fine print" on their labels. Can consumers in late modernity really be blamed for not thinking thoroughly about the consequences of every purchase made? Much of the problem of consumption in modernity as seen in the narratives on public/private space may be traced to existing modes of communications technology that has quadrupled the amount of information delivered to more people within a shorter time-frame. Yet the new found information distributed to consumers worldwide is not any more substantive or anymore analytical. There's merely a larger distribution network. This has three main political impacts on the consumer: (1) more information in less time with less accuracy; (2) costs incurred on new technology are passed directly to consumers; and, (3) the rise of agency-generators that churn out repetitive and dull news-bites of similar views of one issue.

The agents of modernity, viz., the capitalists, administrators, street-level bureaucrats, talk-show hosts, low-level politicians, low-level religious leaders, journalists, and other talking heads mediate public/private spaces with these news bites of analogous messages in different languages, alternative accents, and with absent originals. The public/private world of consumption is Baudrillard's "simulacra". The multiple public/private spaces in Singapore and Malaysia, especially the urban centers, are replete with potentially fractious slices of divergent pieces of the same narratives on modernity. This fragmentary situation presents a precarious public oeuvre for the comptrollers of modernity — the political elite, the big businessmen, the neoliberal capitalist owners of the factors of production, the MNCs and TNCs, the NGOs in Singapore, and Malaysia and the rest of the "advancing" industrial world — and their agents of late capitalist perpetuation (after Jameson). These comptrollers have a common objective of increasing their (profit, wealth, power, and) control over private spaces via public spaces. As the gatekeepers of late modernity, the comptrollers often discover themselves in simultaneous competition for the consumer dollar. The comptrollers of modernity and their agents acquire power and legitimacy with larger market proportions, and lose power and become delegitimized with falling market shares. The overall value of their stock and store of wealth rises and falls within their own arenas of competition.

Consumers and producers are themselves often in search of their own familial origins. This desire and this search often extends into a search for the origins of the goods and services that they purchase. At least some would like to know, "where does this come from?" or "where is this made in?". The influences that are exerted by the (comptrollers and agents working in the) public over the (fragile) private spheres and private realms of thought are clearly seen in searches for the origins of things that cannot be discovered in the first place. This "absence" of an authentic "origin" in modernity suggests that we are mere copies of copies of copies (Baudrillard) wherein which the agents of modernity ensure the regeneration of simulated publics to construct authentic-looking "originals". In seeking an origin of x,

y, or z, we create and construct an "authentic" by the very act of reaching out for it within the public sphere.[1]

The public structures of late modernity — the schools, government offices, the religious centers of worship, the gentrified civic locations, data collection agencies — are equipped to weaken and soften individual resistance against enumeration, collation, and case-study. These agents of modernity seek the homogenization of people so that all tastes, desires, hopes and wants can be predetermined, prefabricated and presented in a productive and an efficient manner, through effective channels. The comptrollers and agents of modernity are anti-thought, anti-representational, anti-relative, anti-emotion, and anti-reflexive. They leave no real choices for consumers although the self-same consumers "appear" to be confronted by more choices today than they did a century ago. Consumers have become so inundated with "plasticized choices" and the fetishization of providing such a multitude of choices that they no longer desire to make decisions: consumers are too exhausted, too weak, and face too much information and too much bland, blankness that it becomes a virtual hassle to think to make these pseudo-choices.

Some points about consumption in late modernity: (1) consumers have a narrower field of choice today than a generation ago; (2) the range of goods and services made available in late modernity have fallen in terms of quality as the owners of the factors of production continue to cut costs and raise profit margins. The implication here is that consumers face a narrower range of lower quality products and services that they did ten years ago; (3) technology does not pay for itself and is primarily driven by hype and media marketing frenzies that promote the modern desire for advancement and progress through the sale and purchase of the latest gizmos and communication tools. The implication is that these products have a very short shelf life, and are virtually out-classed and out-dated by the time they

---

[1] I would like to thank Kathy E. Ferguson for pointing this out at a seminar on feminist theory where we were discussing Foucault, Butler, and Trinh min-ha in 1994. See William Chaloupka, *International Studies Quarterly* (1990), 34 (3): 341-351, and his brief discussion of Baudrillard's "declining social".

reach the furthest markets from which they are produced. (4) The private spaces where we used to make important decisions are now surrounded by the encroaching boundaries of the public. In 1990, for example, Peter J. Katzenstein argued that the "developmental capitalism of East Asia ... predicated on precisely such a political notion of economic life" (Katzenstein, *et al.*, 1990:170). These political notions are equally apparent and operationalized in Southeast Asian economies such as Singapore and Malaysia which have tried, with somewhat uneven results, to foster close economic and political ties with China, and perhaps more successfully, with Japan. We are now increasingly dependent on the agents and agencies of modernity — experts, professionals, *ad hoc* positions, *pro bono* volunteers, technicians, faceless people — to filter and make sense of the world around us for us to survive. This ranges from reading a simple legal document to flying safely on an airplane to our favored holiday destination to hoping that the chosen destination is safe from terrorism, kidnapping, and other heinous crimes. (5) the powerful homogenizing effect of modernity has led to creative and relatively ingenious ways of commodification of virtually all aspects of late modern civilization into goods and services for sale and purchase. The great political theorists and classical economists would never have thought that the 1980s and 1990s would be commodified and sold through the music and media industry and through fashion agencies and through food and nutritional outlets. *How does one package an idea into a container that is portable, functional, cheap and that every other person needs to use?* Perhaps capitalism is indeed the most remarkable consumer product of the 19th, 20th, and 21st centuries.

The theoretical framework of this brief, and limited book on "Modernity" and "Consumption", was built on five-concepts designed under the mRf to analyze family, education, narrative and public space in Singapore and Malaysia. The book involved the production of the family, the rapid evolution of the educational structure, the national security "good", the relationship between narratival space and public space, and the co-dependence between national security and the distribution of wealth. In the Singapore case, education was examined in terms of general, military and national forms of education while in Malaysia education was scrutinized with respect to the National Education System and *Bangsa Malaysia* concept. The analyses were made against the backdrop of quantitative data on consumption patterns and modalities in the two countries. The interplay of politics, policy, and rhetoric in the public sphere constitute hierarchical formations of power based on comprehensive policy output and rigorous policy planning and management as seen in Singapore's "Stop-At-Two" and Malaysia's "Look East" public policies. Within the overarching *public*, "Policy is centrally about classification and differentiation about how we do and should categorize in a world where categories are not given...policy arguments are convincing to the extent that they give a satisfying account of the rightness of treating cases alike or differently".[2] *Singapore One* represents the software hub of the new economy of the island republic. It is too early to speak with confidence about the extent of the impact of software and hardware development technology apart from stating that these are becoming increasingly widespread and only limited by the number of computer terminals. The force of the Intelligent Age of Software will continue to reinvent the nature and patterns of consumer goods and services. New technology-based venture capitalist millionaires with an average age of 24 years in the year 2000 were only matched by equally spectacular results in terms of the greater number of failures of such venture capitalists worldwide. Economic consumption in Singapore and Malaysia is co-dependent with was illustrated in terms of the national security policy and the distribution of wealth as one is dependent on the other. Without national security, the possibility of political and economic instability will be high, making consumption virtually untenable in situations of extreme and prolonged political violence. The importance of distribution of wealth in Singapore and Malaysia are very crucial to the modern quest of economic development as redistribution (1) motivates workers; (2) provides for the relatively fair distribution of the economic pie to all consumers within the domestic market in order to reduce relative deprivation; (3) increases the

---

[2] Deborah A. Stone, *Policy Paradox and Political Reason* (Addison Wesley Longman, Inc. 1991), p. 308.

productivity of the labor force as a whole; (4) inspires investor confidence; (5) marginalizes disconcerted forces pressuring the center for change.[3]

Katzenstein argued over a decade ago that "capitalist markets are politically constructed. Markets cannot be understood apart from states and politics" (Katzenstein, 1990:172). All markets tend towards some form of regulation, while most kinds of market control appear to be centered on the state, the post Cold War era and the New Millennium clearly indicate three major thrusts for capitalist-consumer markets: (1) politics will continue to be the primary mover of people, determining the use of public space, and in this manner, controlling the nature of public space, and the lives of consumers in public; (2) there will continue to be an increasing devolution of economic power away from state control and towards private sector control, meaning that there is more than likely to be increasing control over the economy by multinational investment corporations and financial houses; (3) consumers will increasingly look towards the State for guidance and leadership during economic recessions, and in the continuing battle against international terrorism.

Therefore, Katzenstein's position on the primacy of politics and the importance of understanding markets, states and politics in political and social analyses continues to be an important premise in any work claiming to explain politics and consumption in late modernity. As we have seen, the impact of political consumption in Malaysia was represented through the political narratives of Anwar Ibrahim and Mahathir Mohammed. The comparison with ordinary Malaysians highlighted the differences between powerful actors and powerless ones. It also decried Anwar Ibrahim's fall from high political office as an act of power itself that is represented in the stories that are consumed by the people en masse. The idea of political narratives as consumption goods is defined in terms of consuming images of great and weak actors alike, images that generate wealth for the owners of the mass media and their related corporations. The Malaysian state is itself perceived as an agency that generates narratives as teaching and learning

---

[3] See also the original report from Economic Development Board, *SIN*, 2001.

lessons, cautionary tales of the expected and unexpected as seen in the case of Anwar Ibrahim.

Consumer Culture

The *"depoliticized" Singapore consumer* is stridently different yet ironically similar to the *"politicized" Malaysian consumer*. This is traceable to the historical and political links that Singaporeans share with Malaysia. The former British colony with a strategic geographical location at the nexus of shipping routes, Singapore became the focus of infrastructure and commercial investments since its "modern founding" in 1819. By the time of the Treaty of Pangkor in Malaya in 1878, Singapore had secured a significant position of British commerce in the far East. The British imposed similar divide and rule policies that it had done in its other colonies and in India, and the focus on commercial activities in what was merely an island of swamps became a natural, perhaps logical outcome of its heritage. The large Chinese population in Singapore was primarily interested in saving and returning at some point in time to China. However, the end of the Pacific war in 1945 led to the establishment of a local class of Chinese, Indian, Malay, and Eurasian entrepreneurs. But the Chinese retained their demographic majority. The failure of the British colonialists resulted in the creation of a political class of western educated and Chinese educated businessmen and professional lawyers, physicians, and trade unionists. The failure of Lee Kuan Yew's "Malaysian Malaysia" plan led to the establishment of a kind of secular state in which no religion or ethnic community would be predisposed towards total control over the polity and the economy. However, in reality, the Chinese in Singapore were overwhelmingly the largest ethnic group thereby making their decisions in terms of commercial and political activity supremely important in shaping the politico-economic landscape of the postcolony. The ejection from the federation of Malaysia resulted in a kind of "Garrison State" mentality among the first generation of Singaporean political leaders because of the fear that Singapore would become an economic and political disaster outside the traditional "common market" with Malaysian hinterland. This was not to be the case as the Singapore government decided, perhaps against the theories and principles of third world development at the time, to ensure economic prosperity by way of multi-national investments. The resounding economic success of the small economy with only human resources had two main implications: (1) in order to ensure the economic survival of the country and the people there had to be a strong and credible defense force; and (2) economic development with MNC help and advice from internationally-accredited advisors was to be the way in which its political and economic sovereignty could be fuelled and sustained. Singapore today appears to be paradox of a first world city-state in a third world region. The idea of political consumption as simulacra upon simulacra, representations of first world commercial activities in a third world region has resulted in three main implications: (1) a highly literate and relatively wealthy resident population; (2) a new generation of Singaporeans who have been raised on a generous diet of commercialism, consumerism, and capitalist choices within what has appeared to be a fairly safe and stable political environment; and (3) a continuing support of a single-party dominant state that continues to deliver the economic goods. Official documents that strategize the future in terms of *Singapore, Inc.*, *The Next Lap*, and *Singapore 21*, offer a future for consumers that is directly tied into labor productivity and entrepreneurialism. The New Economy in the 21st century is one made up of consumers who are more likely than not to forego industrial loyalty to the firm and a certain readiness to move on to greener economic opportunities that present themselves as the economy develops. Consumption in Singapore is perhaps best captured by the fact that the seeds of Singapore's economic success are the seeds of its own destruction. The government realized this problem, and with its efficient and surplus driven bureaucracy began inculcating a sense of belonging among Singaporeans "Make Singapore the Best Home Possible". The attraction of foreign talent or global talent to the city-state has always been an important facet of life since its commercial successes began in the early 1900s. every once in a while the state will remind its dutiful citizens of the need to continue to serve the nation and to produce for the nation. The problem is not so much with the first and second generations of Singaporeans but with the future ones, those teenagers in the educational system. The danger stems from the relationship between the city-state's ironic economic successes on one hand and the incremental moves towards a liberal democratic system of government that is so information-dependent it cannot be conceived as being real in any other defining moment without the use and abuse of information as knowledge, truth, and reality. Consumer-driven modernity has led to the inflow of information throughout the world. The control over the media has been a stronghold of government policy since 1965. However, it will become increasingly difficult to control the minds and decisions of future Singaporean consumers in the Age of the Internet. The problem therefore is not when the next generation of consumers recognizes the importance of political freedoms but when the teenagers of today begin to choose and value political freedom over economic wealth. Consumption in Singapore is therefore a complex struggle for the survival of Singaporean consumers who presently continue to enjoy higher per capita wages than their familial relatives and counterparts in the surrounding region. In order for the domestic economy to survive and thrive as it has over the past 36 years, the government must plan to loose many of its citizens to other countries. However, the strategy of choice would clearly be to replace the brain drain with citizens from India, China, Indonesia, the Philippines, Thailand, and Myanmar who will then form over the next twenty years the successor generation of Singaporean and Malaysian consumers. The consumer culture is one that cannot help but be influenced by the juggernaut of modernity through the encroachment of private space by public power. Consumer culture is therefore a net output of the complex interplay of political narratives, social forces, State decision making in public policy, and the politics of a marginalized resistance than cannot exist in the private realm because all the space has been occupied.

Southeast Asian Movements

Within Southeast Asia, there has been over the past seven years from 1995 to 2002, an increasing level of *deregulation, devolution,* and *decentralization* of the mass media, of public policy, and of central control that mirrors and mimics the radical transformation of businesses in mergers and acquisitions and, perhaps with the exception of the Federation of Malaysia, the rapid liberalization of the financial and banking sectors. What used to be popularly perceived as centralized media control is now seen as genuine attempts to genuinely denationalize and farm out the production of public goods and services. In other words, by opening up the systems of control, the Malaysian state equally made vulnerable by exposing the traditional methods in which the cultural reductionism that began with (British) English interpretations of Malay-ness would multiply and be catalyzed by the local and foreign media. By the turn of the millennium, Malaysian media deregulation had resulted in a plethora of news and entertainment agencies that played crucial roles in the popularization of the incumbent political party, United Malays National Organization (UMNO), the 1998 economic recession, the sacking of Anwar Ibrahim, the Deputy Prime Minister and former Minister for Finance, and the 1999 general election victory for Barisan Nasional (BN) and the loss of another state seat to the opposition Islamic party, PAS. Consumption in Malaysia deliberated the ways that political goods and discourses are consumed in Malaysia. The currency speculators that resulted in destabilizing the Malaysian economy was a result of profit-motivation and rent seeking within and without the country. This was why Datuk Seri Dr. Mahathir Mohamad had to step in and re-introduce his concept of "kampong economics", basic economic strategies that simultaneously makes sense to the masses and to the elites. The nature of the public face of consumption in Malaysia has developed sufficient scar tissue so as to be able to stake a relatively modest claim in the international neoliberal political economy.

History as a Sign

The history of consumption in Malaysia has seen the importation of non-indigenous labor from India, Southeast Asia and South China by the British colonial class to work on the tin mines and in the rubber plantations throughout the Peninsula had deepened the division between ethnic Malays, Chinese, and Indians along such racial lines as to make it virtually impossible for what was called the political bargain not to have failed. This pre-1945 "Bargain" referred to an unwritten agreement between the two largest communities, the indigenous Malays and the descendents of transplanted Chinese immigrant laborers and workers. The Malays wanted overt recognition that they were the inherent heirs of the land, the political and sovereign heirs while the Chinese continued to make inroads into the national economy. However, as the domestic consumption thrived before the end of World War II, the Malay communities began stagnating economically while the Chinese ones surged ahead in terms of their penchant for commerce and trading opportunities. This came to a head in various ethnic clashes between Malays and Chinese in the 1950s with the Maria Hertogh riots and the clashes between urban Malay and Chinese workers in the federal capital and sporadically in many towns and villages. The potential disruptions to the domestic economy and domestic consumption were tremendous. By the early 1960s, the failed Malayan Union proposals and the failure of the "Bargain" led to greater intensity of ethnic violence between these two groups. By the time Malaysia was born in 1963, it became clear that there could only be one predominant cultural, economic and political class of indigenous people, and the Malays were unwilling to allow the Chinese to assume this role that had been entrenched by the British colonialists since the Treaty of Pangkor in 1878. Hence, the "common market" of consumers that had been informally established before, during and after the Pacific war was now divided into two commercial zones, the larger Malaysian one in the North and the small Singaporean one in the South. This north-south divide between the two neighbors was itself an extension of the ethnic based differences between the two newly formed postcolonies. The Malay nationalists under Tun Razak would assume command and emergency powers over the entire nation in the period 1969-1970, during which Parliament was prorogued and all political representation was suspended. The high powered committee led by the second prime minister enshrined a new Malaysian Constitution that would guarantee the Special Rights of the Malays and virtual make "second class citizens" of all non-bumiputra Malaysians. The separation of the two sovereign states in 1965 meant that the large Chinese population in Singapore would not create a threatening political imbalance in terms of absolute numbers as there was a very large Chinese population in Singapore.

The separation of the two states meant that the Malay bumiputra would remain the largest domestic consumers communities vis-à-vis the total number of votes. The enshrining of the new Constitution meant that Malays would have the legal and eventually financial power to achieve a higher level of equity within the Malaysian economy as compared to the Chinese, Indian, and Eurasian communities. The outcome of the ethnic-based claims of the Malays within a society that was politically organized along ethnic lines resulted in the affirmation of political representation through political parties steeped in ethnic power. The money supporting these ethnic-based political parties — UMNO, MCA, and MIC — would be derived primarily from their own constituents who would themselves make consumption-based decisions along ethnic lines. Over the years between the 1960s and 1990s commercial activities that were initiated along ethnic lines began to blur the distinctions created by the New Constitution. Positive economic growth meant more goods to share for more people. However, there continues to be much anecdotal evidence of the hardships and difficulties faced by non-bumiputra, non-Malay Malaysians in terms of access to government scholarships, government jobs, places in schools and Universities. Countless newspaper reports and ministerial speeches from the ruling coalition, the National Front, appear to consistently fail to stave off charges of corruption, nepotism, and cronyism from the political Opposition. Despite fears of racial unrest and political violence, domestic consumption continues to remain strong in Malaysia, and generally undisrupted. While there might be, an ethnic-based undertow of suspicion that surreptitiously creates a cultural, linguistic, and political barrier between Malay and non-Malay in Malaysia, these differences are more apparent than real at this point in time at the turn of the 21st century. The conclusion to Part II of this book can only point towards the fracturing of Malay-controlled commercial activities based on legislation and "affirmative action" policies. The signs of weakening among the Malay and non-Malay political elite who often have shared, vested commercial interests that cut across ethnic lines will arise out of consumption-driven modernity. Globalization and capital trade movements are forcing the Malay-Muslim community to fracture into moderates and fundamentalists, those who desire incremental change and slow adaptation to the forces of modernity and those whose preference lies in a return to Malay-Muslim traditionalism when life in the *kampung* or village revolved round the *mesjid* or mosque, the *madrasah* or religious school and the *keluarga* or family. This desire ironically stems from a fear of the fast changing pressures of globalization in which consumerism continues to make inroads into culture, religion and traditional society. Ultimately, the commodification of culture and the commodification of society at large itself will result in a return to ethnic-based claims, and political violence over shrinking access to opportunities within the capitalist structures. The loss of Trengganu and Kelantan, two northern Malaysian states, to the PAS opposition party, and away from the control of the relatively moderate UMNO party, is indicative of the disenfranchisement felt not only by consumers within the non-Malay, non-bumiputra communities but within the Malay community itself. These two northern states have primarily agricultural and farming economies that are too far removed from the wealthy urban centers to have derived direct benefits of the NEP and NDP (Kamal, 1988).

The aim of a national-consumption good is to foster a sense of familial bonding between and among citizens who have never met, yet never need to know each other personally to feel a common sense of belonging to a kind of Andersonian imagined community. The *Bangsa Malaysia* or *Malaysian Culture/Race* as a national-consumption good was reinvigorated in 1995 by Datin Paduka Zaleha Ismail, the National Unity and Social Development minister, with the belief that Malaysians had done well in "propagating the *Bangsa Malaysia* concept...The country's education quota and discounted prices for bumiputras are maintained because they are lagging economically and therefore need some concession. But this will not be forever. When the gap closes, the concessions will be reviewed and they will gradually become a thing of the past". Whether it be the politics of promise or rhetoric, forever usually takes a long time.

Yet the normalization of consumption subsidies on ethnic grounds has continued to prove a thorn in the foot of the Mahathir administration for two main reasons: firstly, the NF or BN cannot remove the bumiputra privileges without a negative groundswell from the Malay Malaysian grassroots especially those who live at or below the poverty level by international standards. The other problem is that the current wave of Islamic fundamentalism or alternatively, Islamic extremism by a minority of Muslims in Malaysia and throughout the world — recently marked by terrorists masked as Muslims but who are really plain terrorists without any conscionable notion of religious fervor, morality, or respect for human life as seen in the 911 episode[4] — has strengthened rather than weakened the PAS-held opposition in the Malaysian states of Kelantan and Trengganu. In order for Datuk Seri Dr. Mahathir Mohamad to win these states back in the next general election, his administration will have to do more than turn away federal aid to these state governments and re-direct aid to the people themselves. Rather, the federal government will need continue to negotiate an ethnic minefield at the center of which is the ageing NEP and NDP that bolster and represent the central economic and consumptive pillars of bumiputraism in Malaysia. Optimists such as Zainal Rampak of the Malaysian Trade Union Congress (MTUC) argued in 1995 in the capacity of MTUC president that "any person who is a citizen of this country and who has sworn his or her undivided loyalty to the King and this country should be considered part of *Bangsa Malaysia*. The question of whether the notion can be achieved does not arise because we have already achieved it" tends towards political naïveté. However, there appears to be hope — albeit moving very slowly, as in 1993, Ng Lip Yong, a former Gerakan Youth chairperson managed to have the word "Malaysian" rather than the word "Chinese" entered in *Keturunan Bapa* and *Keturunan Ibu* categories in his son's birth certificate. But he failed in 1995 when his second son was born. Although he insisted on pure Malaysian categorization, the registration

---

[4] The September 11, 2001 is now known as the 911 episode because of the emergency situation created by the terrorists to which the emergency number is attached as a play on the date itself, the ninth month, and the 11th day.

officer inserted Chinese Malaysian with the rationale that the computer classifications did not have the *Bangsa Malaysia* category.

Consumption in Malaysia as it is in other parts of the world is about the irrational logic and vacuity of modern capitalism. Ironically, it is likely that the continued fracturing and disenfranchisement of the Malay bumiputra community will be a direct result of an equitable stake in the economic pie: the same rights-based claim over a shrinking economic pie that saw political violence in the 1950s and 1960s is likely to return because there will be much less for all consumers in Malaysia to consume. History then becomes a signpost to late modernity.

A Discontented Modernity

This book provides consumers with a variegated set of approaches to understanding modernity and consumption in Singapore and Malaysia. Critics of Modernity's Project have to confront two kinds of opponents: (1) modernists; and (2) dogmatic modernists.

Modernists tend to be happy and optimistic people. They often believe that there is nothing wrong with being hopeful and happy and they are puzzled by inferences and suggestions that the world is a much sadder place that it seems to be. Modernists believe in advancement and progress. They believe that the way forward is through the solutions and resolutions of existing vocabularies of modernity: science, technology, and art to name three main ones. Modernists are in favor of what they perceive as pluralism. They think that plurality is about a widening range of goods and services that are available all over the world and to large extent in the same form as they are available elsewhere. Modernists seek comfort and desire predictability. Modernists are builder and developers. They want to celebrate human life in ways that earn more wealth and generates more income. They are unable to think ironically or at least prefer not to think too much, as Sartre once said, "everything in life has been figured out, except how to live it". Modernists do not take criticism well. When challenged, they become defensive and sometimes suppress their dissatisfaction till they can wreck revenge in a public manner. Suppressed dissatisfaction often leads outbursts in the public realm where they make resounding, logical, and plain speeches that decontextualize the possibility of politics, and elicit the support of the modernist masses. They believe that there is always some critic lurking in the shadows and that shadows are related to darkness, and that darkness is evil. Modernists are unable to think outside the box and often think that creativity can be taught. The kind of creativity being taught then is an in-house, in-box, boxy kind of creativity. Modernists suffer from information overload. They handle information overload by referring to Brand Names. These are the new Aristotelians who hide behind the virtue and virtuousness of the Brand Name because they cant do their own thinking. Once a Brand Name is considered excellent, it remains excellent to a fault. Modernists tend to treat people as digits and data, cases and projects rather than as human beings. Therefore, statistically insignificant persons are often omitted from survey research and data sets because their numbers are too small, never minding or bothering that the survey results will be stilted and skewed from the perspective of humanity. After all, why should they be interested in humanity for all when humanity for the majority is all that can practically be achieved? While the correction of data, the cleaning of data, and the prevention of skewing in quantitative work affords a certain aura of "respectability" and legitimacy, it becomes even more important to make sense of how the data is collected and who is left out of the data. This is where the idea of (conceptual or research) focus arises as rational and a kind of justification for work done: if modernists claim openly and publicly that they are concentrating on one segment of the population, or one slice of reality, then they cannot be blamed for leaving out everyone else. Because there are others who put these diverse sets together, or so the assumption goes.

 Dogmatists, on the other hand, often think that they are being pragmatic when in effect, they are merely effecting a course of action that requires little thought and no criticism. They mistake dogmatism for pragmatism. They desire the control over public spaces and keep calling for more regulations and more control. Dogmatists desire the world to be in black and white; they seek fact to separate fact from fiction; clear directions without change; and a world without irony. They cannot recognize the fact that the world is not simple, but made up of highly complex, transformative, and contingent sets of shifting values, moralities, ideas, and technologies. Dogmatists are modernists by their own "socio-biological programming". They are the likely to reject the modernity/resistance argument because weakens their moral belief system, and delegitimizes their cosmology. The dogmatists believe in stability and conformity without the prospect of criticism. They often use ordinary code in the literal sense "constructive criticism" (only arguments that support their dogma); "the most suitable candidate" (only those who do not delegitimize or challenge their dogma); "value-added" (what's in it for the dogmatist as material consumers); "all suggestions are welcome" (none at all); "the usual suspects"; "hidden agenda"; "perfect solution"; "zero defect"; "conspiracy theory"; "team effort"; "solution partner"; "performance appraisal", "complete agreement"; "final edition", and "united front". For example, between November 2001 and January 2002, the Singapore ISD arrested thirteen male members of the *Jema'ah Islamiah* which is a clandestine network of three terrorist cells linked to the *Al-Qaeda* (the Base). These disenfranchised members of Singapore in late modernity had plans to attack and bomb American military personnel, over two hundred American companies with twenty-one tons of ammonium nitrate. They had also made secret video recordings of the U.S embassy, the Australian High Commission, the British High Commission, the Isreali Embassy, and the Ministry of Defence (MINDEF) (security complex) at Bukit Gombak. The fact that six of the thirteen had performed full time national service in the SAF and were low ranking reservist (NSmen) personnel again raised the sensitive issue in the public domain of Malay-Muslims in the SAF, and resulted in moderate Malay-Muslim leaders adopting a defensive political rhetoric as seen in the words of Mayor Othman (Southeast Community Development Council) and Yatiman Yusof, a senior parliamentary secretary (MITA).[5] These religious dogmatists represent one extreme of the discontented, and disenfranchised markers of modernity. Dogmatists help us think ironically, and make the world an

---

[5] See *The Straits Times*, June 12, 2002, p. 1: H1-H3.

interestingly boring place. Dogmatists like modernists believe in progress, advancement and development but unlike most modernists are unable to conceptualize thought thoroughly because it is too abstract and involves too much thinking. Dogmatists seek to control the world with a single dogma and hope that progress, advancement and development mean no change. The dogmatist believes that there can be no software movement across the globe especially when the idea or concept was invented overseas; and tend to reject technology because they are afraid to be connected with the rest of humanity. The mRf approach has shown that political, economic, and cultural analyses are necessary but not sufficient conditions for the study of consumption because there is too much "slippage" due to the relatively narrower, focal points that makes the three approaches like a horse with blinkers on traveling down a narrow river bed with high embankments on either side at night.

Anamorphic Modernity, the Emptiness of the Public, and Criticism

In 1993, Rosemary Coombe suggests that, "Jean Baudrillard, David Harvey, and Fredric Jameson ... have attempted to theorize the "cultural logic of late capitalism" in terms of the growth of consumer society and modern media technologies. Culture reproduction or image production effaces production in Western societies leading to an immense expansion of "culture" throughout society".[6] But this is the culture of emptiness and worthlessness that is continually mediated by dominant world currencies. This is a discontented culture. But the discontents of modernity I refer to here are different but with similar characteristics. The discontents of modernity — are emptied out of all symbolic value, emptied out of signs, and emptied out of meaning. Consumptions' public discontents are, in effect, to be found in the sites of intellectual resistance — parts of the Academy, parts of the world of Art, and parts of the anti-interpretational Philosophy — and are

---

[6] Rosemary J. Coombe, 1993, "Tactics of Appropriation and the Politics of Recognition in Late Modern Democracies in Language, Recognition, and Freedom", *Political Theory* 21(3): 413.

often lucid in the weak foundational thought of many contemporary political theorists. The public discontentment with consumption has resulted in an emptiness associated with *anamorphic modernity*: the intangible and tangible technological containers of minute, digitized-images of the world that are rapidly condensed, compressed, and suddenly released in large format reality, on the big screen as "knowledge", "truth" and "objectivity" across the globe.

Anamorphic modernity converges public and private space into a single, plural-like, and dominant but fractured space. Anamorphic modernity has radically transformed the old, classical platforms supporting the (i.e. simplistic) platonic fusion of public and private space. Anamorphic modernity has reduced the belief in the public-private divide that we inherited from the enlightenment theorists, and abridged the private into contingent, conditional, ephemeral, and decrepit spaces. The effect of homogenization exerts strong pressures on political, economic, and cultural institutions therefore leading to fragmented sites of resistance across all modes of resistance and consumption. Sustaining our criticism of modernity and consumption in Singapore and Malaysia, indeed, all over the world, makes us aware of the alienation of ourselves from humanity; while its patterns of economic and cultural consumption have tended towards the positive fragmentation of knowledge away from universalism, towards theories of consumer chaos; and the recreation of possible alternative futures. Henri Lefebvre once wrote, 'we are surrounded by emptiness, but it is an emptiness filled with signs'".[7] It is this very critical emptiness that we need to know, and that we need to resist. Criticism is only part of a larger instinct for survival, desensitized through global mediated forms of language, popular culture, hierarchies of political power, earning a living while living an earning and believing narratives that are related to us through thematic expressions of consumption and its discontents in public space. At this end of the book we might tentatively conclude that commodities are merely effects of the process of a "complex and

---

[7]*Ibid.*, note that Coombe cites this in her work which she attributes to Hal Foster's *Recodings: Art Spectacle and Cultural Politics* (Seattle: Bay Press, 1985), p. 165.

dissimulating" commodification while representing condensed sites of social forces (after Wendy Brown). Therefore, the politics of consumption is always to be found in the thing itself, and through thematic expressions of consumer resistance. *Caveat emptor.*

References

Chaloupka, William. 1990. *International Studies Quarterly*, **34** (3): 341-351.

Coombe, Rosemary J. 1993. "Tactics of Appropriation and the Politics of Recognition in Late Modern Democracies in Language, Recognition, and Freedom", *Political Theory*, **21**(3): 411-433.

Economic Development Board. 1976-2001. *Singapore Investment News*. Economic Development Board (various), Singapore.

Jain, M. P. 1997. *Administrative Law of Malaysia and Singapore*. 3rd edition. Malayan Law Journal, Singapore.

Lee, Kuan Yew. 1962. *The Battle for Merger*. Singapore: Printed at the Government Printing Office.

Lee, Kuan Yew. 1965. *The Battle for a Malaysian Malaysia*. Singapore: Ministry of Culture.

Mahathir, Mohamed. 1998. *The Way Forward*. London: Weidenfeld & Nicolson.

Karni, R. S.. 1980. *Bibliography of Malaysia & Singapore*. Kuala Lumpur: Penerbit Universiti Malaya.

Salih, K. 1988. *The New Economic Policy After 1990*. Kuala Lumpur: Malaysian Institute of Economic Research.

Shapiro, Michael J. 1993. "Eighteenth Century Intimations of Modernity: Adam Smith and the Marquis de Sade", *Political Theory*, **21**, 2:273-293.

Shapiro, Michael J. 1999. *Cinematic Political Thought: Narratives of Race, Nation and Gender*. New York & Edinburgh: New York University and University of Edinburgh Press.

Stone, Deborah A. 1991. *Policy Paradox and Political Reason*. Addison Wesley Longman.

Tan, C. H. and Kwan, K. C. eds. 1988. *Handbook of Singapore-Malaysian Corporate Finance*. Singapore: Butterworths.

Bibliography

Anderson, Elizabeth, 1993. *Value in Ethics and Economics.* Cambridge, MA: Harvard University Press.

Anderson, Perry. 1979. *Considerations on Western Marxism.* London: Verso.

Appadurai, Arjun. 1996. *Modernity at Large: Cultural Dimensions of Globalization.* Minneapolis: University of Minnesota Press.

Augustine, St.1963. *De Civitate Dei.* Cambridge, MA: Harvard University Press.

Bachrach, Peter and Botwinick, Aryeh. 1992. *Power and Empowerment : A Radical Theory of Participatory Democracy.* Philadelphia, PA: Temple University Press.

Bamberg, Michael G.W. 1987. *The Acquisition of Narratives: Learning to Use Language.* Berlin and New York: Mouton de Gruyter.

Bauman, Zygmunt. 1999. *In Search of Politics.* Cambridge and Oxford, Polity Press.

Belshaw, Horace. 1956. *Population Growth and Levels of Consumption* (with special reference to countries in Asia). London: Allen & Unwin.

Bianchi, Marina. ed. 1998. *The Active Consumer: Novelty and Surprise in Consumer Choice.* New York: Routledge.

Bickford, Susan. 1996. "Beyond Friendship: Aristotle on Conflict, Deliberation, and Attention." *The Journal of Politics,* **58**(2): 398-421.

Bocock, Robert. 1993. *Consumption.* London and New York: Routledge.

Bordo, Susan. 1993. *Unbearable Weight: Feminism, Western Culture and the Body.* Berkeley: University of California Press.

Bordo, Susan. 1998. "Material Girl: The Effacements of Postmodern Culture", in D. Welton, *Body and Flesh: A Postmodern Reader.* Cambridge, MA: Blackwell Publishers.

Botwinick, Aryeh and Connolly, William E. 2001. *Democracy and Vision: Sheldon Wolin and the Vicissitudes of the Political.* Princeton and Oxford: Princeton University Press.

Botwinick, Aryeh. 1983. *Hobbes and Modernity.* Lanham, MD: University Press of America.

Brennan, Theresa. 2000. *Exhausting Modernity: Grounds for a New Economy.* London and New York: Routledge.

Brown, Peter. 1994. *Restoring the Public Trust: A Fresh Vision for Progressive Government in America.* Boston: Beacon Press.

Brown, Wendy. 1995. *States of Injury: Power and Freedom in Late Modernity.* Princeton: Princeton University Press.

Bryant, W. Keith. 1990. *The Economic Organization of the Household.* Cambridge and New York: Cambridge University Press.

Burk, Marguerite C. 1968. *Consumption Economics: A Multidisciplinary Approach.* New York. Wiley.

Burk, Marguerite C. 1968. *Consumption Economics: A Multidisciplinary Approach.* New York. Wiley.

Campbell, Colin. 1987. *The Romantic Ethic and the Spirit of Modern Consumerism.* Oxford and New York: Basil Blackwell.

Carrier, James G. 1982. "Knowledge, Meaning, and Social Inequality in Kenneth Burke", *American Journal of Sociology,* **88**(1): 43-61.

Carroll, Terrance G 1984. "Secularization and States of Modernity", *World Politics,* **36**(3) :362-382.

Carver, Terrell. 1998. *The Postmodern Marx.* University Park, PA: The Pennsylvania State University Press.

Chaloupka, William. 1990. *International Studies Quarterly,* **34** (3): 341-351

Chan, Angelique. 1996. "How Do Parents and Children Help One Another? — Socioeconomic Determinants of Intergenerational Transfers in Peninsular", *Journal of Population,* **2**(1): 43-82.

Chan, Angelique. 1997. "An Overview of the Living Arrangements and the Social Support Exchanges of Older Singaporeans," *Asia-Pacific Population Journal*, **12**(4), pp. 48-49.

Chua, Beng-Huat. 2000. ed. *Consumption in Asia: Lifestyles and Identities*. London and New York: Routledge.

Connolly, William E. "The Will, Capital Punishment, and Cultural War." Paper presented at the APSA 1998 Meeting, Boston, MA.

Connolly, William E. 1991. *Identity/Difference: Democratic Negotiations of Political Paradox*. Ithaca, NY: Cornell University Press.

Connolly, William E. 1992. "The Irony of Interpretation," in Daniel W. Conway and John E. Seery, eds., *The Politics of Irony: Essays in Self-betrayal*. New York:. St. Martin's Press.

Connolly, William E. 1993. *The Terms of Political Discourse*. 3rd edition. Princeton, NJ: Princeton University Press.

Connolly, William E. 1995. *The Ethos of Pluralization*. Minneapolis and London: University of Minnesota Press.

Connolly, William E. 1999. *Why I Am Not A Secularist*. Minneapolis and London: University of Minnesota Press.

Connolly, William E. *Political Theory and Modernity*. Ithaca and London: Cornell University Press.

Coombe, Rosemary J.. 1993. "Tactics of Appropriation and the Politics of Recognition in Late Modern Democracies in Language, Recognition, and Freedom", *Political Theory*, **21**(3): 411-433.

Dalton, Russell J. 1987. "Generational Change in Elite Political Beliefs: The Growth of Ideological Polarization", *The Journal of Politics*, **49**(4): 976-997.

De Man, Paul. 1986. *The Resistance to Theory*. Minneapolis, MN: University of Minnesota Press.

Dean, Jodi. Ed. 2000. *Cultural Studies and Political Theory*. Ithaca and London: Cornell University Press.

Deaton, Angus. 1992. *Understanding Consumption.* Oxford: Clarendon Press.

Deleuze, Gilles, and Guattari, Felix. 1994. *What Is Philosophy?* New York: Columbia University Press.

DeLuca, Tom. 1995. *The Two Faces of Political Apathy.* Philadelphia, PA: Temple University Press.

Di Palma, Giusseppe. 1970. *Apathy and Participation: Mass Politics in Western Societies.* New York: Free Press.

Digeser, Peter. 1992. "The Fourth Face of Power", *The Journal of Politics,* **54**(4):977-1007.

Dore, R. P. 1964. "The Search for Modernity in Asia and Africa: A Review Article", *Pacific Affairs,* **37**(2): 161-165.

Douglass, M. and Friedmann J. eds. 1998. *Cities for Citizens: Planning and the Rise of Civil Society in a Global Age.* New York: John Wiley.

Economic Development Board. 1976-2001. *Singapore Investment News.* Singapore: Economic Development Board (various).

Eisenstadt, Shmuel N. 2001. "The Civilizational Dimension of Modernity: Modernity as a Distinct Civilization", *International Sociology,* **16**(3): 320-340.

Foucault, Michel. 1972. *The Archeology of Knowledge and the Discourse on Language.* New York: Pantheon Books.

Foucault, Michel. 1977. *Language, Counter-memory, Practice: Selected Essays and Interviews.* Oxford: Blackwell.

Frith, Katherine Toland. 1996. *Advertising in Asia: Communication, Culture, and Consumption.* Ames, IA: Iowa State University Press.

Galbraith, John Kenneth. 1996. *The Good Society: The Humane Agenda.* Boston: Houghton Mifflin.

Glass, D. C. and J. E. 1972. Singer, *Urban Stress: Experiments on Noise and Social Stressors.* New York: Academic Press.

Goldsmith, M. and Villadsen, S. eds. 1986. *Urban Political Theory and the Management of Fiscal Stress.* Brookfield: Gower.

Gopinathan, S. Pakir, Anne, Wah Kam Ho, and Saravanan, Vanithamani. eds. *Language, Society, and Education in Singapore: Issues and Trends*. 2nd edition. Singapore: Times Academic Press.

Gottdiener, M. ed. 1986. *Cities in Stress: A New Look at the Urban Crisis*. Beverley Hills, CA: Sage Publications.

Government of Malaysia. 1969-2001. "Department of Statistics Reports" (various). Singapore.

Government of Singapore. 1971-2000. *Singapore Parliamentary Reports*. (various). Singapore.

Government of Singapore. 1978-2001. "Department of Statistics Reports" (various). Singapore.

Government of Singapore. *White Paper* (various). Singapore.

Green, H. A. John. 1971. *Consumer Theory*. Harmondsworth: Penguin.

Gunnell, John G. 1993. "American Political Science, Liberalism, and the Invention of Political Theory" in James Farr and Raymond Seidelman, *Discipline and History: Political Science in the United States*. Ann Arbor: University of Michigan Press.

Gusfield, Joseph R. 1967. "Tradition and Modernity: Misplaced Polarities in the Study of Social Change", *American Journal of Sociology*, **72**(4): 351-362.

Habermas, Jurgen. 1985. *The Structural Transformation of the Public Sphere: An Inquiry into a Category of Bourgeois Society*. Cambridge, MA: MIT Press.

Henderson, David K. 1993. *Interpretation and Explanation in the Human Sciences*. Albany, NY: State University of New York Press.

Henderson, David. 1992. "International Economic Integration: Progress, Prospects and Implications (in Integrating Economies)", *International Affairs*, **68**(4): 633-653.

Howard, G. S. 1997. *Ecological Psychology: Creating A More Earth-Friendly Human Nature*. Notre Dame, IN: University of Notre Dame Press.

Hughes, Tom E. 1980. *Tangled Words: The Story of Maria Hertog.* Singapore: Institute of Southeast Asian Studies.

Jackson, Stevi and Moores, Shaun. eds. 1995. *The Politics of Domestic Consumption: Critical Readings.* London and New York: Prentice Hall-Harvester Wheatsheaf.

Jain, M. P. 1997. *Administrative Law of Malaysia and Singapore.* Singapore: Malayan Law Journal.

Jameson, Fredric. [1991] 1995. *Postmodernism, or, The Cultural Logic of Late Capitalism.* Durham, NC: Duke University Press.

Jenkins, Richard. 1996. *Social Identity.* London and New York: Routledge.

Kamal, S. 1988. *The New Economic Policy After 1990.* Kuala Lumpur: Malaysian Institute of Economic Research. Malaysia.

Karni, R. S. 1980. *Bibliography of Malaysia & Singapore.* Kuala Lumpur: *Penerbit Universiti Malaya.*

Kateb, George. 1968. *Political Theory: Its Nature and Uses.* New York: St. Martian's Press.

Kateb, George. 1992. *The Inner Ocean: Individualism and Democratic Culture.* Ithaca, NY: Cornell University Press.

Katzenstein, Peter J. 1975. "International Interdependence: Some Long-Term Trends and Recent Changes." *International Organization,* **29**(4): 1021-1034.

Katzenstein, Peter J. 1980. "Capitalism in one Country? Switzerland in the International Economy." *International Organization,* **34**(4): 507-540.

Katzenstein, Peter J., Keohane, Robert O., and Krasner Stephen D. eds. 1999. *Exploration and Contestation in the Study of World Politics.* Cambridge, MA: MIT Press.

Keyes, Charles F., Kendall, Laurel, and Hardacre, Helen. 1994. *Asian Visions of Authority: Religion and the Modern States of East and Southeast Asia.* Honolulu, HI: University of Hawaii Press.

Kierkegaard, Sören. 1980. *Sickness Unto Death: A Christian Psychological Exposition for Upbuilding and Awakening.* Princeton, NJ: Princeton University Press.

Kolb, David. 1986. *The Critique of Pure Modernity: Hegel, Heidegger, and After*. Chicago and London: The University of Chicago Press.

Kratoska, Paul H. 1998. *The Japanese Occupation of Malaya, 1941-1945*. London: Allen and Unwin.

Kritzman, Lawrence. ed. 1988. *Michel Foucault: Politics, Philosophy, Culture: Interviews and Other Writings 1977-1984*. New York: Routledge.

Lee Kuan Yew. 1965. *The Battle for a Malaysian Malaysia*. Singapore: Ministry of Culture. Singapore.

Lee Kuan Yew. 2000. *From Third World to First: The Singapore Story – 1965-2000 – Memoirs of Lee Kuan Yew*. Singapore: Singapore Press Holdings, Times Editions.

Lee, Kuan Yew. 1962. *The Battle for Merger*. Singapore: Printed at the Government Printing Office. Singapore.

Lee, Kuan Yew. 1998. *The Singapore Story: Memoirs of Lee Kuan Yew*. Singapore: Singapore Press Holdings, Times Editions.

Lee, Martyn J. 1993. *Consumer Culture Reborn: The Cultural Politics of Consumption*. London and New York: Routledge.

Lyotard, Jean-Francois. 1993. *Political Writings*. Minneapolis, MN: University of Minnesota Press.

Mahathir Mohamed. 1998. *The Way Forward*. London: Weidenfeld & Nicolson.

Martin, J. K. 1982. *Urban Financial Stress: Why Cities Go Broke*. Dover, MA: Auburn House.

McCabe, Allyssa, and Paterson, Carole. eds. 1991. *Developing Narratival Structure*. Hillsdale: L. Erlbaum Associates.

Miller, Daniel, ed. 2001. *Consumption, Critical Concepts in the Social Sciences*, vols. I, II & III. London & New York: Routledge.

Miller, Daniel. 1987. *Material Culture and Mass Consumption*. Oxford and New York: Basil Blackwell.

Moffat, Robert Scott. 1878. *The Economy of Consumption: An Omitted Chapter in Political Economy*. London: C. K. Paul.

Nietzsche, Friedrich. [1886] 1973. *Beyond Good and Evil: Prelude to a Philosophy of the Future*. London: Penguin Classics.

Nystrom, Paul Henry. 1929. *Economic Principles on Consumption*. New York: Ronald Press.

Orlie, Melissa A. 2001. "Political Capitalism and Consumption" in Botwinick, Aryeh, and Connolly, William E. eds. *Democracy and Vision: Sheldon Wolin and the Vicissitudes of the Political*. Oxford and Princeton, NJ: Princeton University Press.

Pearce, Ivor F. A. 1964. *Contribution to Demand Analysis*. Oxford: Clarendon Press.

Postman, Neil. 1985. *Amusing Ourselves to Death: Public Discourse in the Age of Show Business*. London and New York: Penguin.

Pye, Lucian and Pye, May W. 1985. *Asian Power and Politics: the Cultural Dimensions of Authority*. Cambridge: Belknap Press.

Rappa, Antonio L. 1999. "The Politics of Ageing in Singapore: Perspectives from State and Society," *Southeast Asian Journal of Social Science*, 27(2):123-138.

Rappa, Antonio L. 1999. "Imprisoning the Other," *Peace Review*, 11(1): 157-160.

Rappa, Antonio L. 1999. "Political Pluralism and Governance in Singapore," in Frank Delmartino, Amara Pongsapich, and Rudolf Hrbek, (eds.) *Regional Pluralism and Good Governance*. Baden-Baden: Nomos Verlagsgesellschaft.

Rappa, Antonio L. 2000. "On A Common Currency for East Asia: Some Political Considerations," in *A Common Currency for East Asia: Dream or Reality?* Kuala Lumpur: AIDCOM-Konrad Adenauer Stiftung.

Rappa, Antonio L. 2000. "Surviving the Politics of Late Modernity: The Eurasian Fringe Community," *Southeast Asian Journal of Social Science*, 28(2):153-180.

Rappa, Antonio L. 2000. "Werlin on Wolin: A Misrepresentation of Political Theory," *International Review of Administrative Sciences*, 66 (1): 175-180.

Rappa, Antonio L. 2001. "Urban Political Theory and the Symmetrical Model of Community Power," *Innovation: European Journal of Social Science Research,* **14**(1): 5-16.

Rappa, Antonio L. 2002. ed. Thematic issue on "Modernity and the Politics of Public Space", *Innovation: The European Journal of Social Science Research,* **15** (1).

Raz, Joseph. ed. 1990. *Authority.* Oxford: Blackwell.

Roche, Daniel. 1998. *France des Lumires* (France in the Enlightenment) translated by Arthur Goldhammer. Cambridge, MA: Harvard University Press.

Rorty, Richard. 1989. *Contingency, Irony and Solidarity.* Cambridge: Cambridge University Press.

Sack, Robert David. 1992. *Place, Modernity, and the Consumer's World: A Relational Framework for Geographical Analysis.* Baltimore, MD: Johns Hopkins University Press.

Sandel, Michael J. 1998. *Liberalism and the Limits of Justice.* 2nd edition. Cambridge: Cambridge University Press.

Sarat, Austin, and Villa, Dana R. eds. 1996. *Liberal Modernism and Democratic Individuality: George Kateb and the Practices of Politics.* Princeton, NJ: Princeton University Press.

Shamira, B. A. A. 1998. *The Singapore-Malaysia "remerger" debate of 1996.* Hull: Centre for South-East Asian Studies and Institute of Pacific Asia Studies, University of Hull.

Shapiro, Michael J. 1969. "Rational Political Man: A Synthesis of Economic and Social-Psychological Perspectives", *American Political Science Review,* **63**(4):1106-1119.

Shapiro, Michael J. 1992. *Reading the Postmodern Polity: Political Theory as Textual Practice.* Minneapolis and Oxford: University of Minnesota Press.

Shapiro, Michael J. 1993. "Eighteenth Century Intimations of Modernity: Adam Smith and the Marquis de Sade", *Political Theory,* **21**(2):273-293.

Shapiro, Michael J. 1999. *Cinematic Political Thought: Narratives of Race, Nation and Gender*. New York and Edinburgh: New York University and University of Edinburgh Press.

Shapiro, Michael J. 2001. *For Moral Ambiguity: Theory, Genre, and the Politics of the Family*. Minneapolis and London: University of Minnesota Press.

Shapiro, Michael J. and Alker, Hayward R. eds. 1996. *Challenging Boundaries*. Minneapolis and London: University of Minnesota Press.

Shutz, Eric A. 2001. *Markets and Power: The 21st Century Command Economy*. Armonk, NY: M. E. Sharpe.

Singapore Armed Forces Act. 1995. (Revised). *The Statutes of the Republic of Singapore*, 10, 295.

Sritua Arief. 1980. *Study of Household Consumption in Malaysia and Singapore* Kuala Lumpur: Meta for Sritua Arief Associates.

Sritua, Arief. 1980. *Test of Leser's model of Household Consumption Expenditure in Malaysia and Singapore*. Singapore: Institute of Southeast Asian Studies.

Stone, Deborah A. 1991. *Policy Paradox and Political Reason*. Addison Wesley Longman.

Thumboo, Edwin, et al. 1990. *The Fiction of Singapore*. Singapore: Unipress.

Tiryakian, Edward A. 2001. "Introduction : The Civilization of Modernity and the Modernity of Civilizations", *International Sociology*, **16**(3): 277-292.

Vattimo, Gianni. [1985]1988. *La Fine Della Modernita. The End of Modernity*. Baltimore, MD: The John Hopkins University Press.

Vattimo, Gianni. 1993. *Avventure della differenza. The Adventure of Difference: Philosophy After Nietzsche and Heidegger*. Cambridge: Polity Press.

Wendt, Alexander. 1994. "Collective Identity Formation and the International State", *American Political Science Review*, **88**(2): 384-396.

White, Stephen K. 2000. *Sustaining Affirmation: The Strengths of Weak Ontology in Political Theory.* Princeton and Oxford: Princeton University Press.

Woshinsky, Oliver. 1995. *Culture and Politics: An Introduction to Mass and Elite Political Behavior.* Englewood Cliffs, N.J.: Prentice Hall.

Xenos, Nicholas. 1989. *Scarcity and Modernity.* London and New York: Routledge.

Author Index

A

Abdul Rahman, Tunku, 84, 88, 179
Adorno, Theodore, 78, 120
Aijaz, Ahmad, 33
Almond, Gabriel Abraham, 5, 31
Anderson, Elizabeth, 198, fn. 2
Anderson, Perry, 202
Anwar Ibrahim, Datuk Seri, 179, 201-205,
    fn. 9; 206-207, fn. 10; 209-212, fn. 15;
    216, 225
Appadurai, Arjun, 29, fn. 6; 153
Aquinas, Thomas, 12
Arendt, Hannah, 201
Augustine, 12

B

Bakunin, Mikhail, 127
Bamberg, Michael G.W., 198
Barthes, Roland, 33, 201
Baudrillard, Jean, 64, 201-203, 232-233,
    fn. 1; 248
Bauman, Zygmunt, 29, fn. 2; 39, 78, fn. 17;
    124, fn. 13; 128, 201
Berkeley, George, 4
Berman, Marshall, 128
    All That Is Solid Melts into Air,
        discussed, 125
Berman, Marshall, 65, 201
Bhabha, Homi, 64, 65
Bordo, Susan, 157
Bottomore, Tom, 32
Botwinick, Aryeh, 2, fn. 1; 13
Bourdieu, Pierre, 128, fn. 19
Breckenridge, Carol, 134, fn. 29
Brennan, Theresa, ix, 3, 4, 29, fn. 8; 34, 52

Bronner, Stephen Eric, 120, fn. 8
Brown, Wendy, ix, 3, 4, 13
    States of Injury (1995) discussed,
        19-20
    commodity as a social force, ix
Butler, Judith, 13

C

Canclini, Nestor Garcia, 132, fn. 24; 137
Carver, Terrell, 32
Chaloupka, William, 233, fn. 1
Chan, Angelique, 107, 108, fn. 4
Chekov, Anton, 133, 135, 137
    discussed, 133, fn. 27
    on the masses, 137
    over-burdened donkey, 135, fn. 31
Connolly, William E., ix, 3-4, 10, 13-16, 34,
    115, fn. 1; 129, 147, 150
consumption, 149
leadership, 149
Coombe, Rosemary J.
    on Harvey, Baudrillard and Jameson,
        248, fn. 6; 249, fn. 7

D

Dahl, Robert Alan, 5, 31
Dali, Salvador, 125
DaVanzo, Julie, 173, fn. 4; 173, fn. 6
Davis, Mike
    City of Quartz, discussed, 65
Deleuze, Gilles, 13
DeMan, Paul, 33
Derrida, Jacques, 128, 202
Dumm, Thomas L., 13
Dupre, Louis K., 29, fn. 5

E
Edelman, Murray, 31, 64
enlightened public opinion, 83

F
Fanon, Franz, 64
Ferguson, Kathy E.
    on political theory, 233, fn. 1
Ferguson, Kathy E., 8, 13
Fichte, Johann Gottlieb, 201
Fong, Chan Onn, Datuk Dr., 162
Foucault, Michel, 3, 128, 145, 199, 201-202, 215, 217, 219-220, 222-223, 225-227
    analysis of wealth, 14
    on *Language, Counter-Memory and Practice*, 227, fn. 31
    on multiple power relations, 27-29
    on the *Order of Things*, 220

G
Galbraith, John Kenneth, 32
Giddens, Anthony, 29, fn. 3
Gouldner, Alvin, 31
Guattari, Felix, 13

H
Habermas, Jurgen, 3, 119-120, 146, 164
Harvey, David, 127, 248
Heidegger, Martin, 110, 203
Hobbes, Thomas, and Leviathan (1651), 4
Horkheimer, Max, 78, 120, 127
Horowitz, Daniel, 64, fn. 1
Hume, David, 4
Hussein Onn, Tun, 179
Husserl, Edmund, 201

J
Jameson, Fredric, 125, fn. 16; 134, fn. 28; 137, 202, 232

K
Kamal, S., 154
Kant, Immanuel, 13
Katenstein, Peter J.
    primacy of politics, 236
    developmental capitalism, 234
Katzenstein, Peter J., 225, fn. 29; 228
Katzenstein, Peter J., 31
    analyses of capitalism, 43, fn. 11; 51, fn. 15
Kekes, John, 120, fn. 6
Kellner, Douglas Mackey, 120, fn. 8
Kennedy, Paul, 200
Keynes, John Maynard, 32
Kierkegaard, Sören, 13
King, Gary, 5
Kritzman, Lawrence, 202, fn. 6; 204, 210, 219, fn. 21; 220, fn. 22; 223-224
Kundera, Milan, 135
    The Book of Laughter and Forgetting, 1978, 118

L
Lakoff, George, 65
Larmore, Charles, 13
Lau, Albert, 86, fn. 1
Le Corbusier (Charles Édouard Jeanneret), 134
Lee, Kuan Yew, 85-88
    and "pragmatism", 87
    and narrative, 85

Lefebvre, Henri, 124-125, 128
Ling, Liong Sik, Datuk Seri, 157
Lipsett, Seymour Martin, 5, 31
Locke, J., 4
Lyotard, Jean-Francois, ix

M

Mahathir, Mohammed, Datuk Seri Dr.
    economy, 145, 163
Mannheim, Karl, 201
Maurício, José, 29, fn. 7
Moffat, Robert Scott, 40
Moon, J. Donald, 13

N

Naipaul, V. S., 52, 65
Narayan, R. K., 65
Neubauer, Deane E., 5
Nietzsche, Friedrich, 13, 127, 130, fn. 22; 214
Nik Imran Abdullah, 188, fn. 12

O

O'Connor, James, 32
O'Donnell, Guillermo, 31
Okin, Susan Moller, 13
    on childhood and education, 88
    on marriage, 83
    on textbooks and schools, 88
Ong, Teng Cheong, 74
Orlie, Melissa A., 2
O'Sullivan, Noel, 130, fn. 21; 134, 136, fn. 32; 137

P

Parkes, Graham, 125
Pearce, Ivor, 30
Postman, Neil, 28, 201
    greed and the capitalist, 28

R

Ramasamy, P., 149, fn. 1; 188, fn. 12
Raz, Joseph, 200
Razak, Tun, 243
Ricoeur, Paul, 204
Rorty, Richard, 2, 3, 128-129
    on Foucault, 3
    early Rorty, 202
Rosenau, Pauline M., 124-125, fn. 14
Rushdie, Salmon, 125

S

Said, Edward W., 33
Sartre, Jean Paul, 204
Shapiro, Michael J., 3, fn. 2; 5, 10, fn. 5; 11, fn. 6; 13, 191, fn. 14; 231
    on Jurgen Habermas and critical theory, 3, fn. 2
    on the "Magic Kingdom", 66-67
Simmel, Georg, 64, fn. 1; 125
Skinner, Quentin, 13
Smith, James P., 169
Smith, Sheridan, 201, 210
Sniderman, Paul M., 5, fn. 3
Stallybrass, Peter, 131, fn. 23
Stone, Deborah A., 31, 235, fn. 2

T

Taylor, Charles, 13, 33
Thumboo, Edwin, 118, fn. 3; 119, fn. 5; 122, fn. 9; 123, fn. 11; 125, 126, fn. 17-18
Tomlinson, John, 29, fn. 4

V

Van der Veer, Peter, 134, fn. 29
Vattimo, Gianni, 13, 16-17, 34-35, 52
Verba, Sydney, 5

W

Weber, Max, 227
Welton, Donn, 157
White, Stephen K., 3-4, 6-8, fn. 4; 18
    Sustaining Affirmation, discussed, 8,
      19
Wiggerhaus, Rolf, 120, fn. 8
Wildavsky, Aaron, 125, fn. 15
Wildavsky, Aaron, 5
Wittgenstein, Ludwig von, 127
Wolin, Sheldon, 2, fn. 1; 13

Y

Yeo, Kim Wah, 86, fn. 1

Z

Zhang, Xina, 126, fn. 17

Subject Index

A

Abdul Taib Mahmud, Datuk Patinggi Tan Sri (Dr.) Haji, 149
Ang, Ramli, 214-215, 228
Anwar, Ibrahim, Dato' Seri, 200, 202, 213, 215, 236, 240

C

caliph
    myth of political, 207
capitalism
    irrationality of, 227
Chan Hong Nam, George, Tan Sri Datuk Amar Dr., 149
Chinese
    Development Assistance Council (CDAC)., 91
    Diaspora in Southeast Asia, 92, 104
    ethnic, 84-104
    immigrant, 84
    Singaporeans and loss of cultural heritage, 136
    traditional, 86-89
    university, 91
conspicuous, 174
consumption, 236
    and Malaysia, ch. 6, 145
    and Singapore, ch.3
    agency, 232, 237
    agency-generators, 232
    agents, 234
    consumer culture, defined, 237, 239
    consumption culture defined, 238
    export led, 162
    fear of economic failure, 85
    herd of, v
    nature and pattern and politics, 194-195
    Malaysian family, 169
    traditional impediments, 169
Crisis
    Asian financial (1997-1998), 162
    Asian recession (2000-2003), 163

E

education
    different school types, 102
    economic, 95-96
    general, 99-104
    military, 96-97
    national, 84, 97-99
    in Malaysia, 180-185
    Eurasian, 86, 103-104
    Association of S'pore (EAS), 91
    Catholic, 73
    students, 103

F

Family
    Asian structure of, 88-89
    Western, 104
fantasy, foundational, 108
    and western "decadence", 90
    economic horror, 111
    Faustian image, 110
    success and failure, 84-88
    value of the modern ethos, 104
Fernandes, Jorge, 134, fn. 29
frame of late modernity, 128
fringe community, 155, 165
gender
    and Mahathir Mohammed, 189-190, fn. 13; 191

G
God, 8
Goh, Chok Tong
    and education, 102-104
    and OB markers, 94
    and schools, 102
    National Day Rally Speech, 1996, 116
    vision, 137

H
History as a Sign, 241

I
Indian, 86, 155
    Indian Development Association (SINDA), 91

J
Japanese
    army, 69
    Malayan People's Anti-Japanese Army (MPAJA), 122
    militarism, 127

L
late modernity
    Bintulu, 219
    exclusionary goods, 174, 184
    familial life, 170, 173-176
    inclusionary goods, 168, 183-184
    women, 146-147, 156, 189
Lee, Hsien Loong, 73, fn. 11; 98
    HDB capital appreciation, 116
    National Education, 98
    on "objective" history, 99
Lee, Kuan Yew, 85, 101-102, 103
    fear of economic failure, 85
patriarchal society, & "father-knows best" philosophy, 89

Lim, Kim San, 87

M
Mahathir, Mohammed, Datuk Seri Dr., Bintulu, 163
Malay
    indigenous, 84
    language class, 103
    students, 103
    Islamic values, 136
    The Annals, 117
Malaysia
    analysis of, in Malaysia, 183
    analysis of family planning, 175
    and Mahathir Mohammed, 190
    Bank Simpanan Nasional, 185
    Barisan Nasional, 198
    Bumiputra-Commerce Bank Berhad, 185
    bumiputra, 153-154, 200, 229
    Chinese, 200
    Chinese Malaysians, 155
    Civil Service (MCS), 180
    consumption stories, 148
    Democratic Action Party (DAP), 159, fn. 6
    demography, 171
    family and education, ch. 7, 167
    family and social imaginary, 171
    family life survey, RAND, 173
    family planning, 175
    family, ch. 7, 167
    foreign women & foreign men, 159
    historical narratives, 151
    Indian Congress (MIC), 242
    language policy, 179
    life narratives, 170
    Malay ethnocrats, 154
    Malay hegemony, 155

Malaysian Chinese Association (MCA), 242
modernity and the weakening of tradition, 161
multi-ethnic, multi-cultural and multi-religious, 146
MFLS1, 167, 170, 172
MFLS2, 167
Multimedia Super Corridor (MSC), 182
National Development Policy (NDP), 169, 181
New Economic Policy (NEP), 154, 171, 179, 181
public & private, 164
prime minister, 168, 179-181, 190
race riots, 154
United Malay's National Organization (UMNO), 168, 204, 206
Wawasan 2020 (Vision 2020), 169, fn. 1
work gender narratives, 156
United Malay National Organization (UMNO), 240
Marx, Karl
and the Frankfurt School, 120-121
modern
the fragile, 131-136
modernism 131
Asian and Western, 104, 126
modernity
artifacts of, 133
characterization, **121**
concepts, 33-36
consumer, 147, 150, 152, 158
culture argument, 32-33
discontents, 233
divided, 40-46
economic argument, 32
encountering, 129, 131-133, 137
exhausting, 110
experience of, 134
frame, 121
homologous logic defined, 30
hybrid, 132
juggernaut, 115
metanarratives, 124
metropolises of, 134
narrative and public space, 116
political argument, 31
prison of, 132
rationality, the analyses of, 217
resistance frame (mRf), 33
Singaporean & Malaysian, 36
Southeast Asian, 122
Southeast Asian movements and resistance, 240
sub-hypotheses, 33-34
unfair, 119
war-time, 122

N
narrative
  narratival frames, 136-139
  Singapore, ch. 5, 115
narratives and discursive formations, 147
neo-positivism, positivist political science, 4-11
Neptune Orient Lines, 96

P
Parsi, 103
Peoples' Action Party, 93-94
public arena, 138-139
public good, 137
  collective political good, 150
  inclusionary, 147, 150
  inclusionary goods, 14
public justice, 115

272 Subject Index

public space and private discourse, 130
public space approaches, 116
    and narrative, 116
    and civil society, 122
    institutionalized, 135
    Malay state ethnocratism, 163
    Singapore, 64, 84

R
Rajaratnam, S., 87
Rappa, Kenneth Anthony, 87, fn. 2
rationality, the analyses of, 226
Rhetoric, state and the family, 67

S
signs, 243
Sikh, 103
Singapore
    Airlines, 96
    Authority, Port of, 96
    city-state, 66
    cost of living, 67
    banks, 109
    distribution of wealth, 67, 74-78
    elderly, 106-108
    Feedback Unit, 90
    Housing and Development Board (HDB), 94
    Improvement Trust (SIT), 95
    incorporated, 95
    Legislative Assembly, 84
    Malaysian, 156
    Malaysia-Thailand Joint Authority (MTJA), 162
    national security good, 68-74
    one, 95
    public sector questions on, 101
    SingHealth, 139
    twenty -one, 95
society, instant gratification, 17, 66
space
    interstitial, 64
work gender narratives, 156

T
Tamil, 103
Toh, Chin Chye, 87

W
women, 157-161, 190
    Singaporean, 101

www.ingramcontent.com/pod-product-compliance
Lightning Source LLC
LaVergne TN
LVHW050532300426
837529LV00047B/860